I0820198

FIBER CRAFT *Heritage*

Easy-to-Learn
Textile Techniques from the Stone Age to Today, with 52 Try-It Projects

DORIS FISCHER

Other Schiffer Craft Books on Related Subjects:

The Art and Science of Natural Dyes: Principles, Experiments, and Results,
Joy Boutrup and Catharine Ellis, foreword by Yoshiko Iwamoto Wada, ISBN 978-0-7643-5633-9

Handwoven Tape: Understanding and Weaving Early American and Contemporary Tape,
Susan Faulkner Weaver, ISBN 978-0-7643-5196-9

Weaving Shaker Rugs: Traditional Techniques to Create Beautiful Reproduction Rugs and Tapes,
Mary Elva Congleton Erf, ISBN 978-0-7643-4907-2

Originally published as *Faserwerkstatt* by AT Verlag AG, Munich/Aarau © 2023 AT Verlag AG
Translated from the German by Rachel Joerges

p. 303 (Image Credits) constitutes an extension of this copyright page.

Library of Congress Control Number: 2025930118

Front cover design by Lindsay Hess
Page composition and back cover design by Christine B. Stürmer
Type set in Museo Sans / RecifeText

ISBN: 978-0-7643-6962-9
ePub: 978-1-5073-0624-6

Printed in China

Published by Schiffer Craft
An imprint of Schiffer Publishing, Ltd.
4880 Lower Valley Road
Atglen, PA 19310
Phone: (610) 593-1777; Fax: (610) 593-2002
Email: Info@schifferbooks.com
Web: www.schifferbooks.com

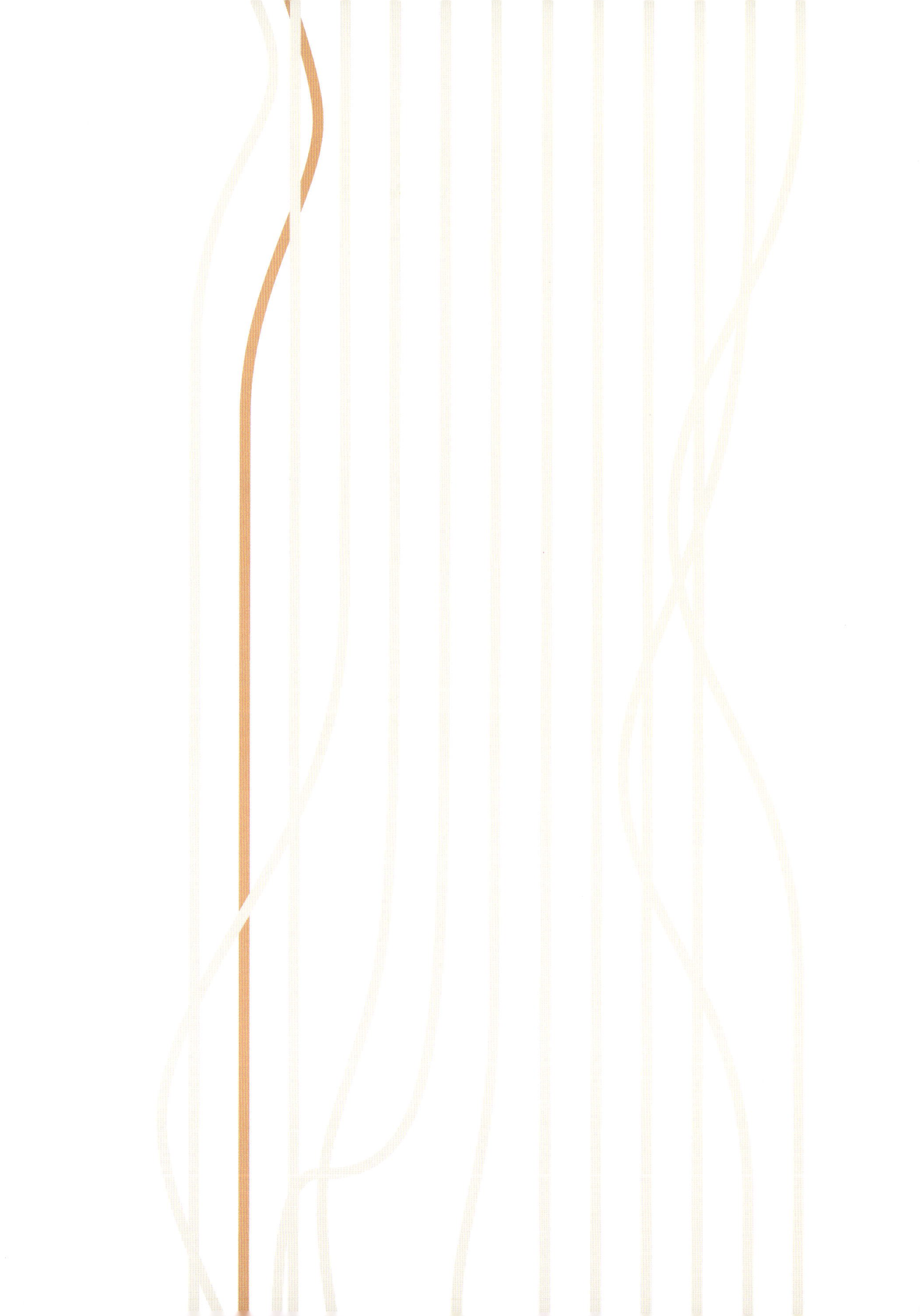

CONTENTS

TOOL WORKSHOP

INSTRUCTIONS FOR BUILDING TEXTILE TOOLS YOURSELF

FIBERS CONNECT US

There are an incredible number of different textile techniques. I love them all. I started with spinning and wool dyeing. The Middle Ages led me to tablet weaving and nålbinding. When I tried to find out more about rarer techniques such as twining or sprang, it became difficult. The minimal literature available consisted of passages in foreign languages in specialty books, in which the craftsmanship itself was mentioned only in passing. I was unable to find a collection of historical textile techniques that also contained practical instructions. That is how this book began.

I originally intended to organize the techniques by region. However, related craft techniques can be found in regions that are very far apart. Slip stitch crocheting, for example, can be found in the Baltic states and in East Frisia, while the fingerweaving from the Swiss Valais looks very similar to that from Scandinavia. Culture has always developed through exchanging, copying, and adapting. And because people are inventive, they often found similar solutions for similar requirements independently of each other. In this respect, a technique may be "typical of this or that region," but it is never actually possible to trace its origins.

We are connected not only across borders, but also across time through craftsmanship. In his book Cræft, British archaeologist Alexander Langlands describes a wealth of experience that stretches from the Stone Ages to his grandfather. Stone Age hunters made spears and javelins from wood. Langlands's grandfather was also a wood craftsman, a gifted maker of golf clubs. He always chose the right woods and could feel when the club was balanced just right. This skill, ability, and feeling for materials and tools had been passed down from generation to generation. When the era of handmade golf clubs came to an end in the 1950s, the grandfather "lost his livelihood and his source of pride, but we, the wider society, lost a direct and tangible link with our ancient ancestry."[1]

1 Alexander Langlands: *Cræft. An Inquiry into the Origins and True Meaning of Traditional Crafts* (New York, 2019), 68.

By learning and practicing traditional textile techniques today, we are making a small contribution to keeping the thread from our past alive. The beauty of it is that it connects us with all the other textile enthusiasts in the world. I experienced this while researching this book. Lots of nice people helped me, and I received practical tips and new ideas, literature advice, and photos. Even though I don't know all these people personally, I feel connected to all of them and am grateful for their support.

And now I would like to take you on a textile journey through Europe—from the Stone Age to the present day.

TRADITIONAL TEXTILE TECHNIQUES

Textile creation is part of our human heritage.

—CAROL JAMES, WEAVER AND SPRANG EXPERT

It is clear to everyone that monuments such as Stonehenge or the Cologne Cathedral are worth protecting. They are large and one of a kind. The countless smaller objects from bygone times, whether they are made of stone, ceramics, wood, or gold, are also preserved and exhibited in museums. All these things are part of our material and cultural heritage. You can see and touch them and marvel at how people could create something so impressive.

There is also the living or intangible cultural heritage, which is at least as important. It encompasses all the practical knowledge and skills handed down by humankind. This includes traditional cooking, songs, and dances, but also the use of plants and all crafts. Of course, it also includes everything to do with textile production.

WHY DID OLD TEXTILE TECHNIQUES DISAPPEAR?

Just as there are red lists for endangered animal and plant species, there are also lists of endangered crafts. Various associations and foundations publish these lists, which also include textile crafts.[2] Some of the techniques presented in this book are part of these lists. The idea behind them is to publicize traditional techniques and encourage modern creative people to engage with them.

Why do these intangible parts of cultural heritage become endangered or forgotten? Traditional techniques were able to survive for a long time, especially in rural areas. It is notable that many disappeared when the products made with them could be bought. Some were made only out of necessity, because there was no store nearby or simply because there was not enough money. As soon as it was available in the local store or from a traveling vendor, people gave up making it themselves. Because, not unlike today, men and women, who were primarily responsible for textiles, always had plenty of other things to do. They lived in the here and now and never lost sleep over their old occupation.

Through industrialization and the mechanized production of clothing, the production of textiles at home was largely abandoned. Until then, it had been an additional source of income in the countryside or even the only way to obtain cash for the necessary purchases outside the rural household. As a result, the knowledge and tradition of a technique often disappeared along with the source of income.

Other reasons are changes in fashion and clothing habits or the replacement of one textile raw material by another. Since people no longer wear knee-high woolen stockings, they no longer need woven garters. When cotton replaced linen, flax was no longer used.

We know which textile craft techniques existed, first because they are still practiced in a few regions today, and second because they can be researched and deduced from surviving textiles. However, they were used mainly for small items of clothing such as belts, gloves, hats, and stockings. These everyday textiles were regularly used and strained and were therefore subject to heavy wear and tear.

2 Among others, the UNESCO lists of Intangible Cultural Heritage; Red List of Endangered Crafts (Heritage Crafts Association, UK); Rødlista Norges Husflidslag; Craft at Risk (Heritage Foundation of Newfoundland & Labrador).

Unlike old priestly vestments with gold embroidery, for example, they were also too common to be preserved in museums and collections. An exception is the very old textiles from the Stone Age, Bronze Age, or Middle Ages that were recovered in archaeological excavations and are now precious documents of earlier craftsmanship.

WHO REDISCOVERED THEM?

Folklore and ethnology have always been concerned with craftsmanship. However, it has tended to be presented in a descriptive, often-romanticized way and with an outside perspective. Archaeology, especially experimental archaeology, should have a much stronger influence on the understanding of special craft techniques.

EXPERIMENTAL ARCHAEOLOGY AND TEXTILE ARCHAEOLOGY

Early experiments on prehistoric techniques focused on the manufacturing of stone tools, metalworking, and house building. In 1973, in his book *Archaeology by Experiment*,[3] John Coles covered the field of textile archaeology in a single short section. In Germany, there was a strong reluctance for a long time regarding experimental archaeology. The open-air museums of the Reichsbund for German Prehistory (Unteruhldingen, Oerlinghausen), in which a constructed "Germanic" life was reenacted, were still a bad memory. The focus was therefore on scientific laboratory investigations. It was not until the 1970s that there were practical experiments carried out in Germany to investigate old craft techniques. Prehistoric wooden houses were reconstructed, and experiments were carried out on Neolithic agriculture. In 1990 in the exhibition *Experimental Archaeology in Germany*, the discoveries were summarized, and further studies were initiated. In the area of textile technology, a working group from the Berlin Museum Village in Düppel, which was founded in 1975, completed groundbreaking work. Their experiments in spinning and weaving in the Middle Ages were published in the accompanying catalog to the exhibition. With the discovery of the glacial mummy "Ötzi" and the analysis of his outfit, the textile techniques of the Stone Age such as twining were brought into focus.

Today, many European museums are conducting research into textile matters. For example, the Vikingeskibsmuseet in Roskilde, Denmark, weaves woolen sails for Viking ships on reconstructed looms. Educational museum programs in which visitors can try out old craft techniques such as spinning and dyeing are now a common feature of archaeological and cultural museums.

A lot has also happened in the field of textile archaeology at universities. Old discoveries are being reexamined and new discoveries from wetland settlements, mines, or medieval cesspools are constantly providing new insights. It is often private individuals who come across a particular technique, become enthusiastic about it, and develop it further. Many also share their discoveries on the internet; for example, on Ravelry or in YouTube videos. Historical working groups and associations are also involved in traditional regional textile crafts, showing them in demonstrations and passing them on in courses. Two examples are the local heritage association in Hochstedt in Thuringia, which demonstrates blue dyeing with woad in its woad museum, and the Wegberg-Beeck local heritage association in North Rhine–Westphalia, which shows flax processing in its own flax museum.[4]

MIDDLE AGES AND LIVING HISTORY

Parallel to archaeology and museums and in a mutual exchange, old techniques have been rediscovered in the medieval scene. People tablet weaving are now just as common at medieval markets as people nålbinding at Viking events. Over the course of time, new insights have increased the demands of artists in terms of materials and equipment. If you want high-quality clothing that is as "authentic" as possible, you can make it yourself. It is easy to buy hand spindles, plant-dyed fabrics, or nålbinding hats from specialty stores.

For those who don't have anything to do with archaeology, the Middle Ages, or living history, they will probably never encounter the historical textile techniques known there. I would like to get these techniques out of their niche and introduce them to a larger circle of people interested in textiles.

3 John Coles, *Archaeology by Experiment* (New York, 1973).

4 Woad Museum: www.waidmuseum.de; Flachsmuseum: www.beecker-erlebnismuseen.de.

WHAT CAN YOU DISCOVER?

In this book you will find a variety of traditional textile techniques from all over Europe. The oldest were developed in the Stone Age. The youngest date back to the nineteenth century. All are little known but easy to learn, and there is no need to buy complicated special tools. Instructions for making simple textile tools can be found in the Tool Workshop [Instructions for Textile Tools: p. 259] where I describe the various techniques so that you can make simple objects yourself. The small projects are ideal for trying out different yarns and patterns, don't take up much space, and are easy to take with you on journeys, to the waiting room, or on vacation. For those who want to work in the traditional manner, natural materials are used: sheep wool, linen, or hemp yarn [Fiber Materials: p. 23], perhaps even with plant-based dyes. Hand spinners will find plenty of ideas for using their own wool—even using wool scraps, small quantities, of the first handspun wool. Most projects in this book offer a wonderful opportunity to use yarn scraps. Many projects are also suited for the use of yarn made from synthetic fibers. For example, there is sock wool made from biodegradable polyamide. For those who do not tolerate wool or do not want to work with natural materials that come from animals, cotton can be used.

Once you have found a technique that you enjoy, you build from this foundation by continuing to learn independently. You can start with tips from experts whom you can find among the instructions. Specialty books offer even more specialized information [Reading Tips: p. 295] The individual working steps can also be found in courses, in museums, or in internet videos.

If you can't wait any longer to discover old techniques, go ahead and get started: With the "Try It!" instructions, you can begin right away. Have fun!

→ Instructions for Textile Tools p. 259

→ Fiber Materials p. 23

→ Reading Tips p. 295

FIBERS AND THREADS

Fibers, threads, cords, and ropes are linear textile structures that are useful for a wide variety of purposes. However, they are also the basic material for flat textiles such as woven and braided fabrics.

HUMANITY'S FIRST THREADS

Threads and ropes are among the oldest structures created by humans. One of the most important tasks facing Stone Age people was to connect different objects together, attach them to something, and hold them in place. This doesn't sound so exciting at first, but it involves such basic needs as warmth, food, movement, and health. Simple or twisted threads are essential for all these purposes.

For a warming fire, firewood was needed, which had to be transported to the storage area—this was much more efficient when the wood was tied into bundles. Clothing could be sewn together from individual pieces of leather or tied from fibers. Berries and mushrooms were collected in woven baskets or containers made from bark. For hunting with a bow and arrow, durable bowstrings were needed, and the arrow fletching was fastened by wrapping a string around it. In warlike conflicts, a rope was useful for tying up prisoners. Fishing line and nets were used for angling and fishing. Rivers could be crossed with tied-up bridge constructions. People even relied on rope to care for the sick; for example, when a broken body part had to be splinted or bleeding had to be stopped by bandaging.

Jewelry, decoration, and art also played an important role from the very beginning. Animal teeth and beads were threaded into necklaces, and snails and shells were sewn onto clothing.

USING NATURAL FIBERS YOURSELF

Over the course of time, people were constantly faced with new problems and challenges that could be elegantly solved with the help of threads, cords, or ropes. If you search an old dictionary for all the words containing "thread," "cord," "line," or "rope," you will be amazed at the number of terms and, above all, the range of uses, especially in agriculture, but also in seafaring, mining, and sport.

Cords and ropes are still important for certain applications. Today they are mostly made of synthetic fibers; for example, fishing lines made of polyamide or sewing thread and ship ropes made of polyester. These materials have many advantages; they are strong, smooth, and easy to care for. The problems arising from the use of synthetic materials are well known. In the private sector, it is therefore a good idea to use threads and cords made from natural fibers. They can be used well in the home, in the garden, and for clothing. They are durable, can be grown or collected yourself, and are easy to dispose of or recycle at the end of their useful life. Below you can see which fibers are suitable and how you can spin, ply, and twist them yourself.

FIBER MATERIALS

In preindustrial times, a variety of plant and animal raw materials were still used for fiber production. Cellulose-containing fibers are found in flax, hemp, nettles, linden and lime bast, seagrass, and wood. For warmer clothing, fibers containing protein such as sheep's wool and other animal hair were used.

Today, modern clothing is of mainly man-made fibers, at best cotton. Technical textiles such as ropes, fishing nets, or fire curtains are also made mainly from chemical fibers. These so-called "synthetic fibers" were initially developed from the plant raw material cellulose. The first was viscose or "artificial silk" around 1890. Since the 1930s, work has been done on completely synthetic fibers. Early synthetic fibers include nylon, Perlon, and Dederon, well-known brands of women's stockings, as well as polyesters made from petroleum components.

When raw materials such as cotton and synthetic fibers became scarce in Germany during the two world wars, textiles began to be industrially recycled in order to obtain sufficient fiber material for textile production. Attempts were also made to revive the processing of domestic fibers. Since the 1950s, however, the cultivation of nettles, fiber flax, and hemp has ultimately become a niche, and with it the knowledge of their processing has also disappeared.

FIBERS CONTAINING PROTEIN

I will only briefly discuss protein fibers here, since their processing is not included when speaking of almost-forgotten textile crafts. Where there are flocks of sheep, hand spinning has never been completely abandoned. As a creative hobby, it was once "in" again in the 1970s and is still popular today. Working with sheep's wool is not so difficult, because the fiber is easily available. Animal hair needs only to be washed and combed or carded before it can be spun. **Sheep's wool** prepared for hand spinning is easy to obtain, and spinning groups and explanatory videos show how to make yarn from it. Rabbit, alpaca, goat, or dog wool is also almost ready to spin after shearing.

Unlike wool, **hair** is smooth and unruffled. Long horse tail hair is ideal for braiding bracelets, decorative cords, or horse bridles. In prehistoric times, horsehair was sometimes used as a yarn for weaving. Fishing lines can also be made from this thin and sturdy material. [Whipcording with Horsehair: p. 95] A special case is human hair, when in addition to the material properties, the connection to the person from whom the hair comes is always important. It can be spun into yarn if it is mixed with sheep's wool. Its stability was used, for example, in knitted work gloves for fishermen. In this way, their wives could also give their husbands a piece of themselves to take with them to sea. [Hairwork: p. 91] The Canary Islands of Tenerife and Gomera have a tradition of twisting ropes from human hair.

Sheep's wool, when clean, can be spun immediately after shearing it.

Silk is the most precious, finest, and strongest of all natural fibers. A lot of money could be made from silk. This was of course enticing, which is why many places in central Europe tried to establish silkworm breeding in the seventeenth and especially the eighteenth centuries. Reeling the silk from the cocoons of the silkworm caterpillars is easy, but breeding the butterfly is difficult because the caterpillars eat only the leaves of the white mulberry tree (*Morus alba*). European silk production was not successful in the long term, mainly because of the unsuitable climate. [Silk: p. 46] Even more valuable than mulberry silk is shell silk or byssus, which was coveted for its golden sheen. It was obtained from the fiber beard of the noble pen shell (*Pinna nobilis*), which is now endangered and strictly protected.[5]

FIBERS CONTAINING CELLULOSE

Fibers from plant stems, the so-called bast fibers, are processed in many individual steps. The bast layer, the phloem, must first be detached from the woody interior of the stem. This is followed by time-consuming cleaning, combing, sorting, and bleaching. The textile use of nettles, hemp, or tree bast has been all but forgotten. Things look a little better with flax. The tools for the individual stages of flax processing are on display in many folklore and local-history museums. However, there are not many people left who have a practical command of flax processing.

With the rise of cotton and, lately, the spread of synthetic fibers after the Second World War, European textile plants became uneconomical. Today, linen and sometimes even hemp clothing is increasingly being offered because it fits in with the current organic trend. In fact, much fewer herbicides and less water are used in their production than in cotton cultivation. More-unusual plant fibers such as bogwood or heather are covered in the chapter "Simple Rope Making." [Raw Materials for Rope Making: p. 68]

→ Whipcording with Horsehair p. 95

→ Hairwork p. 91

→ Silk p. 46

→ Raw Materials for Rope Making p. 68

5 Those who are interested in shell silk can find more information at www.muschelseide.ch.

Stinging Nettle (*Urtica diocia*)

Everyone knows that stinging nettles are weeds and hurt if you touch them carelessly. On the basis of the idea that like can be cured with like, it was used as an herb that burns in the treatment of burning diseases.

Nettle loves nitrogen-rich soil and is therefore also an indicator of human settlements. Because it is often found along fences or in cemeteries, it was thought to have a connection to the world of the dead and spirits.

Very few people today are aware that stinging nettle is a fiber plant. Just like flax, the usable fibers are found around the woody stem under the thin green rind. Nettles are perennial plants that grow permanently in one place. They therefore never had to be cultivated but were simply collected where they grew. Thick, tall stems without many branches are needed for fiber extraction. Experiments have shown that nettles from dense vegetation and shady places produce the best fibers.

However, nettle was never a common raw material for textiles. On the other hand, nettle textiles were an emergency solution when other fibers were unavailable or too expensive. The fiber content of the stinging nettle is only 2 to 4 percent. Up to 66 pounds (30 kg) of nettles had to be collected for a single nettle shirt!

On the other hand, if they were made by hand and not by machines, they were extremely valuable because production was so laborious. One example is Czech bobbin lace made from the finest nettle yarn, which was sewn only onto liturgical textiles or special festive clothing.

In recent years, interest in nettles as a useful plant has grown considerably. Among other things, bush crafters have discovered it as an easy-to-find raw material for twisted cords. Books have even been published that deal exclusively with nettles. [Reading Tips for Stinging Nettle: p. 296]

Nettle fabric is still woven from the Himalayan nettle (*Girardinia diversifolia*) in Nepal today. The Siberian hemp nettle (*Urtica cannabina*) was traditionally used for fiber production in parts of Russia and China.

Today, it is used at most as an admixture to cotton. Another nettle plant is the Asian fiber plant ramie (*Boehmeria japonica*), which is used to make yarn for clothing and indoor textiles.

The oldest thread made of nettle yarn that has been discovered in central Europe to date belongs to the equipment of the Neolithic glacier mummy "Ötzi." The fletching of his arrows was glued on with birch pitch and wrapped in nettle yarn. A bowstring found in Spain also dates to the Neolithic period. The oldest nettle fabric comes from the Danish burial mound at Voldtofte and dates to the Nordic Bronze Age between 940 and 750 BCE. Remains of a very fine fabric made of nettle were found in a bronze urn there. It is particularly remarkable that either the fabric or the fibers had been imported from what is now Austria. The nettle textile from the Viking Age burial ship at Oseberg, Norway, must have been just as precious. Virtually nothing is known about the use of nettle fibers in the Middle Ages. There is evidence of small-scale nettle processing only from the eighteenth century onward.

During the so-called "cotton famine" from 1861 to 1865, as well as during the First and, to a lesser extent, the Second World Wars, nettle was used as a substitute fiber for cotton or as an admixture to other fibers.[6] Fiber nettle, which is bred for high fiber content, is increasingly being cultivated.

Hemp (*Cannabis sativa*)

Hemp was one of the most important fiber plants and was cultivated in Europe, mainly in Russia, Italy, and on the Upper Rhine. Hemp fibers are very tear resistant and can withstand moisture very well. Even the Vikings liked to sew their sails from hemp fabric. However, hemp does not like constant moisture, which is why ropes and cordage made of hemp were often soaked in tar. In archaeological textiles, it is difficult to distinguish among bast fibers such as flax, hemp, or nettle. However, it is certain that the Celts used hemp, since several blankets from the tomb of the Celtic prince of Hochdorf were woven from hemp. In more-modern times, hemp fibers were used to make paper as well as textiles.

Hemp is an undemanding plant that does not require the use of pesticides. The male hemp, fimble hemp, is harvested first. Its fine fibers can be used to make fabrics for clothing. The fibers of the female plants are coarser and are used for ropes and sacks. It is harvested only in midsummer, together with the seeds for the next sowing. Just like flax, hemp is not cut off but is pulled from the ground. The further processing of the harvested plants into fibers is carried out using the same steps as flax processing. [Flax Processing: p. 39]

→ Reading Tips for Stinging Nettle p. 296

6 Detailed history of the modern use of stinging nettle can be found in Václav Michalička, *Die Brennnessel: Kleidendes Unkraut* (Klagenfurt, 2021), 125ff.

Harvesting hemp for fiber at the Center of Traditional Technologies (CETRAT) in Příbor, Czech Republic

Since the 1930s, hemp has been outlawed and later even banned, starting in the USA, due to its content of psychoactive tetrahydrocannabinol (THC) and due to economic interests at the urging of the synthetic-fiber lobby. Today, industrial hemp is once again being cultivated as a food and fiber plant under strict legal conditions. Currently in the EU, only certified varieties from the EU's variety catalog may be grown. In Switzerland, hemp varieties with a THC content of less than 1 percent that are not listed in the EU catalog are also permitted. However, in some cantons there is an obligation to register cultivation.

Linden and Lime Bast

Linden and lime bast is the fiber layer, botanically the phloem, between the wood and bark of varieties of the *Tilia* genus. Compared to other fiber plants, its extraction is relatively simple. In recent years, it has become increasingly clear how important wood bast was as a fiber material in prehistoric times, before people switched to flax and sheep's wool as the main sources of fiber. In Europe, the widest-spread native species is *Tilia cordata*, called lime tree. In North America, the native species include *Tilia americana*, also called linden or basswood.

In 2020, direct evidence of Paleolithic textile craftsmanship was found for the first time: Twisted and knotted fiber remnants had been preserved on a biface from a French rockshelter that had been visited by Neanderthals. They are over forty thousand years old and consist of softwood bast. A particularly beautiful Neolithic find is a spindle with a fine bast thread only 0.7 mm thick, from the Swiss lakeside settlement of Arbon Bleiche on Lake Constance. The Neolithic "pile-dwelling textiles" of the wetland settlements in the foothills of the Alps were "mainly made with the help of wood bast, above all lime bast. . . . The fineness of the young bast from the branches of sticks, when properly processed, was hardly inferior to that of flax fibers."[7] There are even real items of clothing made from lime bast, such as vests, conical hats, or bast shoes. In Neolithic wells, containers made of lime bark with a lime bast wrapping, interpreted as bailer buckets, have been preserved.

A thick rope made from lime bast dates back to the Bronze Age and

Lime bast can be used to make everything from the finest threads to thin cords and strong ropes.

→ Flax Processing p. 39

7 Johanna Banck-Burgess, "Unverzichtbar im Alltag: Textilhandwerk bei den spätneolithischen Pfahlbauern," *Denkmalpflege in Baden-Württemberg* 45.1 (2016): 24–27, here p. 25.

has been preserved in the Hallstatt salt mine. Lime bast ropes are also documented from the early Middle Ages; for example, from the Viking settlement of Haithabu. In modern times, lime bast was used mainly in eastern Europe and Russia. Lapti shoes are a typical product. You can find out how to obtain fibers from processed pieces of linden bark further along. [Extraction of Linden Bast: p. 36]

Flax (*Linum usitatissimum*)

Flax is the plant from which linen is made. The sky-blue flax fields can be seen in mid-June along the coast of the North Sea from Zeeland in the Netherlands to Belgium and the Pas-de-Calais, all the way to Normandy. Other flax-producing countries are Poland, Lithuania, and Ireland. In Germany, Austria, and Switzerland, flax has hardly been cultivated since it was replaced by imported cotton in the nineteenth century.

A distinction is made between tall, branchless fiber flax (also known as common or seed flax) and the low-growing oil flax, with many seed capsules. The flax plant can be used in its entirety, from the roots to the leaves. Its scientific name "the most useful flax" is therefore aptly chosen. Flax oil is pressed from the edible seeds, and the woody stalk is used to make bedding for animals, as kindling, or for building materials such as insulating boards or textile concrete. The bundles of bast fibers, which can be up to 2 feet long (60 cm), can be easily spun into thread. The fabrics woven from them are very durable, are not eaten by pests, and last a lifetime. This also explains why people took on the many different processing steps required.

People from the Palaeolithic Age were already using flax. The oldest discovery of processed flax stalks to date was made in the Caucasus, in the Dzudzuana Cave in Georgia, and is over thirty thousand years old. Some of the flax fibers had been spun into threads and dyed with vegetable dyes. In ancient Egypt, flax was used to make mummy bandages, among other things.

The first flax cultivation in central Europe at the time of the Neolithic Linear Pottery culture probably took place to obtain the seeds as food. Around 4000 BCE, flax textiles can be found in the Neolithic shore settlements of the foothills of the Alps. During this period, flax was the most important source of fiber alongside lime bast.

Sheep's wool was first processed as thread starting in the Bronze Age. Remnants of fishing nets and textiles made from linen were found in excavation sites. It is assumed that flax fibers were deliberately used for

Blooming flax fields invite you to take a trip into the blue.

the nets, since they do not expand when wet. This ensured that the mesh size of the nets remained constant.[8] For the same reason, flax is perfect as a raw material for rope making.

For several thousand years, linen fabrics were an integral part of every household until the nineteenth century, when cotton, which could be grown and processed cheaply thanks to slavery and industrialization, replaced flax (probably for good) as a raw material. The individual steps of flax processing are described further along in the instructions. [Flax Processing: p. 39]

→ Extraction of Linden Bast p. 36

→ Flax Processing p. 39

8 Sabine Karg and Ewald Weber, *Heilsam—kleidsam—wundersam: Pflanzen im Alltag der Steinzeitmenschen,* AiD Sonderheft 15 (Darmstadt, 2019), 51ff.

WHICH FIBER IS IT?

Sometimes it is important to determine the material of the fibers used in a textile; for example, in forensics or when checking whether textiles have been correctly labeled. When recycling used textiles, single-origin fabrics can be processed to a higher quality instead of becoming cleaning rags. Fiber identification is also an important basis for textile archaeology. Every archaeological find is a unique document. For this reason, the analysis should be as nondestructive as possible. Examination with a microscope, in special cases even with a scanning electron microscope, helps here. For a chemical analysis, fibers must be removed and heated in acid or lye.

There may also be reasons for fiber identification in everyday life. Perhaps you want to dye a fabric that you do not know what it is made of. Or you may not tolerate certain fibers due to an allergy. For fiber identification, you can feel the fibers, look at them, smell them, treat them with various substances, or simply burn a fiber sample. This allows you to distinguish whether the fiber is cellulose, protein, or synthetic. If you have ever accidentally burned a hair in a candle flame, you will know the smell of fibers containing protein. It smells exactly the same when you burn sheep's wool or silk. What remains is dark ash. If you hold cellulose-containing fibers in a flame, they burn evenly; that's why candle wicks are made of cotton. It smells like burnt paper, and light-gray ash remains.

For a burning test with synthetic fibers, you should hold only a very small amount in the flame with tweezers and ensure good ventilation due to possible harmful vapors. The smell is unpleasantly "plastic-like." Synthetic fibers melt together to form a hard bead. But please remember: Safety first! Experiment outside or ensure good ventilation, keep long hair and loose clothing out of the way, use tweezers to hold the fibers, use a nonflammable surface, and keep a bowl of water within reach.

Nettle fibers prepared for spinning, with a cross spindle and hand carders in the background

TIPS FROM STINGING-NETTLE EXPERT

MECHTILDE FRINTRUP

- **Natural Retting:** The qualities of the fiber are dependent on the location, climate, and season. The simplest method is natural retting. Nettles whose chlorophyll and sugars have retracted into the root on the stem or have decomposed due to moisture are ideal. When the leaves have fallen off and the stems are no longer green, the fibers easily detach from the wood. On dry slopes or in sunny places, good fiber stalks can sometimes still be found in late winter. However, if the stems are exposed to moisture for too long, the fibers will also decompose.

- **Storage:** Strip or cut off the side shoots and leaves before storing. They will then dry better, cause less dust and dirt, and take up less space. Store in a dry place; otherwise they can become moldy.

- **Fibers in Summer:** In summer it is relatively easy to remove the outer fiber strands from the woody core. The result is moist, green, and long strips. They can be used for cords or for tying up plants. [Splicing: p. 47]

- The fibers tend to tear at the knots of the stem when they are pulled off. Therefore, first pull off the fibers before and after a knot, then remove them with care exactly above the knot. It doesn't work in one go.

- Green stalks can be prepared for spinning by retting the stalks in a similar way to flax. To do this, the stalks are either laid in grass or on a hedge. Or you can put a bundle outside. It is important that the stalks alternate from moist to dry. Dried stems in summer are sometimes also suitable. They no longer need to be retted.

- **Preparing the Fibers:** The fibers removed from about twenty stalks are rubbed between the hands. If you need them for nålbinding [Instructions for Nålbinding: p. 197], it is better to rub them only a little so that they remain as long as possible.

- **Spinning nettle** is best done with a hand spindle. [Spindle Building Instructions: p. 268] As with spinning linen or hemp, the fibers can be twisted together more easily with a little moisture. Short fibers combed with a hand card can also be spun. This produces a slightly thicker, soft thread. Short fibers are also good for making paper.

TRY IT!

HARVESTING AND PROCESSING STINGING NETTLE FOR FIBERS

Look for stinging nettle that has grown as tall as possible. With your hand protected by a work glove or a piece of cloth, grasp the top of the stalk. Now run your hand along the stem from top to bottom. The stinging hairs will fold over, and most of the leaves will tear off. You can now touch the nettle with your bare hands. If you hold the stalk at a distance of approximately 1 foot (30 cm) with both hands and pull it little by little over your thumb or over an edge that is not too sharp (railing, table edge, or similar), the stalk splits into a woody and a fibrous bark part. You can twist the green bast layer between your fingers to form a thread. [Splicing: p. 47]

The woody stem separates from the bast.

The nice thing is that you don't have to grow nettles. Suitable nettles can be found in all kinds of unkept places in the yard or in nature. I let nettles grow in a wild corner of my garden, so that the caterpillars of the peacock, red admiral, and small tortoiseshell butterflies can find something to eat. Various birds pick up the ripe nettle seeds as food. However, there is always enough material left for nettle experiments. If the nettles have spread too much, be sure to save the roots when removing them. You can also use them: Nettle roots dye wool yellow. By the way, nettles are grown to produce food coloring. They contain a particularly high amount of chlorophyll. You can experiment with them in your kitchen and dye powdered sugar or marzipan green, for example. You can find instructions for this on the internet.

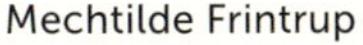

Mechtilde Frintrup
Baden-Württemberg, Germany

Mechtilde Frintrup grew up on a farm. After training and studying in the field of design and advertising, she spent time in the Andes in Argentina, where she was able to learn the Indigenous art of pottery and get to know "life outdoors." She then worked for many years as a media designer and book producer, while also training in medicinal herbs.

Frintrup gives lectures and leads seminars on the subject of nettle (and nettle fiber) and leads nature and herb walks with a practical-artistic focus.

www.andas-werkstatt.com

Book Tip

Mechtilde Frintrup, *Das Brennnesselbuch—Die magische Nahrungs-, Heil- und Faserpflanze* (Aarau, Switzerland, and Munich: AT Verlag, 2022).

→ Instructions for Nålbinding p. 197

→ Spindle-Building Instructions p. 268

→ Splicing p. 47

TIPS FOR EXRACTING LINDEN BAST FROM ARCHAEOTECHNICIAN WULF HEIN

- The bast can be removed from linden and lime trees only in spring, when the sap is rising in the tree. The rule of thumb is early May to mid-June, but this varies from year to year and from tree to tree. Young branchless trees with smooth bark are suitable, up to approximately 1 foot (30 cm) in diameter. An incision is made in the bark at the bottom, and the bark is removed from the tree in long strips.

- These are rolled up and placed in water for three to six weeks, a process known as retting. Microbes break down the bonds between the individual layers of bast, which can then be separated from each other. The soaking time depends on the temperature. You have to try several times to see if the layers are separating. Slightly flowing water is the best, but the bast can also be retted in rain barrels.

- The smell of the soaked bark pieces is very unpleasant, so it is best to wear thick rubber gloves and old clothing.

- After the bast has been separated into individual layers, everything is then rinsed thoroughly with plenty of water and hung in the sun to dry. Now the bast will smell very pleasant.

- The outer layers under the bark are very coarse and best suited for ropes. The inner layers closest to the wood can be used well as thin string when twined. In prehistoric times, lime bast was also used to make items of clothing such as cloaks and hats.

Wulf Hein

Hesse, Germany

Wulf Hein, a trained joiner, has been working in the field of experimental archaeology and archaeotechnology for thirty years. He has played a key role in the construction of several open-air archaeological sites, worked on film and television projects, and is the author of numerous books and articles on archaeological topics. His replicas and reconstructions of prehistoric and ancient finds and features are presented in many international exhibitions and museums.

www.arc-tech.de

Articles on www.academia.edu

Book Tip

Wulf Hein and Marquardt Lund, *FlintHandWerk* (Ludwigshafen, Germany: Verlag Angelika Hörnig, 2017).

TRY IT!

LINDEN BAST PREPARATION

The separated lime bast strips dry in the sun.

Do you know a linden or lime tree that grows next to a busy road? You will almost certainly find branches shredded by car tires on the road, where you can easily recognize the fibers. You can also cut off one of the water sprouts that often come off the bottom of the lime tree trunk. The bark of the sprout can easily be peeled off together with the bast. Although the bast layer is still thin here, it can easily be twisted between your fingers to form a thread sample.

Obtaining bast fibers is very easy if you have linden or lime bark available. It's worth keeping an eye out for fallen branches after a storm. The processing steps are described on the facing page and shown in the photos.

The finished bast strips can be split into even-narrower strips. If you want to do it the Stone Age way, tie several blackthorns together to form a comb and run it through the bast. Alternatively, you can use a brush with metal bristles or a fingernail to split the bast strips. Before processing into threads, cords, and ropes, moisten the bast slightly to soften it. How splicing, spinning, and twining work is described in the next chapter. Even untwisted strips of bast are good as binding material in the garden or for wrapping the individual layers of baskets, using the coil method.

Retting in running water.

→ Spinning Without a Spinning Wheel p. 45

Flax in the garden bed: oil flax in front, fiber flax in the back

TRY IT!

PLANTING FLAX AND EXTRACTING FIBERS

If you want to grow flax, you need special fiber flax, which is grown on long stems. Depending on what you want to use the fibers for, you need different-sized garden beds. In older writings about growing flax, it was said that one needed to plant about a square meter of flax in order to obtain a square meter of fabric. You can use the information on the seed package as reference. There it tells you how much space you need.

Before planting, the earth with be hoed and loosened. The traditional planting day is the hundredth day of the year—the middle of April. In colder areas, you can still plant into May. Once the flax has reached a certain height, it must be supported so that it doesn't break during strong rains. For this, a few sticks can be put in the garden bed, and strings can be run between them.

When the seed capsules start turning brown and the first leaves fall off, the flax can be harvested. The plants are not cut but, rather, pulled completely from the ground. Then the seeds can be removed. If you don't have time to start rippling, the flax can start drying out. The removal of the seed casings, rippling, can be done on a small scale quite easily simply by stripping with your fingers.

Metal combs with coarse prongs were used in farm households, and in some areas, self-made combs out of wood were used. This kind of wooden comb can be easily reproduced. [Instructions for Rippling Comb: p. 266]

A self-made miniature flax break. ›

During the subsequent retting, the firm connection between the flax stem and the bast is separated. There is "dew retting" and "water retting." Water retting is recommended only if your neighbors are capable of suffering or live far away. The smell of the rotting stems is something else. The flax is laid in a cement tub, an old bathtub, a wading pool, or similar. Under high summer temperatures, three to four days can be enough, but in cooler weather, retting can take a couple of days longer. Test if the fibers can be easily separated each day. Careful: Don't wait too long for the stems to become mushy. At this point, the stems have become too decomposed and are no longer intact. Once they have been dried, the stink will disappear.

In earlier times, the pits used for flax retting were established beyond village limits due to the smell. Here are retting pits that are over one hundred years old in Wegberg-Beeck, Germany.

For dew retting, the fibers are spread on the lawn and periodically turned. Dew retting takes at least two weeks.

The old flax hackles from the flea market still work today.

Breaking flax with a meat mallet

Once retted, the flax must be thoroughly dried. Leave your harvest spread out in a sheltered place for a few days and turn it from time to time. It is best to choose a hot summer day for the next step. When the stalks "crack like glass" when bent, as the old instructions say, they are ready to be broken. The traditional method is to use a "crusher" or a "bott-hammer." Alternatively, use a wooden hammer or wooden meat mallet to hit a layer of stalks that is not too thick. A wooden cutting board from the kitchen or a slice of tree can be used as a base. When beating, the woody parts of the stalk, the "shives," detach from the fibers. Residual shives always remain attached. These are removed when combing or hackling. [Instructions for Flax Hackle: p. 267]

Now pull the flax through the nails of the hackle in bundles. Hold the bundle firmly and be careful not to catch the nails. Once this process has been repeated a few times, take hold of the other side and pull through a few more times. Most of the shives should now have fallen off. The fibers that you hold in your hand are the best quality. All other fibers that have fallen off during breaking or hackling are called "tow." In the past, tow was used to make coarse fabrics; for example, aprons and sacks. It was also an important raw material for rope making. Be sure to save your tow. You can use it for simple rope making or for spinning exercises.
[Simple Rope Making: p. 67]

You can find old tools used for processing flax at flea and antique markets. For first attempts, however, self-made tools are more than enough. Now you are ready to process your own flax fibers. You will learn more about spinning and twisting ropes in the next chapters. [Spinning: p. 45]
[Simple Rope Making: p. 67]

INSTRUCTIONS

→ Instructions for Rippling Comb p. 266

→ Instructions for Flax Hackle p. 267

→ Spinning p. 45

→ Simple Rope Making p. 67

TIPS FOR GROWING FLAX FROM THE WEGBERG-BEECK FLAX MUSEUM

- If you want to grow flax only for its beautiful blue flowers, use flaxseed from the supermarket or drugstore. However, it flowers for a period of only ten days, each individual flower for just one day. To obtain fiber, you need to buy special seeds.

- You can easily measure the seeds: one shot glass full is enough for 1 square meter. Incidentally, it used to be said that flax had to be sown so densely that ten grains would stick to your wet thumb when you press it on the ground.

- You can be sparing when watering. As long as the seed is still germinating, the soil should be kept moist. No extra watering is required later on.

Linen cloth begun on a loom in the flax museum ›

- Retting flax works well in an old bathtub placed in the yard. The stalks are weighed down so that they are underwater. When the bast can be easily removed from the stalk, the retting is complete. When drying the flax afterward, be sure to fan it out loosely and turn it often so that it does not rot.

- In the past, the retted flax was dried in ovens or on drying pits before it was crushed. This is not necessary for small-scale flax processing. It is sufficient if the flax is well dried.

Flax Museum
North Rhine–Westphalia, Germany

The flax museum in Wegberg-Beeck ensures that the flax-growing tradition from the Lower Rhine is not forgotten. It is a museum for touching. School classes and other visitors can try the individual steps of flax processing and earn a "flax diploma." The local club Wegberg-Beeck e.V. demonstrates flax processing from around 1850 on historical equipment during external presentations, including at the yearly flax market in Krefeld-Linn.

www.beecker-erlebnismuseen.de

Linen products and literature can be found in the small museum store.

THE DIFFERENCE BETWEEN

SPINNING AND SPLICING

During draft spinning, the fibers, which are prepared in many steps, are continuously pulled out of a fiber bundle and twisted into a single thread. This single thread is stable if it is well spun. [Instructions for Processing Flax: p. 39] In contrast, when splicing, individual fiber strands, which can be freshly pulled from the plant, are overlapped during the twisting process. A thread produced in this way is not stable on its own. It becomes stable only when it is twined (plied) in the same process. This means that spliced fibers must be twined. Splicing is the older technique from which spinning developed.[9] [Instructions for Splicing: p. 47]

9 Margarita Gleba and Susanna Harris, "The First Plant Bast Fibre Technology: Identifying Splicing in Archaeological Textiles," *Archaeological and Anthropological Sciences* 11 (2018): 2329–2346.

SPINNING WITHOUT A SPINNING WHEEL

The simplest spinning method works completely without tools, by twisting the fibers between the palms of your hands or on your thighs. In addition to the well-known hand spindle, there are other spinning tools such as branch hooks, branch whorls, and spinning crosses.

→ Instructions for Processing Flax p. 39

→ Instructions for Splicing p. 47

→ Twining p. 183

→ Slip Stitch Crochet p. 239

→ Silk p. 25

WHY SPINNING?

All textiles consist of short to infinitely long, thin units of flexible material that are joined together. The basic form of the textile raw material is the fiber.[10] Fibers are usually twisted around each other before processing. Depending on the technique, this is called splicing or spinning. However, there are a few techniques in which the fibers can be processed into textiles without being spun. These include twining [Twining: p. 183] and slip stitch crochet. [Slip Stitch Crochet: p. 239] For both, you can use wool "fresh from the sheep" or wool left hanging on fences and bushes. This produces particularly thick and fluffy garments. For most textile techniques, however, spun yarn is required as a starting material.

10 But the willow rods used for basket weaving are also a basic textile material. Woven baskets are technically textiles.

Why are fibers twisted? Natural fibers have a certain length, usually only a few centimeters (exception: silk, see below). [Silk: p. 25] By either splicing or spinning them, it is possible to continually create new fibers.

The new fiber section is clamped in the twist. This results in an endless thread. The thread also becomes more stable because the individual fibers twisted around each other and pressed together act as a single thicker thread (friction, frictional resistance). The twisting prevents them from loosening or slipping. They hold on to each other.

However, a single spliced thread can untwist on its own if it is not under tension. This can be prevented by plying or twining two or more individual threads together in the opposite direction. The result is a twine in which the twist is fixed. At best, it can become loose at the ends, which can be prevented by knotting or by rope splicing. It was also treated with a material that glues the fibers together. In weaving, the longitudinal (= warp) threads were sized on the loom in the case of flax or glued in the case of wool. The size is a thin flour paste, bone glue, or gelatine used for gluing.

Only one natural fiber is almost infinite: **silk**. The thread that forms the cocoon of the silkworm is several hundred yards long, wound up almost endlessly. Silk therefore does not have to be spun, but only unwound from the cocoon. First, at least three cocoon threads are unwound, or more, depending on the desired thread thickness. However, because this thread is still too thin for textile production, several raw-silk threads are twisted together. In the silk trade, the technical term for this twisting is "doubling."[11] Of course, silk from China was not available to ordinary households in Europe; the silk trade was always in the hands of entrepreneurs.[12] In Europe, flax, hemp, and sheep's wool [Fiber Raw Materials: p. 23], all of which belong to the staple fibers and therefore have a limited length, were mainly used.

11 The prerequisite for twisting is that the individual threads already have their own twist (in the opposite direction). In so-called silk mills, the threads to be plied were twisted in one direction during unwinding and were twined in the other direction in the same process.

12 In the eighteenth century in particular, attempts were made to establish their own silk production in various places in Germany. White mulberry trees were planted on mulberry plantations as food crops for the silkworm caterpillars. Ultimately, these ventures failed due to the high costs and unsuitable climate.

In the following pages you will learn how to spin with simple spindles. Perhaps you would like to buy your own spinning wheel later on. The transition will be easy if you have practiced spindle spinning beforehand. But first I would like to introduce you to a yarn-creating technique that does not require any tools at all: splicing with your hands.

SPLICING

Strictly speaking, two operations have to be carried out at the same time during splicing: the actual splicing and the twining (plying). Two strands of a fiber material are twisted or spliced separately in one direction. Only when they are twisted together in the opposite direction—twining—do the two individual strands intertwine, and the spin is fixed. The result is a stable twine, a cord made of two threads.

The two possible directions of rotation are figuratively referred to as the S-twist and Z-twist, with the slanted center of the letters indicating the winding direction. So if each fiber strand is twisted around itself in the S direction, the two strands are twisted around each other in the Z direction.

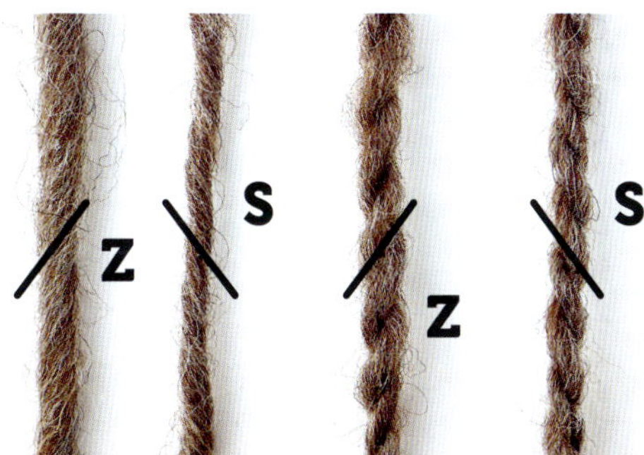

To the left, two single threads; *to the right,* two twined threads.

Splicing is the oldest method of producing yarn from fibers. It is known in all Indigenous societies around the world, on all continents. This includes the San in the Kalahari, the Maya in Central America, and the Salish, Tlingit, and Haida in northwestern America. Until recently, coarse, thicker ropes were also made in this way in Europe. Some examples are the ropes for roofing made from heather on the Hebrides, cords made from lime bast for fastening bast shoes in Latvia, cobbler's twine in

→ Fiber Raw Materials: p. 23

Norway, straw and grass ropes for covering thatched roofs in Schleswig, and ropes made from "bog wood" for covering bedsteads in Ireland. [Raw Material for Ropes: p. 68]

For splicing, you need only

1. the fingers or
2. mouth and both hands or
3. two palms or
4. a palm and a thigh.

It is best to practice splicing and plying with another person first. Then you can try it alone, using only the fingers of both hands. This may not be quick, but it gives you good control over the process. You can hold the twisted end of the yarn with your mouth. Splicing between the palms requires skill, especially because you don't have a free hand to attach new threads to lengthen the cord. The quickest method is splicing on the thigh: either the bare leg or using a piece of leather or sturdy fabric as a base. In the first step, the flat hand is pushed over two strands of fiber, pulling them along slightly and giving them a twist. In the second step, these two strands twist around each other independently when released.

Freshly stripped nettle bast is twisted in.

Twisted and dried nettle cord

TRY IT!

SPLICING AND PLYING IN PAIRS

You may remember this cord twisting from kindergarten. You can either use colorful yarn remnants or any fiber material; for example, stinging nettle or flax.

1 Two people stand across from each other. Each person has an end of a strand of thread in their hand and turns this end between their fingers. You have to decide on a direction; for example, both people turn the strand to their right. You twist until the strand begins to twist in on itself. Don't let go of the ends!

2 One person now grabs the thread at the middle of the strand. The two ends are folded on top of each other and held firmly between your fingers. The end with the fold is now released: The two halves of the strand twist around themselves, and the cord is now plied.

SPLICING AND PLYING WITH YOUR FINGERS

Plying with just your fingers is a very useful technique, since you can quickly twist a string from many natural materials on the side without any tools.

1 Fold a strand of fiber of your preferred thickness in half and hold the folded end in one hand.

2 Using the fingers of the other hand, turn the fiber string ends away from you clockwise and then place it over the other strand in the opposite direction (toward you), so that the two ends have now swapped positions.

3 Now this strand is twisted away from itself and laid over the first one to the front, and the new twist is immediately fixed with the holding hand (see photo above). Spreading the ends of the strands apart promotes a tight twist of the cord.

4 If a strand ends or thins, simply add more fibers overlapping and twist them in. This creates a knotless, endless cord.

Keep all three ends taut while working. The resulting cord can be led around the fingers of the left hand and pinched, just as when knitting. Alternatively, you can hold the end of the cord with your mouth.

→ Raw Material for Ropes: p. 68

SPLICING AND PLYING WITH YOUR PALMS

To practice the movement, you can work with single-thread wool roving or felting wool used for sock felting. However, this purchased wool is already slightly twisted, which must be taken into account when you are plying. If the yarn has a Z-twist (see photo on page 47), work toward you. This twists the yarn more strongly and reinforces the existing Z-twist. If it has an S-twist, the movement of the palm of your hand on your thigh should be away from your body.

[Thread Twist: p. 47]

Materials: Separate a thread of about an arm's length from the ball of yarn. Do not cut it but tear it off. This creates frayed ends that are easier to join together later. Fold the thread in half. Hold it together at the bend with your left hand. Lay it across the thigh so that both strands are barely separated from each other.

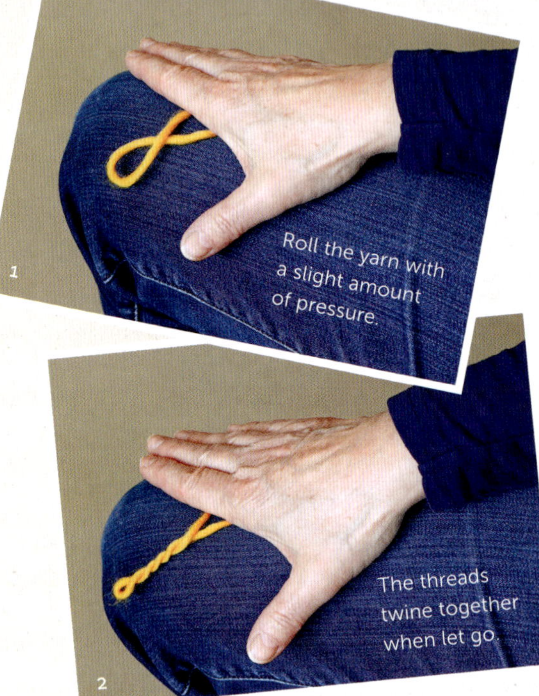

1 Run the palm of your right hand over both ends of the yarn (depending on the direction in which the yarn is twisted; see above). Work loosely, with only a light amount of pressure, is if you were petting, which is easier on your hand.

2 Let go with your left hand—both halves will twine together automatically.

Pull the finished spliced yarn a little farther along the thigh until two individual threads are lying next to each other again. Continue splicing as described.

3 Once the first thread is used up, start two new threads by overlapping. Stagger the points of attachment slightly in height.

4 Continue splicing as described above.

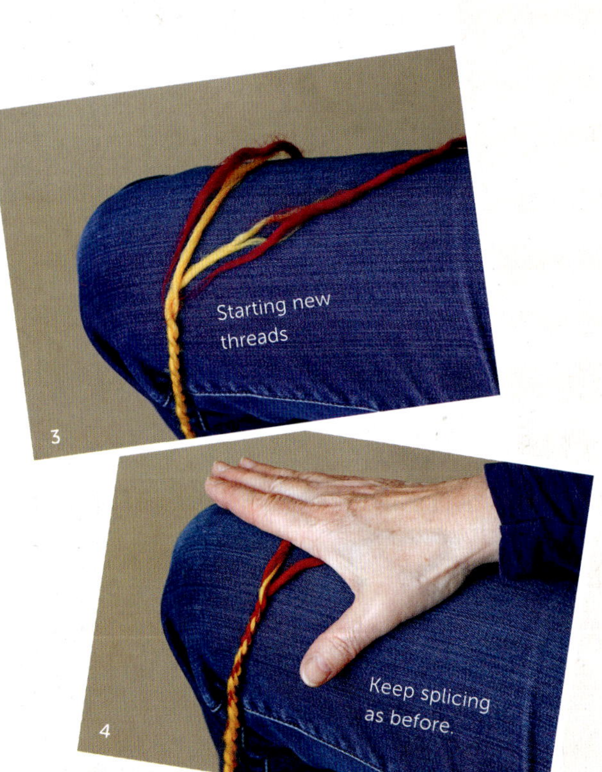

For a better hold, the right "grip," a little moisture in the threads, can help. For this, slightly moisten the wool, using, for example, a spray bottle.

SPINNING

For spinning, you need a tool on which the finished yarn can be secured. The twisting of fibers to a single-thread yarn and the twining or plying of two or more threads are two separate operations. Plying can be done with the same tool as spinning.

A very simple spinning device is the branch hook, which can be carved from any branch fork. [Branch Hook Instructions: p. 268] When spinning, you hold the branch hook loosely in your hand and let it rotate around its longitudinal axis. To make this easier, a modification of the simple hook has been devised in Latvia and Finland: the rotating handle sleeve. A small wooden tube is pushed onto the end of the handle, which is prevented from slipping with a pin. The tube is held firmly in the hand while the branch can rotate loosely around itself in this sleeve.[13] Place the finished thread in figure eights around the branch fork. You can also place the branch hook on your thigh and twist it by passing your flattened hand over it. The branch hook is just as suitable for spinning fine yarn as it is for twisting strong ropes. The branch-hook rope maker works in pairs [Simple Rope Making: p. 72]. Any fiber material can be used.

A further development of the branch hook as a spinning device is the simple hand winch. [Hand Winch Instructions: p. 272] Relatives of the spinning hook are the spinning cross, a longer stick with a shorter crosspiece attached to it (handed down from Finland and Great Britain), and the naturally grown branch whorl, which was used in Slovakia.

It is no longer possible to determine when the branch hook was first used for spinning. However, it is assumed that the technique has been known since the Bronze Age at the latest. The modern use of the branch hook is documented from many regions: from southern Europe (including Corsica), east-central Europe (including Latvia, Slovakia, Ukraine), and Scandinavia (including Sweden, Norway, Finland). The Swedish *snokrok*, for example, was used to twist whipcords from horsehair. The Sami in the Lofoten Islands use the hook to make fishing lines from the same material.[14] In Jølster, Norway, the spinning hook was still being used until the 1960s. The spinning hook was also known in northeastern Africa. The Beni-Amer in Sudan spun wool with a fine wooden hook that was held like a spindle.[15]

13 Martha Bielenstein describes it visually in her book *Die altlettischen Färbmethoden* (Michelstadt, Germany, 1995) (reprint of the 1935 edition), 55.

14 Else Østergaard, *Woven into the Earth: Textiles from Norse Greenland* (Aarhus, Denmark, 2004, 47.

15 Grace M. Crowfoot, *Methods of Hand Spinning in Egypt and the Sudan* (Halifax, UK, 1931).

→ Thread Twist p. 47

→ Branch Hook Instructions p. 268

→ Simple Rope Making p. 72

→ Hand Winch Instructions p. 272

In the Center of Traditional Technologies (CETRAT) in Příbor, Czech Republic, the loosening of sheep's wool is shown with hand cards.

The supposedly ancient metal spinning hooks found in Ephesus, for example, were actually metal attachments for wooden spindle rods. They were used in France, Greece, and southern Italy and date from the nineteenth and twentieth centuries.[16]

16 Margarita Gleba, *Textile Production in Pre-Roman Italy* (Oxford, 2008).

Along with a spindle or a spinning wheel, branch hooks are also used for spinning at CETRAT.

TRY IT!

SPINNING WITH A HOOK

You can simply use any kind of hook-shaped item from your house, such as a clothes hanger. Spinners use the pull-through hook of the spinning wheel. Tie a thread to the hook (a scrap of any knitting yarn will do—pack twine is also suitable for this experiment). Turn the hook in the same direction as the yarn is turned. You will notice how the yarn becomes tighter and wants to twist around itself after a short time.

SPINNING WITH THE BRANCH HOOK

You will need a branch hook [Branch Hook Instructions: p. 268] and a small amount of unspun sheep's wool. It can even be raw, unwashed wool that you found on a fence or a bush. It works just as well with wool bought from shepherds or a spinning supplier. Maybe you even have some leftover so-called fairy wool (combed and colorfully dyed sheep's wool).

1 Pull the unspun wool out to a length of a few inches and twist it into a loose thread with your fingers.

2 Knot this initial thread around the branch hook and pull out more wool (with care—do not tear the wool).

3 Turn the branch hook in your hand or roll it on your thigh. Twist until a tight thread is formed. However, do not overtwist the thread. You will recognize this when it starts to curl and twist around itself.

Wrap the finished yarn in figure eights around the hook. Then continue spinning as described above.

4 When the wool is used up, start new wool. To do this, pull out the end of a lock of wool to a point and overlap it with the rest of the wool that has already been spun. The attachment point can be slightly overtwisted so that it holds better.

SPINDLES

A device that uses an oscillating weight to rotate the fibers attached to it is called a spindle. The technique is basically the same as for the branch hook described above. The finished spun yarn is attached to the spindle rod. Additional fibers are gradually fed in while the spindle is rotated around itself.

There are countless variations of hand spindles. They usually consist of a thin spindle rod and a weight attached to it, which is known as a spindle whorl. Such spindles can be bought, for example, in school supplies or wool stores. Today, the spindle rod and spindle whorl are usually made of wood. However, there are also spindles made of metal, such as the *takli*, the small Indian spindles used for processing cotton. The same applies to Greek iron spindles, which were used for twisting cobbler's thread. These types of spindles can (but do not have to be) released during spinning.

1. If the spindle dangles downward, it is called a drop spindle.
2. When the spindle rests on a surface during spinning, it's called supported spinning. The supported spindle runs on the floor or in a bowl.
3. Spindles can also be rolled on the thigh, like the branch hooks for spinning.

A selection of self-made spindles

→ Branch Hook Instructions p. 268

VARIOUS SPINNING WHORLS

The whorl can be at the top (top or high whorl spindle), in the middle, or at the bottom (bottom or low whorl spindle) of the spindle rod. Modern whorls are usually made of wood, but you can also buy some made of cast resin or brightly colored glass. Traditionally, the whorls were made of ceramic, stone (soapstone, serpentine, tuff), bone, or metal (lead). Some French whorls have an attached, pointed end cap made of sheet copper with a hook or spiral groove. It is known from various Scottish locations that sometimes a potato or an apple was used instead of a spindle whorl.

A spindle whorl does not necessarily have to be circular. In Jordan, there are whorls made from a simple rectangular wooden board. If the whorl consists of two removable pieces of wood attached crosswise, it is a cross spindle. Cross spindles can be found in Turkey and Iraq, among other places. A museum in the Spanish Basque Country also has a cross spindle.[17] In India and Pakistan, cross spindles are used to twist sturdy cords or ropes.

WHORL-ONLY SPINDLE

Various spindles do not require a spindle rod: The Chinese tool for spinning cotton or hemp yarn is very special. Here, a bone with a hole in the middle was used as a swing weight. A small bamboo hook was inserted into the hole, to which the thread was attached. In Scotland, spindles called imp-stones were used. A depression was drilled into round stones picked up on the beach. An iron hook was attached to this hole, and the thread was hung from it. The hook was fixed with lead, a wooden peg, or cork.

Hourglass-shaped wooden spindles, which look similar to a diabolo, were used in China ("spinning hammer"), Bulgaria,[18] and the Basque country in northern Spain.[19] In Basque, this spindle is called *txabila, txatila*, or *txoatile*. It is said to be named after a small black bird named txoa, because it turns in the same way as the txoa does during its mating dance. Tile means wool (i.e., txoatile). Here too, the transverse piece is the actual

17 Museo San Telmo, Catálogo online, Object Nr. E-000232.

18 Christo Vakarelski, *Bulgarische Volkskunde* (Berlin, 1969).

19 Georg Buschan, *Illustrierte Völkerkunde* (Stuttgart, 1926), image 317.

swinging mass, with a hook attached to the top center as a hanger. The txoatile was used by shepherds and farmers for spinning wool yarn for stockings and ropes. The dumbbell-shaped wooden spindle, which was used in China and the Basque country, is similar in its construction. [Dumbbell Spindle Instructions: p. 269]

SPINDLE ROD ONLY

It also works the other way round (i.e., a spindle that consists only of the spindle rod but has no whorl). This is the so-called spinning stick, which is known from Switzerland and the Netherlands, among other places. It actually consists only of a stick. The transition to wooden spindles made from one piece, on which the spindle whorl was turned, is continual. Such one-piece spindles can be found in Russia, Ukraine, and Bulgaria. Identical medieval spindles from France show that this type of spindle is very old. They were found, along with many other wooden objects, during the excavation of the Colletière settlement from the eleventh century. The conical Scottish *dealgan* (pronounced ʤɛləgən or θɛləxən) also has no whorl, but only a thicker and thinner end. Two notches are carved into the lower, thicker end, which cross at right angles. The thread is passed through these and then attached to the thin end at the top. It was used mainly for twining single threads of homespun wool yarn but also works for spinning. The advantage of this compact spindle is that it is indestructible, and the spun yarn can be wound into a ball directly on it, similar to the cross spindle. [Cross Spindle: p. 56] Scottish emigrants brought this spindle shape to North America, where it was still used for a time in Nova Scotia, Canada [Dealgan Instructions: p. 268]

→ Dumbbell Spindle Instructions p. 269

→ Cross Spindle Instructions p. 56

→ Dealgan Instructions p. 268

FROM STONE AGE SPINDLES TO THE HAND-SPINNING REVIVAL

1 The spindle was invented

Spindles have existed since the end of the Neolithic period, initially probably only for plying spliced plant fibers, not yet for actual spinning.[20] Ceramic production, including for spinning whorls, is part of the "Neolithic package" of technological innovations in central Europe starting around 5500 BCE.

2 The spindle is the standard tool for creating thread

From the Bronze Age to the High Middle Ages, the thirteenth century, so more than three thousand years!!

3 The spinning wheel as competition

In the thirteenth century, the spinning wheel with manual operation (spindle wheel) appeared and was viewed critically from the outset: In 1268 the spinning wheel was banned in Paris, and around 1280 in Speyer, only the spinning of weft yarn was allowed with the spinning wheel—the spindle was to be used for warp yarn.

4 Spindle and spinning wheel alongside each other

After the handwheel had become established, it was used for wool. However, flax and hemp continued to be spun with spindle and distaff. From the fifteenth century onward, there is the hand-operated flyer wheel (spinning and winding the thread in one operation) and, from the mid-seventeenth century, the foot treadle flyer wheel. It gradually replaced the spindle. Nevertheless, even in modern times, spindle-spun yarn is still considered to be of higher quality, since it is "stronger, more beautiful, and more uniform."[21]

5 Spindle solely for special purposes

In some places, the spindle is still used for warp yarn and the spinning wheel for weft yarn. In 1865[22] the spindle was used in Saxony "in the Meissen region" to make particularly strong sewing thread from hemp for shoemakers.

6 Spindle obsolete

At the end of the nineteenth century, the use of the spindle was mentioned only as a curiosity: "Yes, in some parts of Germany, spinning is still done with the spindle."[23] Today, this traditional spindle spinning exists only in a few rural regions in Europe, including Bulgaria, Turkey, Italy, Spain, and Portugal.

7 Hand-spinning revival

The hand-spinning revival began at the end of the 1960s in the USA through the back-to-the-land movement. At the end of the 1970s through the 1980s, hand spinning was also modern in Germany. Because the technique of spinning with a distaff had been forgotten here, spinning with a wooden drop spindle without a distaff was adopted from the USA. Today, spinning with a spindle and distaff is used mainly in medieval living history groups.

20 See Gleba and Harris 2018.

21 Erdmuthe Hülfreichinn, *Unterricht für Hausmütter* (Vienna, 1807).

22 *Die kulturwissenschaftliche Sammlung des Hofraths Dr. Gustav Klemm in Dresden*, Teil 3, *Das Ausland* 38 (1865): 345–349.

23 Richard Andree, *Braunschweiger Volkskunde* (Braunschweig, Germany, 1896), 223.

^
The bobbin winder for winding the yarn for the loom has almost the same design as the medieval spindle wheel.

›
In Sweden, Josefin Waltin spins as it was done in the Middle Ages.

SPINDLE SPINNING

Building instructions for various spindles can be found in the Tool Workshop. [Spindle-Building Instructions: p. 268] You can use flax tow as fiber material for your first attempts. These fibers are relatively thick. This makes it easy to recognize and understand the principle of spinning. Unfortunately, this rough material is not particularly skin-friendly. If you have sensitive skin, it is therefore better to start with sheep's wool. You can order easy-to-spin wool from specialty dealers (ask for wool for beginners!). Local sheep farmers will also be happy to supply raw wool. You have the best chance of getting good spinning wool if the shepherds also spin wool themselves and can therefore assess the suitability of the material. Coarse impurities, especially burrs, thistles, and straw, must be removed from the wool before spinning. If the wool is clean, it does not necessarily need to be washed. Choose the most beautiful and cleanest wool. The wool grease (lanolin) gives you free skin care while spinning.

Diabolo and dumbbell spindles are whorl-only spindles. They are used as drop spindles, meaning they hang below the yarn supply. With the *dealgan*, you can choose to spin in the medieval way (i.e., with a distaff and spindle held sideways in your hand). Or you can use it as a drop spindle. [Dealgan: p. 57]

It is easiest to learn spinning when being shown by a spinner. Instruction videos on the internet can also be a big help.[24] As a preliminary exercise, you should first try spinning with the branch hook. [Branch Hook: p. 54] Then spinning with a spindle will come much more easily.

24 For example, Lois Swales shows spinning with different spindles in her videos, with and without distaffs. In *Spin Like You're Scottish*, she demonstrates spinning with the dealgan. The videos from Chantal-Manou Müller, alias chantimanou, are also very informative about various themes revolving around spinning.

SPINNING WITH A WHORL-ONLY SPINDLE

1 Secure a short yarn remnant as your starting thread on the spindle hook. You can also make the beginning thread yourself—for this, turn the end of a wool lock between your fingers to make a thread and knot this on the hook.

2 Pull a small tuft of fibers from the fiber supply, twist it into a loose thread with your fingers, and knot it to the starting thread. If you started at step 1 with a self-twisted starting thread, you can skip the knotting. You then start spinning directly at 3.

3 Hold the fiber supply in your left hand. Slowly turn the spindle with your right hand. Remember the direction of rotation: You must maintain this during spinning; otherwise the thread that has already been spun will unravel again.

Always turn the spindle in the same direction.

Pull out more fibers.

4 Pull out more fibers before the twist is transferred to the fiber supply. Pull the fibers with care; do not pull them with too much force. The connection to the supply must not be torn off. To prevent the spindle from turning in the opposite direction when pulling out the fibers, simply hold it against your stomach to stop it. Then you can work on the fiber supply without any time pressure.

5 When the thread is so long that you can no longer reach the spindle with your right hand, pick up the spindle. Wind the finished thread around the spindle. Hook the end of the yarn into the hook. The spinning starts again.

→ Spindle-Building Instructions p. 268

→ Dealgan p. 57

→ Branch Hook p. 54

TIPS FROM SPINNER

ULRIKE CLASSEN-BÜTTNER

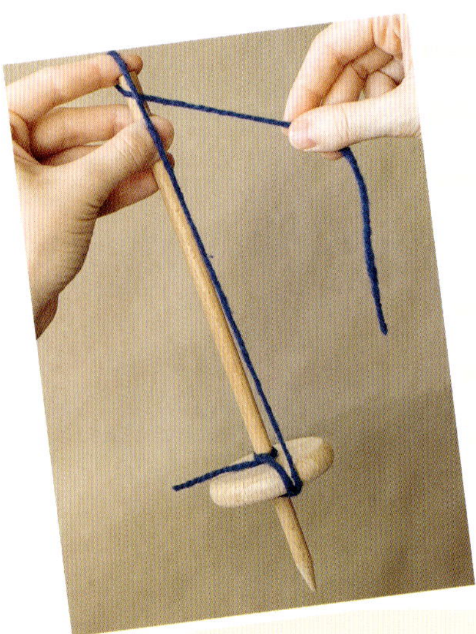

Ulrike Claßen-Büttner
North Rhine–Westphalia, Germany

Ulrike Claßen-Büttner has busied herself with prehistoric textile techniques since getting her archaeology degree in Cologne. For the Römer und Bajuwaren Museum in Kipfenberg, she developed the interactive exhibition *Spinnst Du?*, which was subsequently shown as a traveling exhibition in various museums. The book accompanying the exhibition was followed by further publications. In addition to textile technology, her topics include creative upcycling and positive psychology. She gives courses and runs stalls at museum festivals and craft markets. She is currently planning to open a creative workshop with a studio and gallery.

www.ulrikeclassenbuettner.de

Book Tips

Ulrike Claßen-Büttner, *Spinnst Du? Na klar! Geschichte, Technik und Bedeutung des Spinnens von der Handspindel über das Spinnrad bis zu den Spinnmaschinen der Industriellen Revolution* (Books on Demand, 2009).

Ulrike Claßen-Büttner: *Nålbinding—What in the World Is That? History and Technique of an Almost Forgotten Handicraft* (Books on Demand, 2015).

- Sheep's wool for spinning can be bought either combed (combed top) or carded (roving). Carded wool is recommended as a starting fiber, since the individual fibers are still intertwined. This prevents the thread from breaking so quickly. Once you have had some practice, you can try the parallel fibers in the combed yarn, which allow you to pull out the wool very finely and evenly.

- First, a few "dry runs" with the hand spindle: Knot a scrap of thread to the spindle, guide it around the spindle as shown in the image in the top left, and hook it at the tip or tighten it with an inverted loop. Now leave the spindle hanging on the thread and turn it at the top of the spindle rod with the other hand. Spend a few minutes practicing both the even twisting and the correct winding of the finished yarn onto the spindle.

- You should also practice drafting—pulling the wool out of the fiber supply—in advance without a spindle. Take a handful of wool loosely in one hand and pull out a few fiber tips with the thumb and forefinger of the other hand: The so-called drafting triangle is formed. The fibers pulled out can now be twisted between the fingers to form a first piece of thread.

• To start, perform the following steps with the hand spindle, one after another. The smooth transition will appear following a little practice.

1 To connect the loose wool with the secured starting thread on the spindle, fray the end of the thread in a fan shape.

2 Place this fan on or in the loose wool and hold this area firmly while you turn the spindle hanging on the thread. You can also knot the wool to the starting thread (see photo on the right).

3 When the spindle has built up enough twist in the thread, stop it and lean it against your leg so that it does not turn back in the other direction.

4 Now draw out some loose wool together with the fan and let the twist formed by the turning run into this fiber triangle. The initial thread and wool supply are now connected. If there is still a lot of twist in the thread, you can pull out another drafting triangle and let it run in. If not, the spindle must be turned again.

5 To do this, the transition area between the loose wool and the start of the thread (drafting zone) is held firmly again, so that the spindle can be left hanging and given a new spin. If the newly spun thread is too long, it must be wound onto the spindle rod. From here, the steps are repeated.

6 Once you have mastered this step-by-step spinning technique, you can move on to drawing out the new fibers and letting the twist run into them while turning the spindle again and again in parallel.

SIMPLE ROPE MAKING

The spinning of coarse threads and turning together of single threads (plying, twining) with winches, cranks, and rope-twisting paddles.

Rope making is the twisting of fiber materials around their longitudinal axis. Twisting makes the end product more stable and flexible than the original material. During the twisting process, new material can be constantly fed in and incorporated. The result is a long linear textile that is created without having to knot short pieces. A rope is twined together from many individual threads. In the technical language among rope makers, individual strands are "laid up" into a rope. If there are only a few threads twisted around each other, it is called a cord or a line. Anything over a centimeter in diameter is usually called a rope. The thickest ropes are used in seafaring, where they are called cables and hawsers. However, there is no standardized regulation for these gradations.

Professional rope makers were already organized in guilds in the Middle Ages. They made ropes for hoisting loads on building sites, for example, which had to meet special requirements. Simple ropes, which could easily be made by themselves, were sufficient for the rural household. This home rope making saved a lot of money. On the farm, ropes were used as reins, well ropes, and washing lines. The grain harvest was tied together with sheaf bands, and thatched roofs were secured with straw ropes. In the home, homemade cords were used to cover chair seats or bed frames.

RAW MATERIALS

The range of materials that can be used for spinning ropes is far greater than that for spinning fine yarns. Ropes must be strong and able to withstand tension, and they shouldn't wear easily. However, a particularly soft feel is not important. The raw material can therefore also be rough and hard. The main thing is that it can be twisted without tearing. The bast fibers of the hemp plant (*Cannabis sativa*) are particularly strong and can be over 1 yard long. In addition, cultivation is possible on moist soils in central Europe without any problems. For centuries, hemp fibers were therefore the most important raw material for professional rope making. With the exploitation of overseas colonies, sisal, jute, and coconut were added.

Rural rope making, on the other hand, has always used whatever was suitable, cheap, and available locally. Farm animals also had to make their contribution to domestic rope making. Suitable materials of animal origin include horse tail and mane hair, cow tail hair, donkey tail hair, rawhide, leather, sinew, and, of course, sheep's wool (preferably rough, second-choice, short-fibered wool).

Today, the industry almost exclusively processes synthetic fibers and metal wire into ropes. Asbestos is an inorganic raw material. Even in ancient times, asbestos fibers were spun into threads and woven into fireproof textiles. An asbestos rope found in Bryggen indicates its use in the Middle Ages. The danger of asbestosis was not recognized until around 1900.

PLANT-BASED RAW MATERIALS FOR ROPES PREVIOUSLY AND CURRENTLY USED IN EUROPE

- **Bogwood**, bog deal, became important as a raw material in Ireland when deforestation in the sixteenth and seventeenth centuries meant that wood from forests was no longer available. Bogwood ropes were used for roofing and as bed cords on which the straw sack was placed for sleeping.

- **Cattails:** Cattail leaves were woven into ropes to bind harvested tobacco together.

- **Club-rush** (*Schoenoplectus*), also known as bulrush. Used in Ireland for *rush-ropes*. The rushes were beaten soft before processing.

- **Common reed** (*Phragmites australis*)

Willow bark cord, made by Jörg Nadler

- **Corn leaves** and corn husks. Used in Hungary as twine for vines and for washing lines.

- **Crowberry** (*Empetrum nigrum*), Danish *revling*. In Skara Brae, Scotland, a fragment of crowberry rope was found, dated 3200 to 2400 BCE. In Denmark, it was used for ropes for tethering animals and for thatching roofs.

- **Eelgrass** (*Zostera marina*) was used in Austria and Ireland to make ropes.

- **Esparto grass** (*Lygeum spartum*) and halfah grass (*Stipa tenacissima*) are found in the Mediterranean region and are particularly well known in Spain for ropes, bags, mats, shoes, and paper.

- **Evergreen clematis**, traveler's joy, old man's beard (*Clematis vitalba*). On Lake Constance, it was used to make ropes on which fish baskets were lowered into the lake.

- **Flax.** For rope making, tow, the short fibers that are not suitable for high-quality yarn, could also be used. [Flax: p. 30]

- **Hay** (dried grass). Hay ropes were used to hold the mown hay from the fields together while drying.

- **Heather** (*Calluna vulgaris*) was used instead of wood where wood was too valuable for binding purposes (e.g., for fixing thatched

→ Flax p. 30

→ Hemp p. 27

Old bogwood in Ireland that is thousands of years old

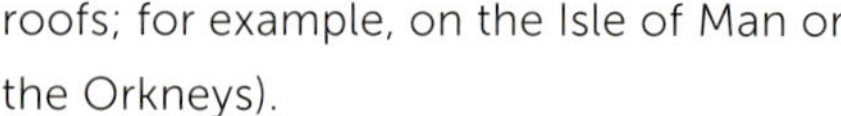

roofs; for example, on the Isle of Man or the Orkneys).

- **Hemp.** The classic material for rope making. [Hemp: p. 27]

- **Marram grass**, beach grass (*Ammophila arenaria*) for ropes for roofing ("Rooper" on Sylt, "Reepen" on Amrum, "simmens" on the Shetland Islands; also on the Hebrides and in Ireland).

- **Moss:** Hair moss (*Polytrichum commune*), also known as common haircap, is resistant to moisture. Twisted moss ropes have been used for waterproofing boats since the Bronze Age. Many medieval rope discoveries, including from Aachen, Duisburg, and Einbeck (all thirteenth century), as well as from Shrewsbury, London, York, and Perth.

- **Quaking grass sedge** (*Carex brizoides*). Ropes were made from quaking grass for thatching roofs. In modern times, quaking grass ropes were also used for packaging purposes: They were spun and unraveled to produce a crimped padding material, similar to wood wool (excelsior).

- **Recycled materials**; for example, leftover twine made from hemp or sisal, which was used in agriculture to bind straw or hay.

- **Rush** is not very stable. Compact rush, *Juncus conglomeratus*, was once used to weave cords and tie bunches of herbs together.

- **Stinging nettle.** Rather rarely used, but a raw material that has been used since the Neolithic Age at the latest. [Stinging Nettle: p. 26]

- **Straw** from rye, oat (used on the Orkneys), black oat (*Avena strigosa*), and wheat.

- **Tree bark**; willow is the most suitable. The bark was left over from basket weaving. Willow bark ropes were used to catch reindeer in Sweden or as lines for fishing nets on the Lower Rhine.

Beach grass from the North Sea island of Juist

- **Tree bast**, especially linden or lime, elm, and willow. There is also evidence of the prehistoric use of oak bast, including from the Stone Age settlement of Çatalhöyük. Remains of an oak bast rope were found on a bailer in a Roman box well from Erkelenz-Kückhoven. Experiments in rope making with oak bast have not been very successful so far, however, because oak bast is brittle and breaks easily when twisted. [Linden Bast: p. 36]

- **Tree roots.** In Lapland they made spruce root ropes.

- **Wood.** Branches and twigs were twisted into withes, especially birch (*Betula*), willow (*Salix*), and also juniper (*Juniperus*); for example, on the Faroe Islands for ropes needed for roofing.

- **Wood shavings**. In Sweden, pine wood, or alternatively spruce, was heated and the shavings were removed and twisted. These pine ropes were made for fishing and boats. In the "bastabinne" technique, cords are made in a similar way, from which bags are tied. [Bastabinne: p. 198, 208] Wooden shaving ropes have been documented in Schleswig from the eleventh to fourteenth centuries. In more-recent metal foundries, wood wool ropes were used to produce clay cores for casting.

→ Stinging Nettle p. 26

→ Linden Bast p. 36

→ Bastabinne p. 198, 208

ORIGINS OF SIMPLE ROPE MAKING

The world's oldest evidence of intentionally twisted fibers dates to around forty to fifty thousand years ago. These are thread remnants stuck to a Neanderthal hand axe from the Abri du Maras site in southern France. A tool that was presumably used for Paleolithic rope making has also been discovered. This stick with holes was made of mammoth ivory and found in the Hohle Fels cave near Schelklingen, which was visited by early humans. Experiments with a replica of the tool proved that it could be used to twist ropes. Cord imprints in clay can be found in the Lascaux cave, and imprints in ceramics can be found in the Japanese hunter-gatherer culture of the Jomon. Such imprints were the basis of the name of the type of decoration found in Neolithic Corded Ware culture. Also from the Neolithic period, a twisted flax cord was found about 22 inches (56 cm) long, dating to the fourth millennium BCE, which was excavated from the Etton earthwork site in Peterborough, England.

Tools and Technique

Our hands are an important tool for rope making. On the Scottish Hebrides, ropes made from heather were twisted "just like that" with our hands. The same applies to ropes made from sedge (*Carex*), which were used to thatch roofs in Holstein.[25] There is also no need for special tools when twisting several individual cords together to make a thicker rope. Two or three threads wound on a stick or a branch hook are laid around each other in the opposite direction to the spinning direction. Of course, it is quicker with a suitable tool. Sometimes the same simple tools were used for spinning finer threads; for example, the branch fork or the spinning hook. However, there were also special tools that were used only for spinning thicker cords and ropes, in particular the rope-twisting paddle and the hand winch.

Rope-Twisting Paddle

The rope-twisting paddle consists of an axle with a loosely attached elongated weight. The axle is held in the hand, and the weight is swung around in a circle. This circular movement twists the knotted threads around each other. The process of winding the individual threads into a thicker cord is called twining or plying. However, you can not only twine but also spin loose fibers.

The scientific documentary film *Making a Rope with the "Slingholt"* (*Tauherstellung mit dem Slingholt*), from 1966, documents the work process. Farmer Lüders uses the tool to recycle leftover sisal twine.[26] Traditionally, two people work with the rope-twisting paddle. This makes it easier to make very

25 Arnold Lühning, *Drehen von Hartgras-Stricken zum Reetdachdecken* (1962), *Encyclopaedia Cinematographica*, E 540/1963. IWF-Film, Schleswig 1963. Online on the TIB AV-Portal: https://av.tib.eu/media/26337.

26 Arnold Lühning, *Tauherstellung mit dem Slingholt* (1966), *Encyclopaedia Cinematographica*, E 1460/1971. IWF-Film, Göttingen 1971. Online on the TIB AV-Portal: https://av.tib.eu/media/11609.

Spinning cord with
the twisting paddle

long ropes. Otherwise, like farmer Lüders, you have to walk backward when spinning until the rope is long enough. Or only a short piece is spun at a time and wound onto the tool again and again, which is very cumbersome.

Rope making with the twisting paddle was already known in ancient times. The oldest pictorial representation comes from Egypt. A wall painting in a tomb in Thebes shows several men making a papyrus rope. In Europe, there is only modern evidence of this tool. Apart from northern Germany, it was also known in the Lower Rhine region and in Holland.[27] On ships, the device known as a "woit" in sailor's language was used to twist nautical yarn from rope remnants. In the southern part of North America and in Central America, the twisting paddle is known to have been used for rope making. Horsehair, agave fibers, and Spanish moss were used. The tool has various names, including *tarabilla*[28] or simply *rope twister*. It is assumed that the Spanish conquistadors brought the technique with them. Today, the tradition has been revived in the USA. A small, modern version of the device is sold there as the *Mayan spindle* and is intended for spinning sheep's wool.

[Instructions: Rope-Twisting Paddle: p. 270]

Hand Winch

This device looks like a reel for winding up washing lines or kite string. It consists of an axle with a handle. A frame is attached to the axle. This is used to hold the rope and can be rotated. When spinning, the device is held in the right hand. The fibers are pulled out of the fiber supply with the left hand, while the right hand swings the winch in a circular motion. The fiber supply can be tied to a distaff, hung on a hook, tucked into a belt, clamped under the arm, or placed on a table and weighed down with a heavy object. When so much yarn has been spun that the right arm has to be stretched out, it is wrapped around the frame. The next section can then be spun. The principle used here to twist the fibers together with a swinging motion corresponds to that of the simpler twisting paddle (see above).

You do not need to build a winch to try out this spinning technique. You can use a clothesline winch for this purpose. Regional names for the hand winch are *Weife* (Thuringia, Mark Brandenburg), *Weefe* (Saxony), or *håndten* (Denmark).[29] In Cornwall, the device called wink was used for making straw rope used for thatching roofs.[30]

Instead of holding the axle in your hand, you can secure it somewhere; for example, in a hole in the wall or in a beam. A version of this technique can be seen in a wood carving from the fifteenth century.[31]

An axle with two cross-shaped end pieces is rotatably mounted in a stand. The rope maker holds one end of the rope in his hand; the other is wound around the axle. He keeps the carousel in motion with continuous swings of the rope. Martha Bielenstein described this construction as a "Latvian mill."[32]

The hand winch was used for the production of fine and coarse threads or ropes made of a variety of fibers, especially for recycling fiber remnants. In a documentary film from Schleswig,[33] you can see how twine left over from bundling grain is processed together with horsehair. Elsewhere, coarse sheep's wool, hemp, or flax were used. Cords were twisted from bulrush to cover chair seats. Fishermen also used a winch to make cords for their own use. The cord produced must be strong enough to set the winch in motion without breaking.

Hand Winch with Bracket

Another type of hand winch also consists of a handle and a rotating yarn holder. Here, however, there is a U-shaped or rectangular bracket in the upper crosspiece, which has a hole for the axle at the bottom center. You can find the building instructions for a winch with a square bracket in the Tool Workshop. [Winch Instructions: p. 272]

Only one very old hand winch has been found: In the Hanseatic quarter of Bryggen from the Middle Ages in Bergen, Norway, the handle of a yarn winch made of yew wood was found, which dates back to the thirteenth or fourteenth centuries.[34]

There are a few images from the late Middle Ages that show cross-shaped winches. In addition to the abovementioned "The Eight Mischiefs" ("Die acht Schalkheiten") from the fifteenth century, this design can also be seen on the rope pictures of the Mendel Twelve Brothers Foundation. A cross-shaped device is pivoted at the top in a vertical post. The rope maker turns the rope from the supply of fibers around his waist as he walks backward.

In modern times, the hand winch has been handed down from Scandinavia, the Baltic states, Poland, and England. In Germany, the winches were known in Schleswig-Holstein and Lower Saxony. The hand winch was also used in Russia.

In his book on prehistoric fishing equipment, Eduard Krause shows a spinning device called a *maktii* from the Ainu on

27 According to Eduard Krause, *Vorgeschichtliche Fischereigeräte und neuere Vergleichsstücke* (Berlin, 1904), 141ff.

28 Universität Innsbruck, Institut für Archäologie, Arbeitsgruppe Bekleidung Textile Techniken (ABT), *Spinnen grober Fasern und Seilherstellung in Amerika*. Online: https://www.uibk.ac.at/archaeologien/forschung/arbeitsgemeinschaften/abt/spindeltypologie/seilherstellung/seilherstellung_amerika.html.de.

29 Carl Jensen, *Bogen om Siv* (2002; reprint from 1941).

30 Thomas Hennell, *Change in the Farm* (Cambridge, UK, 1936), 154.

31 *Die acht Schalkheiten: Der betrügerische Seiler.*

32 Bielenstein 1935/1995, 57.

33 Arnold Lühning, *Spinnen mit dem Spinnhaken* (1966), *Encyclopaedia Cinematographica*, E 1461 / 1971. IWF-Film, Göttingen 1971. Online on the TIB AV-Portal: https://av.tib.eu/media/11611.

34 Ingvild Øye, *Textile Equipment and Its Working Environment: Bryggen in Bergen, c. 1150–1500*, Bryggen Papers, Main Series, vol. 2 (Bergen, Norway, 1988), 55: The wimble.

→ Twisting-Paddle Instructions p. 270

→ Winch Instructions p. 272

Top: Rope-twisting paddle made from wood scraps; see instructions, p. 270

Bottom: Rope-twisting paddle built by J. Nadler according to an antique model

Sakhalin.[35] This type of winch, **reptrilla** in Swedish, was also used in Swedish pine rope making. In Slovakia, spinning with simple tools, including the hand winch, is called *druganie* or "coarse spinning." In Slovenia, the practice does not seem to have been completely forgotten, as a modern photo on the internet shows. Drawings from 1957 with details of the hand winch can be found on the pages of the Slovenian Ethnographic Museum.

Branch Hooks

Multistrand ropes can be produced with a simple branch fork. Using a branch hook, three to four cords of flax tow or hemp are twisted separately. The cords are then attached to a hook, and the ends are pulled through a small board with three or four holes. The board looks like a weaving tablet but is much larger. [Tablet Weaving: p. 149] The other end is attached to a branch hook. One person then turns the hook in the opposite direction of the original spinning direction, while the other slowly moves the boards toward the wall.[36] Incidentally, the same technique is assumed to have been used for the stick with holes that was found, dating to the Paleolithic period (see above).

Spinning Crank

Twisting the rope is more convenient with a crank than with the branch fork. The branch fork must be swung around in a circle. With the crank method, on the other hand, you can hold one hand still while the other turns the crank in a small movement. This is less strenuous in the long run. Traditionally, the spinning crank was used to make straw ropes. These rough ropes were needed for thatching and reed roofing, for fastening the thatched roofs of grain barns, for metal casting of cannon barrels, for chair seats, or for wrapping pottery for transport. Straw rope cranking is described as typical work on rainy days or in winter. Later, these ropes were twisted using a special machine.

Simple spinning cranks were made entirely of wood. Ash or another easily bendable type of wood was used. A further improvement is a sturdy crank made of metal, with only the handles made of wood.[37] There are pictures and descriptions of the spinning crank mainly from England and Scotland, where it was known as a rope twister, wimble, or thraw hook. In Germany, the crank was used to twist straw ropes, while in Austria quaking grass sedge (*Carex*) was processed.

These tools were generally made on the farm itself.

35 Eduard Krause, *Vorgeschichtliche Fischereigeräte und neuere Vergleichsstücke* (Berlin, 1904), Tafel XV.

36 August Bielenstein, *Die Holzbauten und Holzgeräte der Letten* (Petrograd, Russia, 1918), 573.

37 Described this way in Herbert Remmel, *Von Köln nach Ballinlough: Eine deutsch-irische Nachkriegskindheit* (Pinnow, Germany, 2016), 133: "A bucket handle bent into a crank, which had previously been inserted into a hollowed-out elder branch."

→ Tablet Weaving p. 149

TRY IT!

USING A SPINNING CRANK

A simple crank can be bent from a strong wire (e.g., fence wire). It is more convenient to use an old brace and bit hand drill. Instead of the drill bit, clamp a hook bent from wire to the front. Knot a thread (yarn remnant) to the hook. A second person holds the end of the thread. If you crank in the same direction in which the thread is twisted, you will notice how the twist becomes stronger until the thread wants to twist around itself.

To practice spinning, knot fibers to the hook. Again, a helper holds the end. A thread is formed through cranking.

SPINNING WITH THE SPINNING CRANK

[Spinning-Crank-Building Instructions: p. 271]

Materials: Straw, long hay from the meadow, or long grasses from the field

Before spinning, the grass or straw must be slightly moistened so that it doesn't break. In the past, it was placed in the cowshed for a few days for this purpose.

Two people always work together. One person sits next to the straw (or hay) supply. The first straws are twisted by hand into a short piece of rope, folded in the middle, and laid on top of each other. The beginning is hung on the protruding end of the arch. The second person turns the spinning hook and slowly moves backward as the rope grows.

The first person constantly adds new material. When a sufficient length has been spun (or the person spinning has reached the wall of the house and cannot go any farther back), the person sitting down winds the rope into a ball. The person with the spinning hook must not let go of the rope; otherwise it will unravel again. They slowly approach the person winding the rope until the whole piece of rope is wound up.

TIPS FROM FISHERMAN AND ROPE MAKER

JÖRG NADLER

- Stretch the twisted rope strongly several times. The best way to do this is for one person to hold one end while the second person jerks the other end. The stretching pulls the rope to its final length

- The rope should be slightly overtwisted so that it interlocks well. This excess twist can be removed by soaking the rope in water overnight before use.

- Loops at the rope ends are sometimes practical. They are created by splicing. To do this, the end of the rope is unraveled slightly, and the individual strands are wound into the rope following the course of the twisted rope.

- And another special tip from the fisherman: Never tie knots in dry hemp rope on the boat. The fibers swell up and the knots can no longer be untied!

Jörg Nadler

Schleswig-Holstein, Germany

Jörg Nadler from Schleswig, who works mainly as a fisherman on the Schlei, demonstrates fishing techniques from the Stone Age through the present day as a "historical fisherman" in museums and at events. The photo shows him as a Roman rope maker in the LVR Archaeological Park of Xanten. His presentation focuses on rope making and net making, for which he also gives courses upon request.

www.historischerfischer.de

Book Tip

Carl Pause, ed., *Fisch Land Fluss–eine Zeitreise durch die Fischereigeschichte am Niederrhein* (Neuss, Germany: Clemens Sels Museum, 2020).

→ Instructions: Building Spinning Crank p. 271

BANDS AND BRAIDS

Ever since people were technically able to make bands and braids, they have had in mind more than just a practical purpose. Especially with bands that were intended for clothing, people experimented with colors and patterns when weaving or braiding.

There are different ways of referring to long, narrow textiles. If they are thin, they are called strings or cords. If they are slightly wider, they are referred to as narrow fabrics, which include bands, braids, and edgings. Bands include the activity of tying. Bands are incredibly versatile: Bands can be used to tie off, tie on, tie down, tie up, tie around, or tie together. When there were no zippers, safety pines, Velcro fasteners, or elastic bands, you couldn't go without woven bands and straps. They were needed practically everywhere: on clothing such as belts, suspenders, shoelaces, cords, apron strings or garters; as straps for sleeveless shirts; for tucking up long skirts and protecting the hem of skirts; for tying hoods; and for tying bags. In the home, pillows and comforter covers had to be tied up and towels hung up. Bag and pouch handles were made from woven bands, as were wicks for candles and lanterns. Diaper bands held cloth diapers together, and a cradle band stretched back and forth secured the baby in the cradle. The Shakers in North America even made chair seats from handwoven bands. Bands were also indispensable in agriculture. They were used to tie up large cloths in which fodder grass or hay was carried from the meadow to the barn, and to tie up sacks of grain, fodder, and seed. Short straps sufficed as hangers for tools. Sturdy straps made of flax tow, hemp, or sisal were woven to carry baskets or haversacks. Horse reins and saddle girths were part of the horse tack.

There are many different techniques for production. You can braid, weave, whipcord, knit, or sprang. Multiple techniques can also be combined to form one band.

WHIPCORDING

The weaving of cords from four weighted strands has been known since the Middle Ages at the latest. Whipcording is a textile technique that can be learned in just a few minutes. It promotes a sense of rhythm as well as hand-eye coordination and is great fun, especially in pairs.

Any reasonably tear-resistant material is suitable for whipcording, from fine hair to strong cords. If you use very thin yarn, however, a little patience is required. It is not for nothing that the Northern German word for whipcording (*tundeln*) was another word for dawdling around.

A thin cord of buttonhole silk and silver Madeira embroidery thread at the top. The other cords are made of wool.

TECHNIQUE

For whipcording, or tontle (Fresian), four strands are crossed in a certain order to create a round cord. A weight is attached to each thread. These weights ensure even thread tension. [Construction of a Whipcord: pp. 98–99] Whipcording is done either alone or in pairs. The threads must be attached in such a way that the bobbins can swing freely. This can be done with a hook on the ceiling, for example. The cord forms from the suspension downward. In the past, women usually did whipcording alone, either standing or sitting. Men stood in pairs facing each other and threw the bobbins to each other crosswise. If you want to be mobile while working, you need a portable suspension for the bobbins. One such holder in the shape of a cross can be seen in the painting *The Education of the Virgin Mary* by Baroque painter Guido Reni. It is particularly suitable for weaving fine cords with light bobbins.

Different patterns are possible by combining different colors, using yarn of different thicknesses in a braid, or by changing the sequence of crossing the bobbins. If a core—the so-called soul—is braided from strong yarn or wire, a very stable cord is created.

FLAT AND ROUND BOBBINS

A bobbin set always includes four weights. The traditional bobbins are turned, sometimes also carved, and 6 to 8 inches long (15–20 cm). They are bottle shaped or consist of a rod with a ball at the lower end. To distinguish them from the similar-looking but smaller and lighter lace bobbins, they are sometimes referred to in the literature as "fist bobbins." In Norway, wooden weights in the shape of an axe or a key are also found. In Denmark, the bobbins were sometimes additionally weighted with small lead weights attached to them.

The yarn is tied to the bobbin or wrapped around the bobbin stem and attached with a holding loop. Many of the old bobbins have a metal hook at the top where the thread can be wrapped. This allows a single bobbin to also be used as a spindle for spinning yarn. [Spinning Instructions: p. 61]

Turned *slingrestokk* from Norway

For thicker cords or those with complicated patterns, more than four bobbins can be used. Danish textile researcher Margrethe Hald references the Tolvtottaband from the Faroe Islands, which is made up of twelve individual strands (*tolv* = 12). On the North Sea islands, wide bands were woven with even eighteen or more bobbins.

→ Construction of a Whipcord pp. 98–99

→ Spinning Instructions p. 61

FIST BRAIDING

You can also braid four-strand cords without tools, using only your fingers. Sailors refer to the technique as "four-strand round plaiting." Since relatively heavy hemp or synthetic fiber yarn is used for cordage braiding, no weights are needed to tension the threads.

Fist braiding is the traditional technique for making slingshots in many locations, including Peru, Iran, Palestine, and parts of Central Asia. In Anatolia, it was used to join the loose warp threads at the ends of tablet-woven bands. [Tablet Weaving: p. 149] Today it is also used to weave so-called survival bracelets from paracord synthetic fiber cords.

BRAIDING TABLES

Japanese strand braiding, *kumihimo*, is braided over a special wooden frame. This weaving stand is called *marudai* ("round stand"). The silk yarn wound on small bobbins hangs over the ends of the stand. The finished cord is pulled down through a hole in the middle of the stand by a counterweight. This is the opposite of whipcording, where the finished cord is at the top and the yarn supply at the bottom. The four-thread cord, for which you will find instructions below, can also be braided using the *kumihimo* technique. In Japanese it is called *Maru Yotsu Gumi* (*maru* = round, *yotsu* = four pieces).

Strand braiding was also known in Europe with braiding tables. Posament or lace makers made their cords on a semicircular tambour (drum) or on a high braiding table. In the city of Brasov in Transylvania, Romania, several hundred families earned their living two hundred years ago by making cords for uniform trimmings (găitanele). The tools used were a semicircular piece of wood called a troci and four to twelve wooden bobbins, or "mallets."

Man at a braiding table, from Mark Campbell's *Self-Instructor in the Art of Hair Work*, New York, 1875

In the eighteenth and nineteenth centuries, corded watch straps and brooches made from human hair were popular as friendship or mourning jewelry to remember loved ones. The Swedish town of Våmhus in Dalarna was famous for its hairwork called *hårkullorna*. In Switzerland too, there are now a number of craftsman and women who weave hair ornaments on the knotting board called a *jatte*. The tail hair of horses is used instead of human hair. [Human Hair as a Fiber Material: p. 24]

→ Tablet Weaving p. 149

→ Human Hair as a Fiber Material p. 24

WHIPCORDING HISTORY

It is difficult to say how long cord braiding with bobbins has been around. You can't necessarily tell from a strand found during an archaeological excavation how it was braided. The result of fist braiding [Fist Braiding, p. 90] (see above) or whipcording with weights is the same. The discovery of the tool used would be reliable evidence of whipcording. So far, only one original bobbin has been found that is older than early modern period. It comes from the archaeological excavation of the German Hanseatic base Bryggen in the Norwegian city of Bergen. The discovery dates to the late Middle Ages and is therefore the oldest bobbin found to date. A four-thread braided leather cord from the Krogens Mølle bog near Brovst in North Jutland, Denmark, could indicate that the technique is possibly significantly older. It was made between 500 BCE and the turn of the millennium and thus belongs to the Nordic Iron Age.

Other cords that were possibly made using bobbins come from the Middle Ages. A well-known textile discovery from the Middle Ages is the well-preserved clothing from Skjoldehamn in Norway. On the hoodlike head covering of a woman buried in the eleventh century, there were two four-thread braided woolen cords with a greenish-brown spiral pattern sewn on.

In medieval London, on the other hand, precious silk was used as a braiding material. Some eight-thread braided silk strands were found there, which may have been made with weights. These cords, which were used as drawstrings for cloth bags or as cords for closing garments, were also braided using the loop technique. [Loop Braiding, p. 101]

Modern Whipcording

In more-recent times, since the eighteenth century, whipcording is well proven through scattered written references and well-preserved bobbins. As with many textile techniques that can be quickly learned, child labor also played a role in whipcording. In the middle of the nineteenth century, children were taught how to make woolen cords at industrial schools in Baden Württemberg to "earn a living." Cord making was also recommended as a pastime for young ladies.

The most important application for these cords was to protect skirt hems. The cords were attached to the lower edge of the long women's skirts worn at that time. If the hem of the skirt was worn through, you had to replace only the border and not the whole skirt. In northern Germany, women also made wider bands to tie up their skirts "because of the work in mud and water."

The "Tuntel sticks" were no longer used once the braids became cheap to buy. Skirt cords were also made much farther south; namely, in Switzerland. Here, the activity was called *dünteln*; the tool, *Düntel* or *Tündel*.

This modern period axe- or key-shaped wooden bobbin looks almost exactly like the medieval find in Bergen.

→ Fist Braiding p. 90

→ Loop Braiding p. 101

^
Cords made from fine linen yarn, made with lace bobbins. Blue and white cord as a cushion closure (*on the left*), brown cord for a medieval wool dress lacing (*on the right*).

›
Norwegian woman whipcording. The threads are attached to the roof overhang of her house.

In Nord-Østerdalen in Norway, the binding cords for tobacco pouches were made from human hair. Operating cords for spinning wheels (*rokkesnor*) were also made in Norway. Other uses for whipcording included curtain cords and fasteners for pillows and comforter covers. The whipcorder in Guido Reni's painting (see page 88) is making a cord for a pillowcase, as can be seen in the center of the picture on Mary's lap, while the other young women are busy cutting and sewing the fabric.

> Cords of twine are twisted by the women with four cones or bobbins, one span long made of wood, of white, sometimes also blue and white twine looped into each other, and used for pillows, blankets, and bedcovers in order to tie them up with it.
>
> UNIVERSAL LEXICON, 1743

Corded Fishing Lines

In Norway another type of whipcording was known. With wooden weights shaped like an axe or a key, special fishing lines were made by the fishermen themselves. [Fishing-Line Bobbins: p. 93] For this, two men always worked together. The material for the lines was linen or hemp. They were needed for line fishing.

In Scotland, fisherman made this type of fishing line, known as a leader, themselves. Here, however, the material was not linen but horsehair, and the fishing lines were spun with the help of a stone spindle whorl. [Stone Spinning Whorl: p. 56]

Viking Technique?

When the technique of whipcording was almost forgotten, it was revived by the Danish Viking and medieval scene. It was probably triggered by an article by textile researcher Margrethe Hald in her book *Olddanske Tekstiler* from 1950, in which she describes *snorefletning* (cord braiding) and mentions that Danish children had mastered it "until recently." Whipcording was revived in the Viking scene in Denmark in the 1990s. It is now demonstrated by various Viking groups at markets or museum events. However, there is no evidence to date that the technique was known at the time of the Vikings (i.e., in the early Middle Ages), or even earlier. However, braided cords have certainly been around since prehistoric times.

→ Fishing-Line Bobbin p. 93

→ Stone Spinning Whorl p. 56

TRY IT!

BRAIDING ON CARDBOARD

Cut four threads of not-too-thin wool or cotton yarn of the same length and knot them together at one end. Attach the threads to a beer coaster or a piece of cardboard. To do this, cut a hole in the middle of the cardboard and cut six slits in the edge: N, NNE, E, S, WSW, W. Hang the knotted thread into the hole and hold it in place. Distribute the four threads over the slits.

1 Exchange the first thread pair: Thread "South" to thread "NNE."

2 Thread "N" to "S."

3 "NNE" switches to "N."

4 Exchange the second thread pair: Thread "E" to "WSW."

5 Thread "W" to "E."

6 "WSW" switches to "W."

7 Now "S" back to "NNE," etc.

If you cut more slits, many more patterns are possible. That is the Japanese technique called kumihimo (see above under "Braiding Tables"). [Braiding Tables: p. 90]

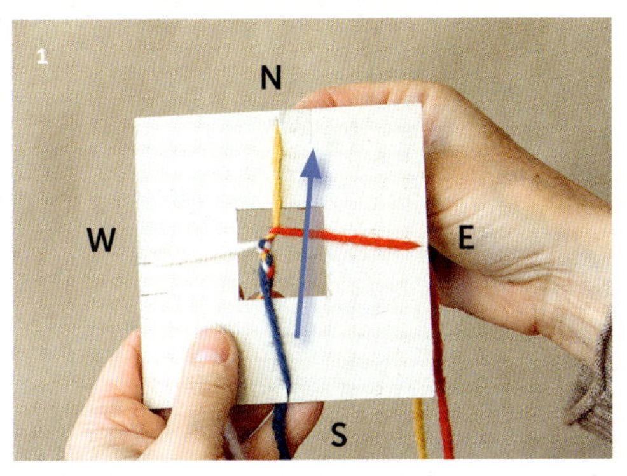

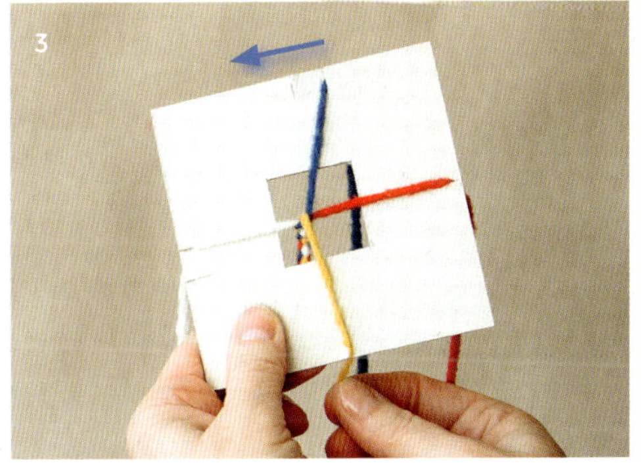

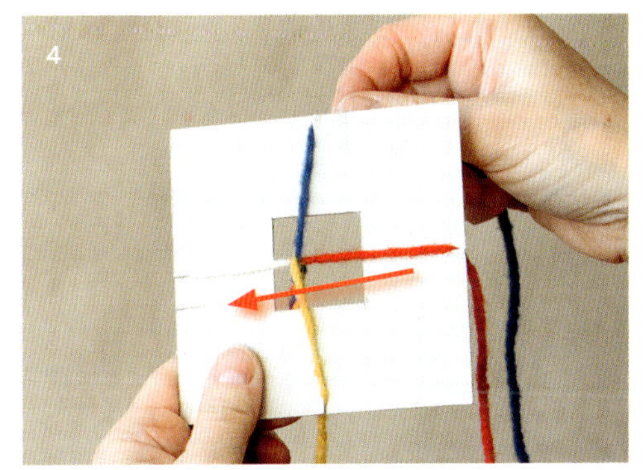

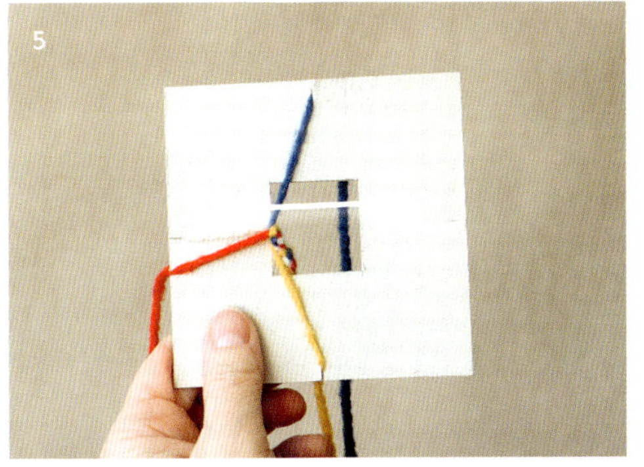

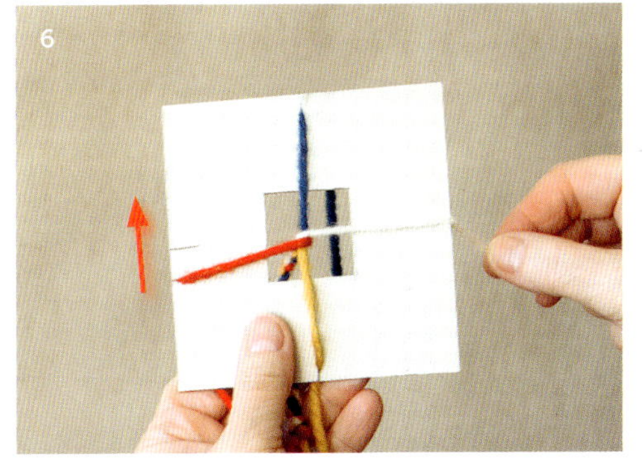

→ Braiding Tables p. 90

WHIPCORDING

BOBBINS

- Turned bobbins are sold in certain Danish museum shops and at Viking festivals. Those who can turn wood can of course make them themselves.

- An alternative is making bobbins from everyday objects: four uniform weights, for example, wooden cones from a skittles game, small plastic bottles filled with water or sand, or holed rocks from the last Baltic Sea vacation. [Bobbin Instructions, pp. 276–277]

Materials:
Stable wool, linen, or cotton yarn. Different types of yarn should not be used together in a strand because they stretch differently. Then the bobbins would start to hang at different heights, which makes them hard to grip.

Silk yarn looks best when used in fine lacing bands; for example, for homemade medieval clothing. Choose appropriately light bobbins for thin yarn.

Two-Colored Pattern from Four Threads
Select two thread colors. Cut and knot 6.5 feet (2 m) of yarn for each bobbin. Thin yarn can also be doubled over. If bobbins are used with an option for winding the yarn, the thread can be longer. In this case, gradually unwind the yarn supply.

Knot all threads together at the top so that the bobbins hang at the same height. Attach at a height of approx. 6.5 feet (2 m) (to a swing frame, tree branch, nail in doorframe, overhanging sun or market umbrella stand, floor lamp stand, etc.).

Now two people stand opposite each other. Each person is given two bobbins with different colors of yarn. Swap the bobbins crosswise with a slight swing. The right hand swaps with the partner's right hand, and the left hand swaps with the left. (It is also possible to do this without a partner. However, to prevent the cord from becoming too loose, the threads must be pulled tight after every second bobbin exchange.)

Stripes: Like colors are swapped.

Spirals/Crosses: Different colors are swapped.

Secure the end of the finished strand with a knot. Do not cut the excess threads too close.

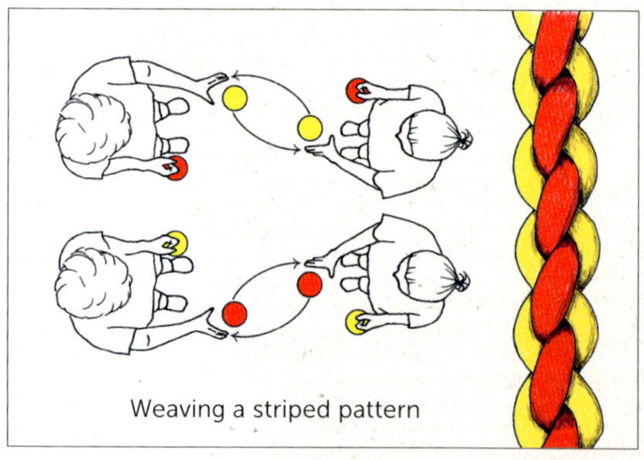
Weaving a striped pattern

TIPS FROM THE BAND-WEAVING AND WHIPCORDING EXPERT HILDEGUND HERGENHAN

- Secure the thread wrapped around the whipcording bobbin with a double twisted, folded loop to prevent sliding (see bottom right picture).

- If the whipcording process has to stop now and then: Prepare a piece of cardboard with four slits where the four threads can be inserted.

- One pair of whipcording woods (two diagonally opposite bobbins) is swapped clockwise, the other counterclockwise! If you swap both pairs in the same direction, you get two individual cords twisted around each other instead of a single cord.

Hildegund Hergenhan
Schleswig-Holstein, Germany

Born in 1938 in Stettin, Hildegund Hergenhan, a band weaver and pattern designer from Kiel, learned about weaving as a child on her grandparents' farm. After training as a technical designer and having a family, she is, as she says, "completely immersed in band weaving." She regularly demonstrates old handicraft techniques, such as whipcording, at the Molfsee open-air museum in Schleswig-Holstein. She also runs seminars and creates exhibitions on textile techniques.

In 2021, Hildegund Hergenhan was awarded the Medal of Merit of the Federal Republic of Germany for her commitment to old craftsmanship and traditional costume research.

www.bandweben.info

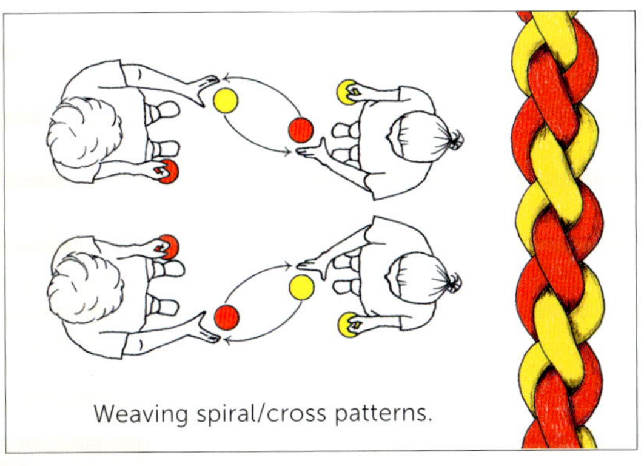

Weaving spiral/cross patterns.

→ Bobbin Instructions pp. 276–277

FINGERLOOP BRAIDING

Fingerloop braiding is known mostly in living history and medieval reenactment groups. The oldest finds of fingerloop braids possibly date back to prehistory. In the Middle Ages, this braiding technique was widespread. There are even written instructions that can be found, starting from the late Middle Ages.

THE TECHNIQUE

For fingerloop braiding, you don't need any special tools, just your own fingers. To do this, hang doubled threads with their loop ends over the fingers of both hands. One finger remains free as the working finger. With each braid, a loop is lifted from the other hand with the free finger. Once you have familiarized yourself with the process, braiding progresses quickly. The threads move back and forth between the two hands in a certain rhythm. The order in which the fingers are passed through the loops when lifting determines the appearance of the finished braid. Simple braids, round or square cords, braided eyelets, or flat bands are created.

The loops can be transferred from hand to hand in different ways. Either each pair of threads in a loop is treated as a single thread, just as in normal braiding, or the working finger first passes through one or more loops of the same or the other hand (or both) before lifting a loop. This technique is what makes loop braiding so special and opens up many possibilities for structures and patterns.

When braiding, the palms face each other. One finger normally carries a loop, but not every finger has to be occupied. Three pairs of threads are sufficient for a simple braid. With just two more loops, you can braid many different cord designs. The variety of patterns can be increased by working with even more loops and several braiders at the same time. The braiders then swap a loop with each other according to a certain system and at the right place so that the individual braids join together.

The length of a cord is limited because only a certain length of thread can be pulled tight with the outstretched arms. However, if one person braids and the other fastens the braided crossovers (i.e., presses them tight), very long cords can be braided.

One variation is the fringed border. This is worked in pairs. One crosses over the loop threads and the other passes an extra thread first through the braid and then around a thin wooden stick. When the stick is pulled out, a border of fringed loops is formed.

The finished cords and bands can be used for all kinds of purposes. In the past, loop-braided cords were used to tie and bind garments. They were also used to close small cloth bags or as sealing strings. Flat braided bands were sewn onto clothing as decorative borders or to reinforce fabric edges. Braided from colorful wool, they were used as garters to prevent stockings from slipping. In a more rustic version made of sturdy yarn, they could also be used as straps for carrying loads.

MEDIEVAL "LACE OF BOWES"

It is not easy to determine the braiding technique used for finished braided cords. However, there are certain clues that can be used as a guide. If you find a narrow band with loops at the ends, where the individual threads are not twisted around each other and run parallel over a certain distance, it was mostly likely created by fingerloop braiding. Surviving prehistoric pieces that could possibly have been done by fingerloop braiding are sparse, but they do exist. The oldest piece analyzed so far is a bracelet woven from cow hair. It comes from a Bronze Age (1730–1600 BCE) burial in Whitehorse Hill, Dartmoor, Great Britain. A special feature of this jewelry is the pewter beads inserted into the braid at regular intervals.[38] The special braiding technique of two braided fragments from the Hallstatt mine in Austria was also initially questionable. Both bands are made of brightly dyed wool yarn and date to the early Iron Age, around 800 to 400 BCE. Textile archaeologists have discovered that the bands could have been fingerloop-braided by two people working together.[39]

Linen, Wool, and Silk Laces

The earliest finds date back to the Middle Ages, when the technique became an important and common textile art.[40] The bands and cords were used to close money or relic bags or as the edges of hairnets. They were also important for lacing items of clothing. So that they could be easily threaded through the embroidered eyelets in the fabric, a tip made of rolled-up sheet metal, the aglet, was sewn onto the end of each cord. Particularly fine cords were woven from silk, such as the looped bands from the twelfth to fifteenth centuries that were excavated in London. The preserved cord remains from Lengberg Castle in Tyrol, on the other hand, were almost all made of linen.[41] The descendants of the Vikings, who lived on Greenland until the middle of the fourteenth century, also knew loop braiding. They used the wool of Greenland sheep as a material for woven fabrics and braided bands.[42] Not only surviving braided bands, but also contemporaneous illustrations give us clues to the medieval fingerloop braiding. A fourteenth-century fresco in the "Haus zur Kunkel" in Constance shows two women who are probably working on a looped band. The depicted activity can be clearly recognized on an altarpiece from Saragossa, Spain. Here the Virgin Mary can be seen loop braiding.

38 Celia Elliott-Minty, "Exploring the Construction of a Bronze Age Braided Band from Dartmoor, UK," *Archaeological Textiles Review* 62 (2020): 56–64.

39 Karina Grömer et al., "Iron-Age Finger-Loop Braiding. Finds from the Hallstatt Salt Mine," *Archaeological Textiles Review* 57 (2015): 33–40.

40 Katrin Kania, *Kleidung im Mittelalter. Materialien, Konstruktion, Nähtechnik: Ein Handbuch* (Köln Weimar, 2010) 61; Beatrix Nutz, "Drgens sn wir vs nvt schame," *Estonian Journal for Archaeology* 18.2 (2014): 116–134, here p. 118; and Grace Crowfoot et al., "Fingerloop Braids," in *Textiles and Clothing, 1150–1450*, Medieval Finds from Excavations in London 4 (London, 2018), 138–140.

41 Nutz 2014, fn. 3.

42 Østergård 2004, 106ff.

Lacing made from linen, braided to match the pillow material

Written instructions for loop braiding have existed since the late Middle Ages at the latest. The description for a braid called "dragon lace" (*lintwurm portlein*) from the fifteenth century has unfortunately not been preserved in its entirety. It begins: "wiltu dringen ein portlein" (Will you braid a lace). Instructions for loop-braiding "laces of bowes" can also be found in two English manuscripts from the fifteenth century.[43]

English-language instructions with glued-in braiding samples were published in the seventeenth century. These show mainly braids that could be made by only several people, including interwoven

Above center: Flat braided cord from linen yarn

Directly above: Close-up of a five-loop cord made from horse tail hair

43 See Kania 2010, 62; *The Tollemache Book of Secrets*, 16th century.

letters. These were no longer simple utility bands, but elaborate bands with complicated patterns. Gold and silver threads were also used for braiding, as a border with loops on the robe of the Danish king Frederik II from the middle of the seventeenth century shows.

Fingerloop Braiding in Asia, America, and Europe

Evidence for fingerloop braiding in North Africa is an illustration from 1809 showing an Egyptian braider working on a device with which he can tighten and attach the braided band. Fingerloop braiding was also used in Asia. The samurai of the Japanese Middle Ages used loop-braided silk cords to lace their armor. In Japan, the technique is called kute uchi. On the South American continent, fingerloop braiding was known in Bolivia and Peru, among other places. Indigenous communities in Venezuela and Guyana are known to have used their big toes to tighten the loops during braiding. Today, the Colombian Wayúu still use this technique. They are known for their high-quality textile craftsmanship and produce mainly crocheted bags for the souvenir market. The bands used to close these bags are sometimes created with fingerloop braiding.

In German-speaking countries, the name became virtually unknown over time along with the knowledge of the technique. In Europe, fingerloop braiding lasted longest in various regions of Scandinavia, where simple loop braids were still being made for household purposes in the last century. In the 1970s, the technique spread to the USA as slentre braiding, thanks to an American woman who had learned loop braiding in Denmark. There it was still practiced in workshops and summer camps for young people. Today it is still known there as slentre or fingerloop braiding. In Scandinavia, where it was never completely forgotten, loop braiding found its way into the Viking scene. While simple loop braids are now well known in medieval living history, the more complicated patterns—for example, from the Harley MS 2320 manuscript—are still a specialist area. The Swiss textile designer Noémi Speiser analyzed the old English instructions and thus made them accessible to a wider circle.[44]

44 Noémi Speiser, *Old English Pattern Books for Loop Braiding: A Monograph Critically Comparing English Instructions from the 15th to the 17th Century* (Arboldswil, Switzerland, 2000).

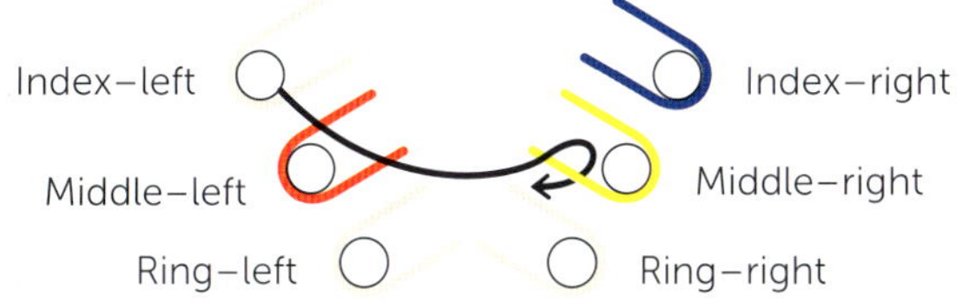

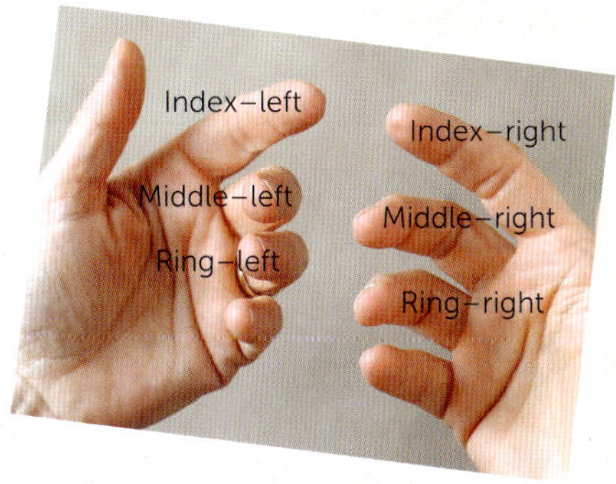

TRY IT!

BRAIDING FROM LOOPED THREADS

To practice the movement and hand position, we first braid a normal plait.

Cut three threads of the same length and fold each one over.

Knot the six open ends together.

Attach the knot to a fixed point (such as a shelf or table leg). The big toe will also work. To prevent the threads from cutting into the skin, you can tie them to a key ring or large plastic ring that you put over the toe. Find a well-lit place where you can stand or sit comfortably.

Pull the loops onto your fingers: one loop on the middle finger of one hand, the other two looks on the index and middle fingers of the other hand.

Braiding: Extend the free index finger and remove the loop from the middle finger of the other hand.

Free the index finger of the other hand (the loop moves from the middle finger to the index finger as the index finger goes into the loop and the middle finger is pulled out).

Extend the free index finger again and retrieve the middle finger loop, and so on.

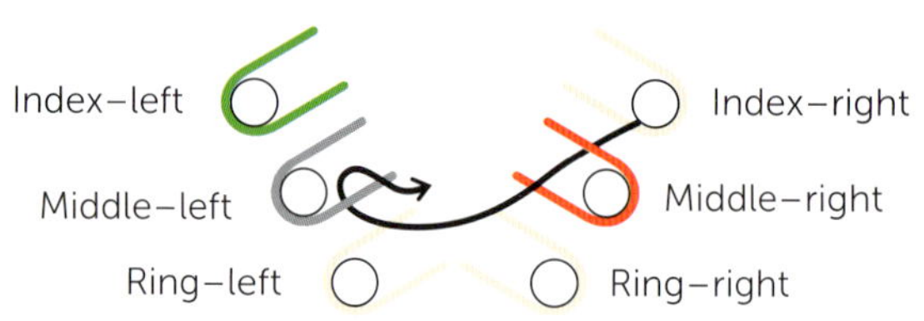

THREE-LOOP CORD

With three folded threads you can braid not only a simple plait, but also a real loop cord. Depending on how you lift the loops, either a single cord or two separate cords are formed.

Materials: Leftover yarn in three different colors, with the same stretchiness, not too fluffy, not too thin.

Preparation: Cut yarn: approx. 3 feet (1 m) per thread. The finished cord is approx. 1 foot (30 cm) long. For a bracelet, 30 inches (80 cm) is enough. You can easily measure this length by wrapping the yarn around your thumb and elbow, like winding a clothesline.

Hold each thread in the middle and fold them in half. Knot the six open ends together. It is important that all the threads are the same length (i.e., all the loops are at the same height).

One loop on the left, two loops on the right

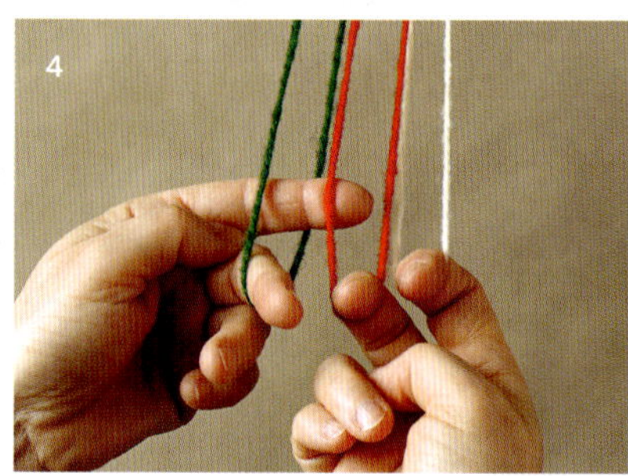

Left index finger grabs the lower thread from the right middle finger.

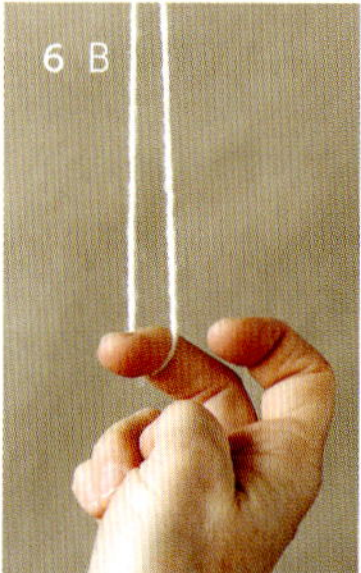

Release right index finger.

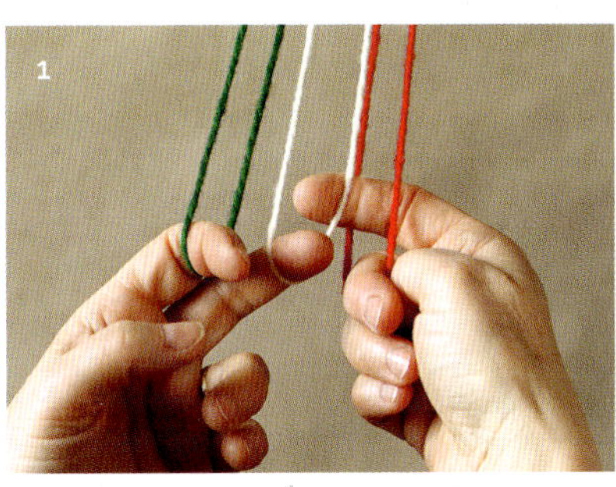

Right index finger grabs the lower thread from the left middle finger.

The loop moves from the left index finger to the left middle finger.

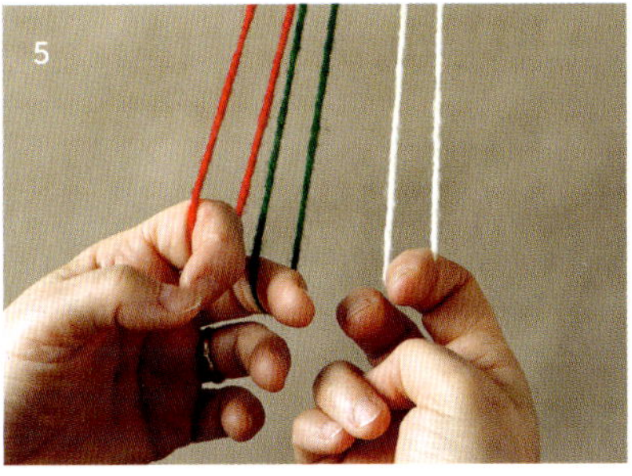

Two loops to the left, one loop to the right

Pull the cord tight.

Tie the knots to a secure point. Put the loops on the fingers (see the photo on page 107 for the finger labels):

Put one loop on your left middle and index fingers and one loop on your right middle finger. Keep your hands vertical so that your palms are facing each other. While braiding, there should be a slight tension to the loops.

1 **Braiding begins:** The right index finger is not holding any loop and becomes the working finger. The right index finger goes through the loop being held by the right middle finger and grabs the lower thread from the left middle finger. Do not insert the index finger into the loop on the middle finger, but grab the middle finger loop from the bottom (outside). This twists the loop and creates an undivided cord.

2 Now on the left hand there is only one loop remaining, and two on the right hand. Stretch both arms out in order to pull the braid tight.

3 Release the left index finger by moving the loop from the left index finger to the left middle finger; the left middle finger goes to the left index finger in the loop. The left index finger goes out, and the left middle finger takes over. The left index finger is now the working finger.

4 The left index finger goes through the loop on the left middle finger to pull the lower thread from the middle right finger through.

5 Now there are two loops on the left hand and only one on the right.

5 Release the right index finger; the right middle finger takes over the loop on the right index finger. The right index finger is now free, and you are back at the starting position.

7 Don't forget to pull tight!

FIVE-LOOP CORD

This simple cord can be braided by elementary-school-aged children. The result is an oval band with colored areas in high contrast to each other.

Materials: Cotton or linen yarn in two contrasting colors. A wool yarn that is not too rough can also be used.

Preparation: Measure the yarn and tie off the bundle of threads as described above for the three-loop braid.

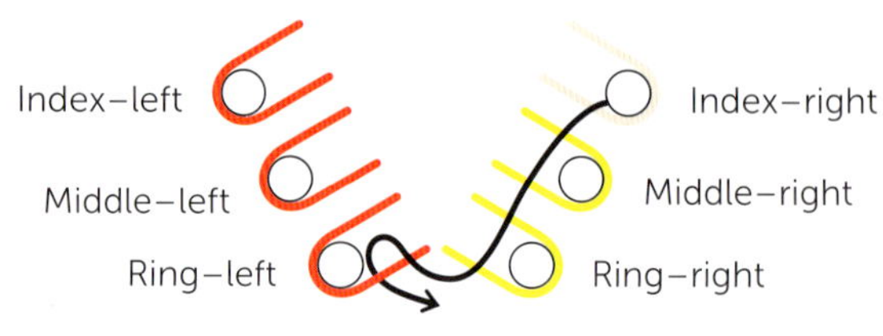

1 Three loops of one color on the left index, middle, and ring fingers. Two loops of the other color on the right middle and ring fingers.

2 **Braiding begins:** The right index finger passes in front of the right middle and ring fingers,

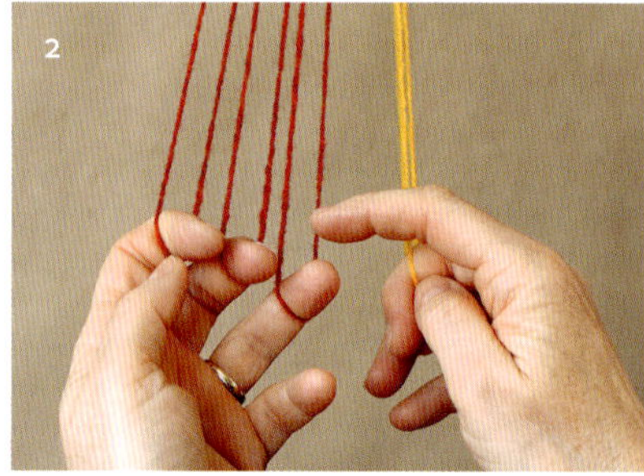

Stretch out the right index finger and take the loop from the left ring finger.

3 to go through the loop on the left ring finger and grab the lower thread. Spread the arms apart to tighten. Repeat this tightening after each thread change.

4 The loops of the left hand move downward—the left index finger is free.

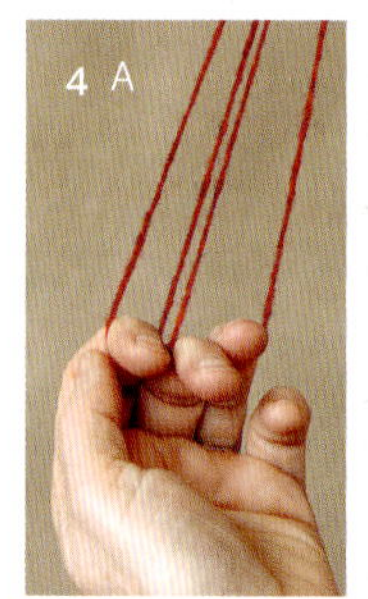

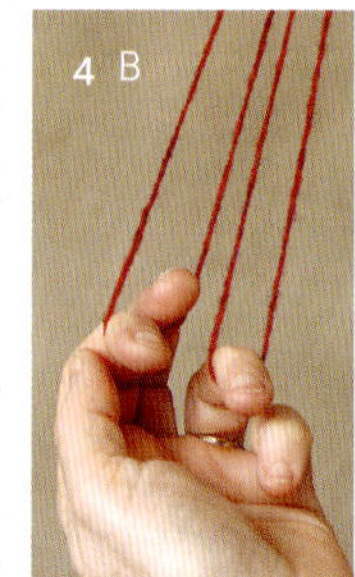

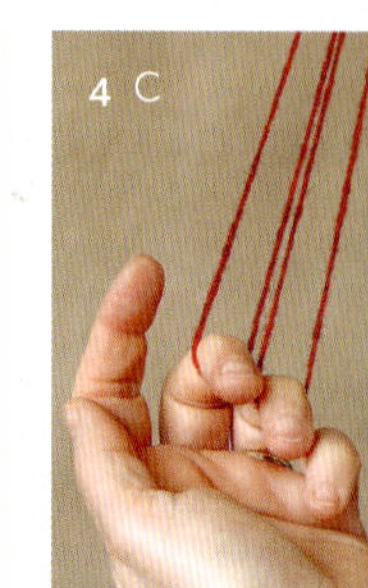

A to C: Release the left index finger.

5 It works the same on the other side: The left index finger passes in front of the left middle and ring fingers,

6 to go through the loop on the right ring finger and grab the lower thread.

Three loops to the left, two to the right

7 The loops of the right hand move downward—the right index finger is free.

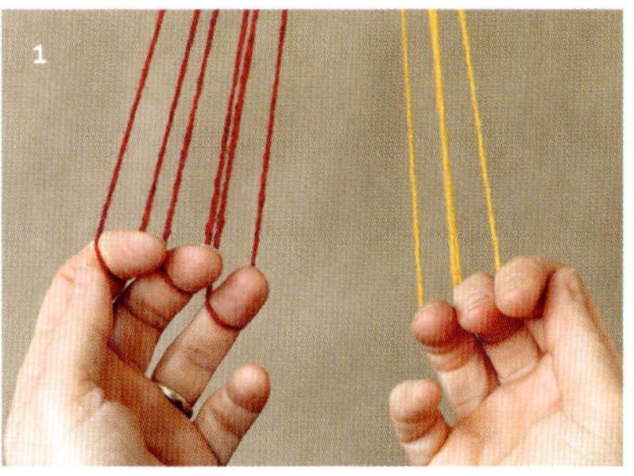

Three red loops to the left, two yellow loops to the right

Two loops to the left, three to the right

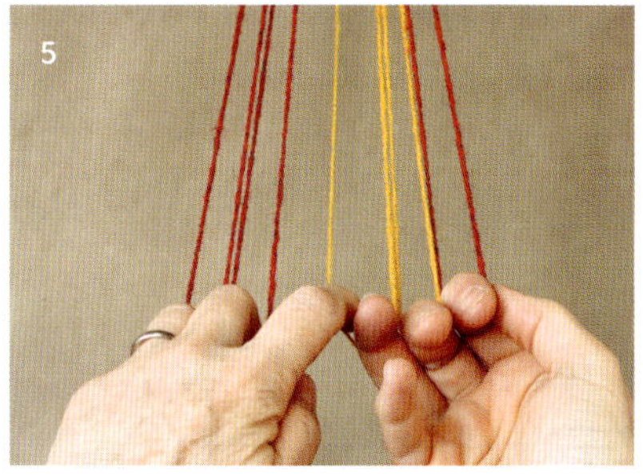

Left index finger takes the loop from the right ring finger.

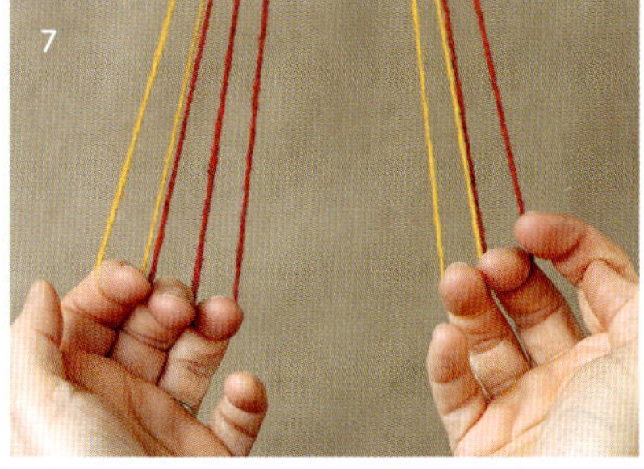

Right index finger is released.

Keep repeating steps **2 to 7**. After ten passes, you will have the initial distribution of colors on your hands again—in our example, three red loops on the left and two yellow loops on the right.

The thread loops are secured so that they do not get mixed up during **a break** or when transporting a work in progress. To do this, slide the loops onto the teeth of a comb in the correct order and use an elastic band to prevent them from slipping off. A strip of cardboard with slits is also practical.

When the loops become too short to braid, slide them off your fingers. Secure the end with a knot.

The distribution of five loops in two colors as can be seen in photo 1 is a good starting point for different patterns. The instructions to the left result in a flat band. When the working finger is led *through* one or two fingers on the same hand before the loop is taken from the ring finger, oval, square, split, or flat bands and cords can also be braided. Countless further patterns can be found online when you search for *fingerloop braiding*. Or you can just experiment yourself by varying the amount, color, and paths of the loops. A template for creating your own patterns can be found on my website www.ausgraeberei.de.

TIPS FROM TEXTILE ARCHAEOLOGIST AND FINGERLOOP BRAIDER KATRIN KANIA

- To ensure that the band tightens as evenly as possible, it helps to wiggle your fingers and little and turn your hands slightly when pulling them apart; for example, with your palms facing upward or downward. When braiding two separate braids at the same time, one often becomes slightly longer than the other. This is normal and difficult to prevent, but wiggling your fingers and turning your hands helps.

- As the loops become shorter, all the angles change when tightening, and the strap becomes much tighter than at the beginning with the long loops. It helps to deliberately tighten at the beginning and loosen toward the end to make the strap more even.

- Made a mistake—for example, because a loop fell off? This sometimes happened to weavers in the Middle Ages. It is usually very difficult to correct a mistake in loop braiding—so it is best to simply ignore it and carry on. There are a few very good examples of bands with braiding errors that were nevertheless used—to the great delight of researchers, since the loop-braiding technique can be proven with certainty only by using these errors.

- With bands like the three-loop cord, two bands are created when all the loops change hands untwisted, a closed band when all loops are exchanged while twisted, and a wide band when the loops are twisted with one hand and taken untwisted with the other. The principle works just the same as with the five-loop cord when adding more loops, when the working finger grabs through both loops of "his" hand.

- Beautiful color varieties can be created from two-colored loops. For this, single threads of the same length are measured in two colors and tied together at one end. The loops created in this way are then tied together at the other end and are braided. The two-colored loops also help when "taking twisted or untwisted loops" causes confusion—and with them, two bands in different colors can be braided at the same time.

- In instructions, sometimes the letters A to D are used to label the fingers. When that causes problems in the beginning, it can help to label your fingers with the corresponding letters.

- The loops sit best in the small crease between the first and second finger joints when the fingers are slightly bent. With more complicated bands where two loops need to be on the same finger, the second loop needs to sit in the crease between the second and third finger joints. But be careful; this is where they like to slip out!

Katrin Kania

Bavaria, Germany

Katrin Kania has a PhD in medieval archaeology. As a textile archaeologist she tries to answer the question "How did it used to be done?"

The main focuses of her work lie in historical spinning techniques, tablet weaving, and medieval tailoring. She also presents and teaches various other techniques such as fingerloop braiding, making hairnets, embroidery techniques, and many more.

Katrin works as a freelance textile archaeologist. She reconstructs textiles and clothing for museums, teaches courses, and offers a selection of material and tools for historical textile techniques at exhibitions and on her online shop.

www.pallia.net.

Book Tip

Katrin Kania, *Kleidung im Mittelalter: Materialien–Konstruktion–Nähtechnik; Ein Handbuch* (Köln: Böhlau, 2010).

FINGERWEAVING

When especially flexible bands were needed in earlier times, such as for belts or garters, fingerweaving was the first choice. With the fingers as the only tool, braids with diagonal, checkered, or arrow-shaped patterns are created.

Fingerweaving can be found all over the world. The materials can be comparatively hard, such as palm leaves or flat wood shavings in basket and mat braiding, or soft and smooth, such as wool and silk. Fingerweaving with different yarns was used mainly for textiles where a certain amount of stretch was required. Elastic bands were not yet available. Traditionally, narrow garters and apron, neck, wrap, and ankle bands were fingerwoven. Belts or colorful edgings were also made using this technique, as were the carrying straps for the roomy peasant's or shepherd's bags woven in checkered patterns in Romania. With a correspondingly large number of threads, very wide braids are also possible. This was used in the Swiss Valais and in French Canada for sashes worn around the hips. [Swiss Sash Ouacoo: pp. 123, 131]

→ Swiss Sash
Ouacoo
pp. 123, 131

THE TECHNIQUE

Just like with normal hair braiding, you don't need anything other than the braiding material and your own hands for fingerweaving, with an additional option of having a place to secure the threads. You can either tie them off or have someone hold them while you are braiding. A fingerweave can be recognized by the course of the threads, which move as diagonal lines from side to side through the structure.[45] These lines are created by the fact that each individual thread is led across through the remaining threads.

Braiding from one side to the other

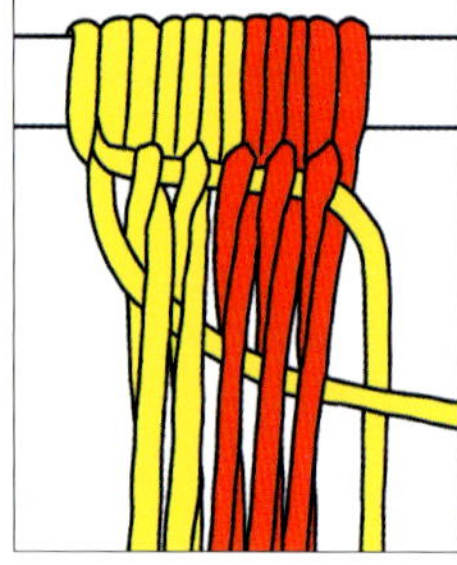

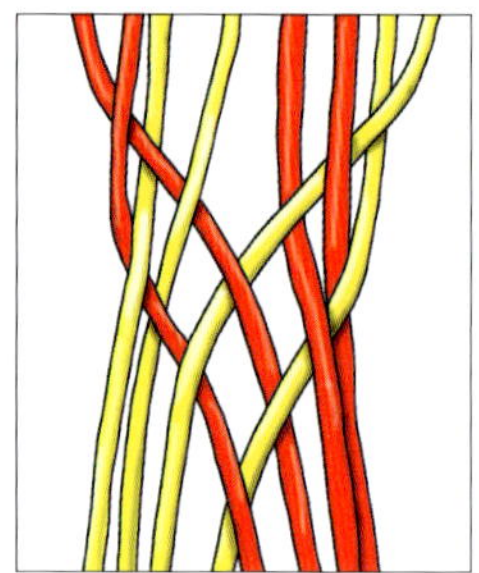

Braiding from the outside to the middle

BRAIDING OR WEAVING?

In German, the term *Diagonalflechten* (diagonal braiding) is used. In English, the technique is often known as fingerweaving, and the French is *tissage aux doigts*, which means fingerweaving. From a technical standpoint, this is not really accurate because it has to do with a braiding technique, not weaving.[46] When weaving, there are passive, meaning fixed, taut threads (warp) and active threads (weft). The warp threads run vertically, and the horizontal threads (wefts) at a right angle to the warp and to the edge of the weave. When fingerweaving, the functions of the threads change. Each thread is sometimes a warp and sometimes a weft thread. So both thread systems are active, and the path of the warp and weft is slanted compared to the edge of the textiles.

When weaving, it is possible to lift many warp threads at the same time to guide the weft thread through the resulting shed—think of the loom when the shuttle with the yarn spool is flicked from one side to the

Braiding machine in the Technical Museum of Band Weaving Großröhrsdorf

other.

While braiding, on the other hand, the individual wraps are carried out one after the other. Mechanization is therefore difficult because different systems have to be moved. However, such braiding machines were developed at the time of early industrialization, and many were in operation in Wuppertal in western Germany. Shoelaces and straps are examples of machine-produced fingerweave.

As with traditional weaving, different structures are also possible with fingerweaving. The appearance of the structure depends on how tightly it is braided. A loose braid produces a plain weave[47] (i.e., the weft thread runs alternately above and below a warp thread). The upper sections of warp and weft are visible. However, if the weft thread is beaten upward, it is practically invisible because it disappears under the warp threads. In this case, we speak of a warp-faced or warp-emphasized textile.

45 Swiss textile artist Noémi Speiser explains this visually in a talk with the Museum der Kulturen Basel at the exhibit *StrohGold*, 2020, online at https://www.museumsfernsehen.de/strohgold-kulturelle-transformationen-sichtbar-gemacht-im-museum-der-kulturen-basel/. Also see https://www.mkb.ch/de/ausstellungen/2014/strohgold.html.

46 Annemarie Seiler-Baldinger, "Systematik der Textilen Techniken," Basler Beiträge zur Ethnologie 32 (Basel, 1991), 46ff.; see Reading Tips at the end of this book.

47 More complicated weaves, such as alternating over two and under two threads or a twill weave, are also possible, but rather uncommon.

Bands braided on the basis of old patterns from different countries.

PATTERNS

When working with different colors in one braid, different patterns can be created, depending on the working method. **Diagonal stripes** are the simplest pattern. They are formed when you always braid in the same direction. For example, always from the left to the right edge. When braiding from two sides, the typical V-shaped arrow or **chevron patterns** are created. You can work from the edge to the center (arrow pointing up) or from the center to the outside (arrow pointing down). Traditional names for fingerweaving patterns are spruces (Lithuania); flames (Norway and Germany); fishtails (Baltic states); herringbone (Norway); arrowheads (Canada); scissors or gussets (Hesse, Germany); and diamonds, lattices, wives' teeth, or witches' teeth (Norway). Checks are created by working with threads in different colors so loosely that the warp and weft are visible. As described above, this creates a plain weave. Diagonally checked tartan patterns are also possible (see below), but they are easier to make using the sprang technique with loose thread ends. [Interlaced Sprang Band: p. 234] You can also braid horizontal stripes, vertical stripes, and ladder patterns. Different patterns can also be combined in one braid with a single set of threads.

FIXING THE THREADS

Traditionally, the braiding threads were often tied to a branch fork or inserted into a stick split at one end. This meant that the person braiding was mobile. The branch could either be stuck into the ground or supported by the person's own stomach when working in a sitting position. The branch fork method was practiced in Latvia and by the Finnish Sami, among others. The technique may also have been known in Italy. The ethnologist Eugenie Goldstern brought back from a research trip a "device made from a naturally grown branch fork with three ends for braiding tapes"[48] from the Italian Aosta Valley. Unfortunately, it is not known what the braids made with this device looked like. However, they could well have been fingerwoven. In other regions, for example in Sweden, the branch fork was used for band weaving. [Branch Fork for Band Weaving: p. 135] In the Swiss Valais, the split stick was used for braiding. This is documented in several older illustrations. For example, in a drawing by the Swiss artist Henri van Muyden (1860–1936), a young shepherdess from the Savièse region can be seen tying her braiding to a stick and working on it standing up.

→ Interlaced Sprang Band p. 234

→ Branch Fork for Band Weaving p. 135

48 *Ur-Ethnographie*. Die Sammlung Eugenie Goldstern. Kataloge des ÖMV, Band 85.

Prehistory and Early History: Sparse Fragments

Fingerweaving in Europe is at least three thousand years old, but material evidence is sparse. It seems to have been a sporadically used technique for when a narrow and flexible band was needed for a special purpose. On some Bronze Age woven fabrics that have survived, the edges were fingerwoven. There are examples from Denmark and Hallstatt in Austria. The find from the Rieserferner glacier, which dates to the Iron Age, contains a narrow band sewn into the side seam of a woolen legging, probably to make it stretchier.[49]

The medieval finds are not much more abundant either. A few fingerwoven textiles from the Viking period were found, such as a fragment just a few centimeters in size in a grave in Birka. Remains of bands were found in the Danish grave of Mammen on Jutland and in York in Anglo-Scandinavia. A leather braided oar fastening from the Oseberg ship is fingerwoven. A blue-and-white checkered wool braid from the Merovingian period (sixth century CE) was recovered from the Morken burial ground in North Rhine–Westphalia. In late medieval Sweden, the technique was used on objects for liturgical use and, quite profanely, on a purse.

Modern Age: Colorful Stockings and Wide Sashes

In the modern era, fingerweaving suddenly became widespread, or so it seems to us. The most important use is now for garters. However, it takes a bit of sleuthing to find evidence of fingerwoven garters. Collectors or ethnologists who were not familiar with the technique often described them as "woven" or just generally referred to them as "braided." They have been handed down from various regions within Scandinavia, Germany, Switzerland, the Baltic states, Russia, and Spain. The technique of garter braiding also reached North America with European immigrants.[50] In Quebec, Canada, wide woolen belts were produced in addition to garters after some time. These sashes, first mentioned in 1777, were wrapped around the fur coat to keep the body warm. Traveling traders, the voyageurs, spread them throughout the colony. They gradually became a symbolic piece of clothing for French Canadians. Even for Indigenous people who already knew the braiding technique and were introduced to the sashes by the traders, they were a status symbol.

49 Grömer, *Prähistorische Textilkunst in Mitteleuropa* (Vienna, 2010), 388. Available in English; see Reading Tips, p. 296.

50 In *Prairie Farmer* from April 3, 1889, 220, there is a lady from Dansville, New York, who gives short instructions for braided garters out of twenty to thirty wool threads that "our grandmothers used to wear." Can be found online in the Illinois Digital Newspaper Collections.

Part of an arrow sash of the Mi'kmaq (McCord Museum Stewart, Montreal, Canada).

GARTERS AND SUPERSTITION

Apart from brides, garters are now used only by people wearing traditional garb. In the past, when there were no elastic bands, they were indispensable for preventing knitted stockings from slipping. Various techniques were used to make the garters: knitting, band weaving [Band Weaving: p. 133], luceting, or sprang [Sprang: p. 215]. However, fingerweaving is particularly suitable because it produces elastic bands.

Garters are associated with special rituals: a garter braided from nine colors is a Russian folk remedy for chills. You are supposed to tie the band around a tree and recite a special saying against the fever. Tie a knot in the band each time you recite it. In East Frisia, fever could also be transferred to the tree by tying a garter around an elder bush. To banish cramps, people in the Ulm region laid the garters crosswise on the table in the evening. And in the Rhineland, the saying went, "If my garter comes loose, someone is thinking of me." In northern Hesse, special color codes revealed a lot about the wearer of the garters. Red with green stood for single women, while blue or purple with green was for married women.

Fingerweaving Today

In some regions of the world, fingerweaving has not yet been completely forgotten. Similar wide sashes like the ones referred to above in Canada also belong to the traditional men's costume of the Savièse in the Swiss Valais. They are known as *ceinture ouacoo* and are about 5 inches (12 cm) wide and up to 11½ feet long (3.5 m). The pattern is composed of consecutive Vs, as one knows from the standard pattern of many garters. In the past, simple carrying straps made of linen or hemp yarn and colorful stocking and cradle straps were braided in the same way. The latter were clamped in a split stick during weaving.

Ouacoo of the traditional costume group from Savièse, at the Swiss Dance Festival in Langnau

Garters are still or once again braided in Norway and the Baltic states. In Norway, braided garters are part of traditional bunad clothing. Each traditional costume region has its own colors and patterns, the correct use of which in clothing is strictly monitored by a state bunad council, Norges Husflidslag, also known half-jokingly as the "bunad police." In Lithuania, where braiding returned to fashion with the revival of the national costume at the end of the twentieth century, fingerweaving is on the list of intangible cultural heritage, which shows that the value of this textile technique has been recognized.

In Asia, there is another use for the flexible bands: the Hunza people in Pakistan and the Indian Punjab braid drawstrings for shirts and pants made of cotton or silk. These bands, known as *azarband*, *kamarband*, or *nada*, are made using the sprang technique [Sprang: p. 215] as well as fingerweaving. After the craft technique was almost forgotten because people preferred to buy machine-made bands, various projects are now trying to bring it back to life. You can also find numerous tutorials on the internet.

→ Band Weaving p. 133

→ Ouacoo Instructions p. 131

→ Sprang p. 215

TRY IT!

FINGERWEAVING WITH SIX THREADS

Begin with a total of six threads in two colors (three strands per color) from thicker, not-too-slippery yarn. Cut the threads to arm's length.

A rod can be used to attach the threads. This can be a round piece of wood, as shown here, or simply a pencil, knitting needle, or chopstick. Attach the stick at both ends so that it hangs horizontally. You can tie it to the back of a chair, for example. You must be able to sit comfortably in front of it without getting back pain. You will find further fastening suggestions in the next instructions. [Tying Threads: p. 127]

1 Fold the threads in half and hang the middle of the thread over the rod. Pull both ends of the thread through so that they hang down the same length.

2 Push the threads together on the rod.

3 Form the shed (= opening for inserting the cross thread): Starting with the left index finger, lift the first thread to the left, place the second thread to the back, etc. Six threads are in front of the index finger, six behind it.

4 Grasp the leftmost thread with your right hand and place it as a weft (= cross thread) in the shed created. Hang the end of the thread upward over the rod.

5 Form the new shed: Starting from the left, pull the back thread forward with your left index finger and push the front thread back (or pull it back with your left middle finger).

6 Six threads are in front of the finger, five behind the finger.

7 Remove the weft thread from the rod and place it at the back: six threads at the front, six at the back. Now pull the leftmost thread through the shed again from left to right and hang the thread end on the top right, out of the way.

8 Continue working according to this pattern.

9 After each row, tighten the braid by pushing the threads upward against each other or tapping them upward with your finger. A pattern of diagonal strips running from right to left will automatically form.

10 Continue braiding until the thread ends are too short to hold. At the end, either wrap the remaining length of thread tightly with a thread, loop it into a knot, or braid it into individual plaits. Further decorative end treatments are presented on page 130.

9 Hand the threads over the rod.

2 Push the threads together.

3 One thread is always to the front, and one to the back.

4 Pull the cross thread from left to right.

5 Form the new shed, starting on the left.

6 Six threads in front, five in the back

7 Pull the cross thread through the shed.

8 Form the next shed.

9 Tighten the braid.

10 Continue until the threads are used up.

→ Tying Threads p. 127

FINGERWEAVING A CHEVRON PATTERN

Yarn recommendation: Pure new wool yarn

Colors: Not too many; preferably clear colors that are contrasted. For a symmetrical pattern, mirror the color order, starting in the middle. Example: Total of twelve threads (four green, four white, four light blue).

Determining thread length or yarn consumption: The length should be 30 percent longer than the finished band. (You lose length through the braiding itself. In addition, the last 6 inches [15 cm] can no longer be braided, since they slip through your fingers and can no longer be held.) If you want to braid a belt, measure an existing belt. Finished length for a garter: 40–47 inches (1.0–1.2 m) (it is wrapped around the calf twice). Cut all threads to the calculated length. The ends hanging down must be open—no loops should form.

Calculate number of threads: Lay the threads next to each other on a ruler to a width of 1 cm and push them close together. Count the threads in 1 cm. Multiply this number of threads by the desired width and divide by 2.

There are many options for **securing the threads**. Try them and see which option is most comfortable for you.

Sit on the floor with the loop around your foot and your leg providing tension.

Secure on your pant leg with safety pins.

Tie to the back of a chair.

Pin to a cushion (similar to bobbin lace braiding).

Hang on a screw clamp that is clamped to the tabletop, for example. Think up a base (such as cardboard) for the clamp so that the table is not damaged.

Tape a small stick—for example, a pencil—to the tabletop with adhesive tape that does not leave any sticky residue, such as masking tape.

Attach directly to a belt buckle or snap hook (if it is to become a belt or bracelet).

Use a clipboard. Weigh it down with a sand-filled bag or a doorstop.

Tie to a tree trunk.

Tie to a simple wooden frame. [Instructions for Sprang Frame: p. 290]

→ Instructions for Sprang Frame p. 290

THE FINGERWEAVING

1 Fold the threads in half and wind the middle of the thread once around the rod. The color order is 2 green, 2 white, 4 light blue, 2 white, 2 green.

2 Starting on the right, form a shed as described above, but with only half of the thread pairs: pull the first green thread in the back to the front and the first green thread in the front to the back, the second green thread in the back to the front and the second green thread in the front to the back, the first white thread in the back to the front, and so on. Now on the right index finger there are 2 blue threads, 2 white, 2 green.

3 Use the outermost green thread on the right (lies on the top of the finger) as the weft through the resulting shed, and let it hang in the middle. The weft coming from the right now belongs to the warp threads of the left side. The right index finger can stay in the shed. On the right index finger there should now be 2 blue threads, 2 white, and 1 green.

4 Then continue building the shed with the second half of the threads, starting on the left and working toward the center. The first green one in the front moves to the back, the first green one in the back to the front, etc. There are now 2 green threads, 2 white, and 2 blue on the left index finge

5 The outermost left thread (lies below the finger) is inserted as the weft thread. On the finger there should now be 2 green, 2 white, and 2 blue, and the green weft from the right that became a warp thread.

6 Now it continues from the right again. The first green thread in the back comes to the front, the single green thread in the front goes to the back, the second green thread in the back comes to the front, etc.

7 Continue according to this pattern. After each row, push the weft thread upward with one finger and pull both halves of the braid down slightly, carefully, so that it becomes denser.

Control: The weave pattern (plain weave = the weft thread always goes alternately over and under one warp thread) must continue in the middle. This happens automatically if you always bring the outermost thread to the front on the right and the outermost thread to the back on the left. To keep an overview, sort the threads before you decide which one has to go to the back and which one to the front. This works better if you don't work too tightly.

If you need a break: Using an overhand slipknot, combine all threads that are currently lying together in a group. Pulling on the open end releases the knot.

1 Hang the threads sorted by color over the rod.

2 Form the shed on the right half.

3 Pull the cross thread from the right to the middle.

4 Form the left shed.

5 Pull the cross thread from the left to the middle.

6 Again from the right, one to the front, one to the back, etc.

7 Tighten the braid.

Please note: The loose ends of the braiding threads twist around each other during braiding. This is not a problem, so don't worry about it; just untangle it if you can't otherwise continue working.

Variation: A plaid or tartan pattern is obtained when the work is so loose that the cross threads are also visible in the braid. The plain weave is then visible. To do this, braid from the edges to the center as described above, but keep both halves of the braid wide apart on both sides. Push each row firmly upward with your index finger. Do not pull the braid down!

DESIGNING THE ENDS

End tassel

Knots and fringes

One or more braids

Colorfully patterned fabric strips (like the Estonian wedding bands)

Stringing beads

Wrap several threads tightly around each other.

Splice the thread ends and twist them until they start to wrap around themselves. Then fold them in half and let go. The resulting doubled thread/twist is then secured with a knot.

Mini pom-poms (instructions on the internet)

Clamp buckles for belts made from belt webbing are available to buy as sewing accessories. These can also be attached to braided belts.

TIPS FOR A OUACOO SASH

FROM ALEXANDRE SOLLIARD

- The traditional ouacoo (see picture on page 123) is made with wool yarn. It is important to use plied yarn. If you use pure wool yarn, you should make sure that no knots (pilling) form when braiding. Otherwise, it would be better for you to pick a wool/acrylic mix.

- Depending on the width of the ouacoo, you need between 120 and 140 threads.

- For a sash 11½ feet in length (3½), you need threads that are 16½ feet long (5 m). A traditional ouacoo always has six different colors.

- Braiding begins in the middle of the sash. Sort the threads in mirror image: the right and left must be the same sequence of colors. The work is clamped under a wooden strip to hold it in place.

- Work from the outside toward the center. Whenever four to six rows have been braided, the fabric is compacted (press upward with your thumb or index finger) and leveled.

- When one half is finished, turn the work over and start on the second half.

- Plan on about 120 hours to braid a sash that is 11½ feet (3½ m) in length.

- The threads at both ends are braided into thin three-strand braids. The sides of the ouacoo can be crocheted with a jagged edge made of matching colored yarn.

Alexandre Solliard
Valais, Switzerland

Alexandre Solliard is a primary-school teacher and textbook author. He learned fingerweaving from his mother over thirty years ago. He passes on this special textile technique in creative handicraft lessons at school and in adult education courses. He presents his self-braided sashes, belts, and webbings at craft exhibitions, including at the Ballenberg open-air museum in Switzerland.

Alexandre is involved in the Société des costumes et des patoisans de Savièse. You can find more information about costume, traditions, and language in Valais on the association's website.

www.costumesdesaviese.ch

Book Tip

Le Costume de Savièse–patrimoine vestimentaire de 1860 à nos jours Savièse, Switzerland: Fondation Anne-Gabrielle et Nicolas-V. Bretz-Héritier, Éditions de la Chervignine, 2011).

BAND WEAVING

With a simple wooden grid or a simple weaving box, you can make sturdy belts from hemp or linen yarn, as well as colorful patterned bands and braids from the finest cotton or silk threads.

WEAVING WITHOUT A LOOM

Bands and belts can be produced with different textile techniques, including through braiding, whipcording, or weaving. Each technique has its pros and cons. For flat and simultaneously tough, strong bands, band weaving is most suited. For bands that are even more robust, the tablet-weaving technique is available. [Tablet Weaving: p. 149] Each warp thread is passed through perforated tablets and twisted together during weaving from several, usually four, individual threads. Weaving tablets can also be used to produce the band fabrics described here: Only two holes of a tablet are covered at a time, and the stack of tablets is tilted back and forth to form the shed.

In weaving, the threads are joined by overlapping and underlapping to form a flat textile. You may be familiar with this technique from weaving bags in kindergarten or from the school weaving frame in textile lessons. The simplest structure in weaving is the plain weave. The long threads stretched lengthwise (the warp threads or warp) are crossed at right angles by the transverse thread (the weft thread or weft).

→ Tablet Weaving p. 149

Woven bands based on American pieces from the nineteenth century

The weft thread passes alternately over and under a warp thread. To enable the weft thread to pass through in one go, a device was invented that automatically lifts every second warp thread: the rigid heddle. Half of the threads are guided through small holes in the heddle and thus fixed in place. Every second thread runs through a slit and can move freely in a vertical direction. If you now move the rigid heddle up and down, an upper and a lower shed open alternately.

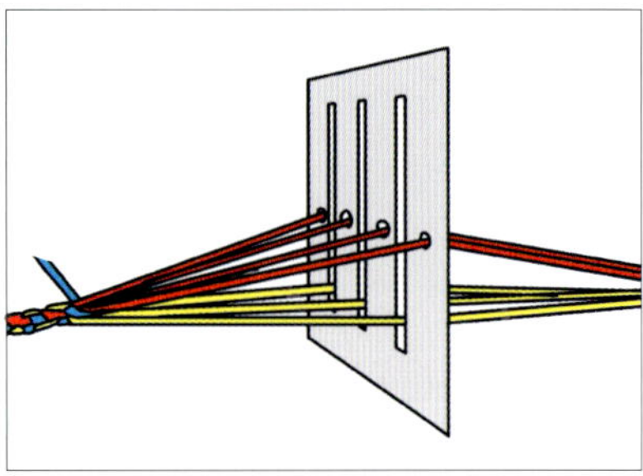

When the heddle is lifted, the threads going through the holes move up as well.

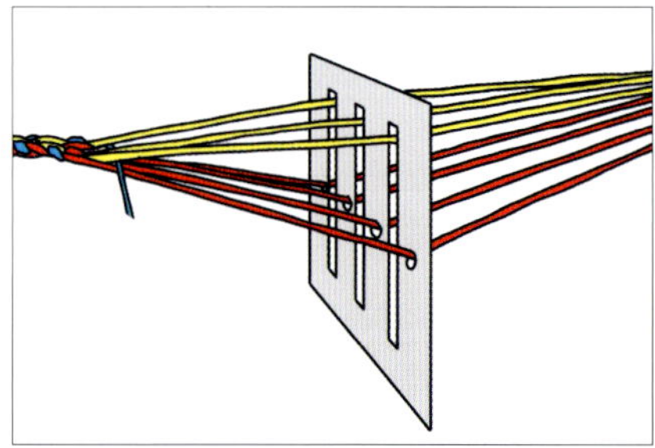

When the heddle is down, the threads in the slits are on top.

The warp threads must be tense. There are various ways to do this. You can use your own body and tighten the threads between your big toe and hip, neck, or hand. It is also possible to stretch between the hip or back of the knee and a fixed point (door handle, table leg, post, tree trunk). In Latvia, Poland, and Sweden, as well as among North American Indigenous peoples, a semicircular bent branch (bow loom) was used as a band-weaving device. The warp yarn supply was wound onto the fork of the branch at one end. The bow kept the warp under tension. In Lithuania, a branch bent into a circle or a vertical branch fork with horizontally fastened pieces of wood was used as a portable band loom to bind the warp yarn. The box tape loom is a special band-weaving device. It consists of a small wooden box with a vertical rigid heddle mounted on the narrow front. Here, the shed is not formed by moving the heddle up and down, but by moving the bundle of warp threads up and down.

Box band loom at the Ratzenried local history museum

In addition to this box loom, there were also band looms with shafts and foot pedals mounted on a simple wooden bench. Others looked like a miniature version of the large loom. They were even available as Jacquard band looms with punched cards. In modern band weaving in the hobby sector, the warp is usually mounted on a wooden band-weaving frame *(inkle loom).*

Three different patterns, each made of five orange and five green warp threads

Band with pick-up pattern. Warp made from cotton yarn in two thicknesses.

THE WARP DETERMINES THE PATTERN

In order to weave a stable band, the warp threads must be pushed close together; otherwise the result is a rather loose plain weave. The resulting strong fabric is a warp-faced band, which means that only the warp threads are visible. The weft thread peeks out only a little at the edges. Patterns can be influenced by the colors of the warp threads. Horizontal stripes are created when one color is pulled through the holes and the other through the slits. Then one color alternates with the other on top. Vertical stripes are created when several threads of one color are pulled in next to each other.

In order to achieve patterns when weaving with the rigid heddle that do not automatically result from the order of the warp threads in different colors, you can raise or lower certain threads before threading the weft thread through. In this way, individual colors can be exchanged as desired. This technique is called pick-up bandweaving. Traditionally, thinner linen or cotton yarn is used for the base color, and thicker wool in a contrasting color for the pattern. In this way, complicated patterns and even letters can be woven.

FROM THE ROMAN RIGID HEDDLE TO THE MODERN BAND LOOM

The weaving technique used with the rigid heddle could have been used over three thousand years ago. Remains of Bronze Age band weaving were found in the Mitterberg copper-mining district in the Eastern Alps. In the Celtic period that followed, there are multicolored bands in repp weave that were discovered in the Iron Age mine in Hallstatt. However, since no rigid heddles were found, it is also possible that these Bronze and Iron Age bands were woven using string heddles.[51] [String Heddle Weaving: p. 141] The same applies to a find from the medieval fortress at Lõhavere in Estonia. The remains of bands made from white-, red-, and blue-dyed wool were found in a birchbark box. They have simple dot and zigzag patterns and may or may not have been woven with a rigid heddle.[52]

There is reliable evidence of band weaving with the rigid heddle in antiquity from several Roman finds, including those from Pompeii, London, Xanten, and Enns in Austria. These heddles are made of wood, bone, antler, or bronze. The next most recent discoveries date back to the Middle Ages. During the excavation of the German Hanseatic settlement of Bryggen in Bergen, Norway, a fragmented narrow wooden rigid heddle (late twelfth century) and a complete piece of elk antler (thirteenth or fourteenth century) were found. Another small rigid heddle made of antler dates from the Swedish Väskinde on Gotland and is dated to the late Middle Ages.

Band weaving also appears in medieval illuminations. The famous Manesse manuscript from the fourteenth century shows a rigid heddle mounted on a column (in combination with hexagonal weaving tablets). There are even depictions of looms from the fifteenth and sixteenth centuries.[53] [Box Looms: pp. 133, 136]

Modern ribbon weaving continues up to more-recent times. Even up to the beginning of the twentieth century, band weaving with the rigid heddle was still widespread. It is known in regions in middle, eastern, and southeastern Europe, Alpine regions, and around the Baltic Sea. Carved rigid heddles, colorfully decorated with patterns and figures, were often given as gifts to express love. They were not necessarily intended for everyday use but were kept and displayed as a status symbol "for show." Many folklore museums still have such beautifully decorated rigid heddles.

Bands were not only made for one's own personal use. In Slovakia, for example, simple woven bands are known as *cigánske tkanice* (gypsy bands). They were sold by their producers or exchanged for other goods. The material was leftover warp yarn

51 This is something that both Karina Grömer and Ronja Lau determine: Grömer 2016, 93; and Ronja Lau, *Studien zu kammgewebten Borten: Eine experimentelle Nachstellung von mittelalterlichen Borten aus dem Baltikum* (Berlin: Bachelorarbeit FU, 2017).

52 Silvia Laul and Ülle Tamla, *Peitleid Lõhavere Linnamaelt* (Tallinn, Estonia, and Tartu, Estonia, 2014).

53 A collection of medieval depictions of box band looms. www.larsdatter.com/weaving.html.

^
Norwegian rigid heddle, approximately 8 × 8 inches (20 × 20 cm) in size

›
Late medieval rigid heddle from the church in Väskinde, Sweden

→ String Heddle Weaving p. 141

→ Box Band Looms pp. 135–136

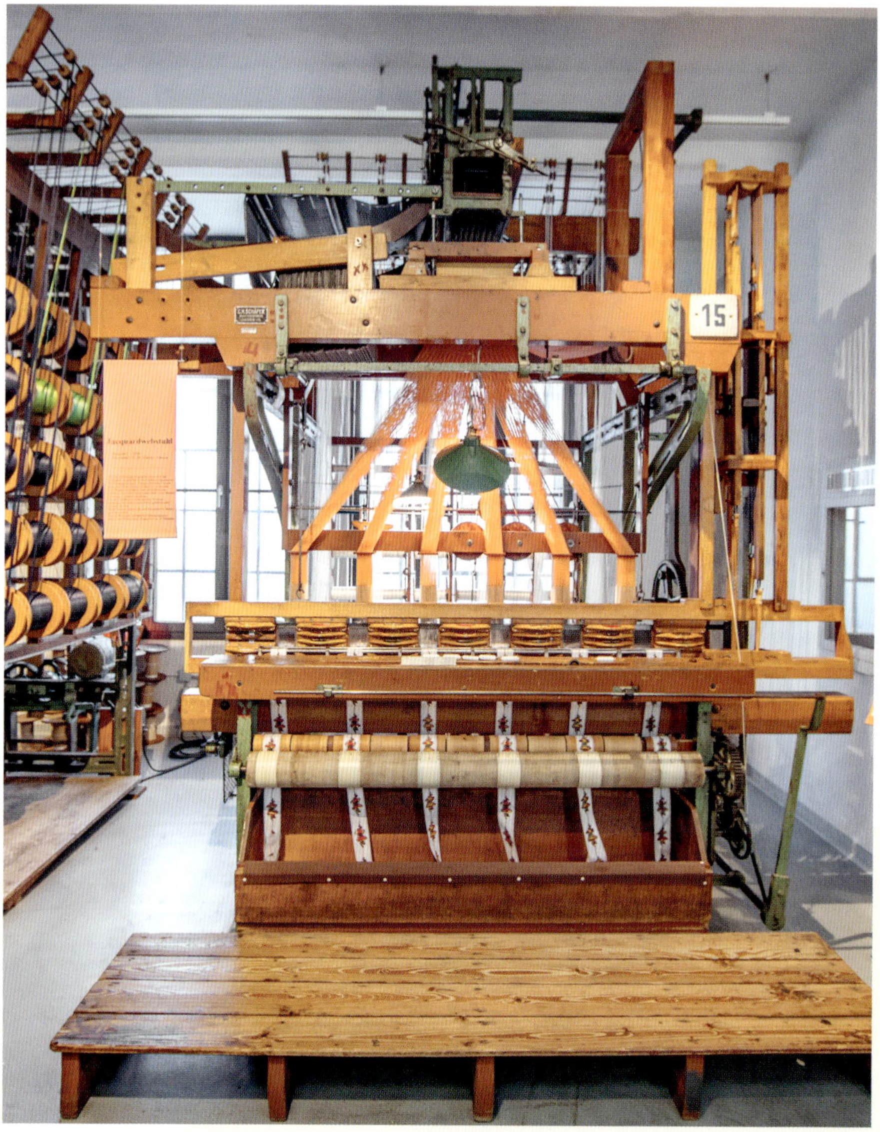

^
Jacquard band loom

›
Mechanical band loom from around 1900 in the Technical Museum of Band Weaving in Großröhrsdorf

from the loom, made from hemp, linen, or cotton. In the Austrian Waldviertel region, band weaving became established in the eighteenth century, using the putting-out system. Families wove ribbons at home and delivered them to their merchants, who supplied them with the raw material. They were sold by itinerant "Bandlkramer." Band weaving was also recommended as a relatively easy-to-learn craft technique as an occupation and a way of earning a living in "children's homes."

Band weaving became continually more industrialized. The centers included Krefeld on the Lower Rhine, the Bergisches Land, Lusatia, and northwestern Switzerland. At the end of the nineteenth century, there were simple so-called "pick" or "girth" looms, multishaft "band looms" or "band mills" for patterned borders, as well as jacquard looms controlled by punched cards. The weavers or "ribbon weavers" used these to produce their narrow weaves. The looms were initially operated with foot pedals, later even with steam engines.

Today, we deal with machine-produced bands every day. You surely have encountered band-woven textiles in everyday life, whether as a seat belt, window blind strap, a carrying strap on a backpack or travel bag, or as trim on an item of clothing.

STRING HEDDLE AND FOOT WEAVING

A shed can also be created without a special device, by tying every second warp thread to a thread loop (heddle) and then using a loop or heddle rod to pull all the loops up or down at the same time. This technique of string heddle weaving is used all over the world.

On the Irish Aran Islands and on Inisheer, wide colorful belts, *crios*, were woven in this way, with the warp stretched between one hand and one foot. This made it possible to work comfortably while sitting down, and the weaving work could be transported. Today *crios* are popular at weddings and are wrapped around the hands of the bride and groom during the wedding ceremony. However, they are woven on modern looms or inkle looms.

Iceland also has an old tradition of foot weaving called *slynging*. It is a combination of weaving and sewing used to reinforce the edges of woven or knitted textiles.

Until recently, band weaving on a ground loom was still widespread in Turkey. The warp is stretched horizontally just above the ground. The stick with the thread loops is attached to a wooden tripod.

Band weaving is a fascinating craft with countless possibilities and variations. I can give you only a small introduction here and have selected an unpatterned strap and a two-colored band in a checkerboard pattern as simple models to get you started. If you would like to learn more about the different patterning techniques, you can find corresponding tutorials on the internet. Of course, it is even better to learn how to weave in a course.

Here are a few ideas on how you can use your self-woven bands: bookmark, key chain, USB drive strap, dog leash, hat ribbon, decorative band (for example, for a door wreath), gift ribbon, bracelet.

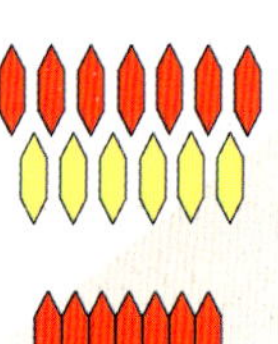

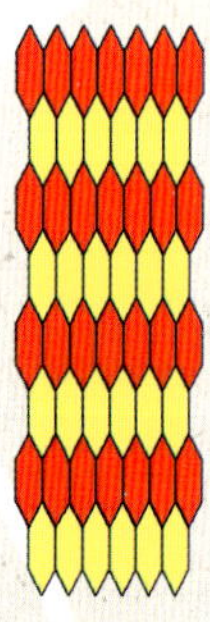

Explanation for pattern drawings can be found on the top of page 143 and on the left on page 146.

TRY IT!

BAND WEAVING, BEGINNER SAMPLE

Material and Tools: First you need to make a rigid heddle. For first try, glue a heddle from popsicle sticks or wooden spatulas, which works quickly. [Instructions: Rigid Heddle: p. 280]

In the beginning, weaving works the best with a smooth yarn. Cotton crochet yarn in two contrasting colors is well suited. A few yards from your scrap supply are enough. In addition, you will need a belt.

Lift the heddle.

Push down the weft with your finger.

Knot the warp yarn together and thread through the warp threads.

Let the heddle hang down. Lead the weft thread through.

Lead the weft thread through.

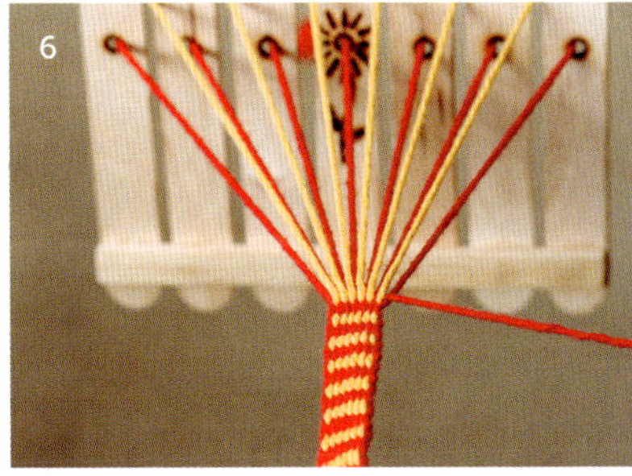

A pattern of horizontal stripes is formed.

1 Cut the warp yarn: a thread for each hole and slit in the heddle. The length for each can be, for example, 5 feet (1.5 m). Knot the ends of the warp yarn together and thread the warp in the holes and slits. One color for the holes, and the other in the slits.

Secure the knots on a fixed point, pull the warp threads tight, and secure the other end with a knot.

Tie these knots on your belt. Position yourself so that the warp is continuously under tension. Make sure that you maintain a comfortable posture so that back pain doesn't ruin your weaving fun. If you need a break, take off the belt and put down the weave. Don't worry, nothing will happen. You can resume work on your band at any time.

2 Let the heddle hang down for the first row or push slightly down so that a shed opens. Lead the weft thread through the shed.

3 Lift the heddle. The second shed will open.

4 Lead the weft thread through to the other side.

5 After each row that you weave, pull the weft thread carefully and push down with your finger. The weft thread should not be visible in the weave. The warp threads lie close together.

6 Continue weaving until the warp yarn is used up. Cut the band. Pull the beginning and the end of the weft thread through the band with a needle.

→ Instructions: Rigid Heddle p. 278

The finished belt strap

WEAVE A BELT STRAP

Material and Tools: You can use the simple rigid heddle described in the previous section. Instructions for other sawn and carved models can be found in the Tool Workshop [Instructions: Rigid Heddle: p. 278] as well as a template for a small shuttle. [Weaver's Shuttle: p. 281] Twine made from hemp or linen is suitable for a sturdy belt. A softer strap can be made from cotton yarn. Wool yarn looks very good but may stick to the wood due to the protruding scales, so I do not recommend it for the first attempt.

Set up the warp.

The warp threads are lead through the holes and slits.

PREPARING TO WEAVE

1 Setting up the warp: Total the number of holes and slits in your rigid heddle. This is how many threads you need to cut off. On a wide rigid heddle, you do not have to use the full width. Decide for yourself how wide your first band should be.

To calculate the correct length, take the preferred length and add anywhere from 15 to 20 percent for the excess on the ends and the contraction or shrinkage due to weaving.

Wrap the warp thread around two fixed points at a determined distance from each other. This works well with two screw clamps that have been attached to two tables. Do not use force to tighten the warp. Pull just tight enough so that the strings do not hang down.

2 Thread the strings through the rigid heddle. If necessary, use a needle or a crochet hook to pull through the holes. Use a strip of cardboard to push in slits.

Knot the warp threads together at one end and attach them to a secure point. Grab the loose end and pull the warp tight. While weaving, pull the warp threads taut with your body. Because of this, make sure you have a comfortable place to sit.

The rigid heddle hangs down—the weft thread is pulled through the shed.

The rigid heddle is lifted up—a new shed is formed.

Push the weft down with your finger.

THE WEAVING

3 Let the rigid heddle hang or slightly push it down. The threads in the slits form the top of the shed; the threads in the holes are down. Pull the weft thread from right to left through the shed while letting the beginning of the thread slightly hang over.

For a neat start, you can place a narrow strip of cardboard in the first shed.

4 Now lift the heddle. The threads in the holes are now up, and the threads in the slits are down. Lead the weft thread from left to right through the new shed. The thread needs to be pulled tightly—only the warp threads should be visible in the finished band.

5 Push the weft thread down toward yourself with your finger.

6 Continue weaving according to this pattern. Once a few inches have been woven and you have the feeling that your arms are too short for weaving, bring the rigid heddle closer to yourself. To do this, loosen the band at the belt, pull it farther around the belt, and clamp it (with a special clamp) or secure it with a loose knot.

Continue until the band is long enough or the warp threads are too short to form a new shed. Cut off the band. The ends of the weft threads should be pulled through the weave with a needle. The ends of the warp threads should be knotted or tied together with a short thread.

→ Instructions: Rigid Heddle p. 278

→ Weaving Shuttle p. 281

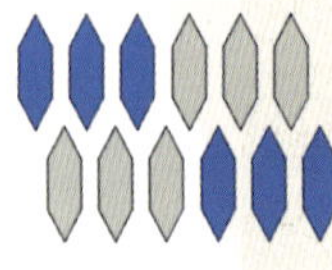

WEAVE A PATTERNED BAND

In band weaving, patterns are created by the colors of the warp threads. The weft thread is there only to hold the warp threads together. The warp threads that are on top in the shed are the ones that form the patterned row. For example, if there are only red threads on top, there will be a red horizontal stripe as seen in the instructions "Try It Now." If over the course of many rows, red and yellow stripes alternate in the threads on top, there will be vertical red and yellow stripes after weaving. [Vertical Stripe Pattern: p. 142] Each pattern, except for the pick-up patterns, is formed by two alternating woven rows. The pattern descriptions therefore show only two rows: one for the slits and one for the holes. It doesn't matter which row you use for the slits and which one you use for the rows. A template for creating your own patterns can be found on my website: www.ausgraeberei.de.

Material and Tools: Rigid heddle and weaver shuttle [Instructions: Rigid Heddle: pp. 278–280] [Weaver Shuttle: p. 281]; belt for securing the warp; yarn in different colors. Cotton crocheting yarn, linen yarn that is uniformly thick, or wool that isn't too fluffy works well.

Draw out your pattern or work according to a finished pattern design.

Preparing to Weave: Prepare the same way as described above for the belt strap.

Setting Up the Warp: If you want to know how to prepare the warp so that the threads do not get confused, look for information in a book about weaving or on the internet. For simple bands, it is fine to measure the colorful warp threads separately and then to pull through the holes and the slits of the rigid heddle according to the pattern drawing.

This time we will use a **weaver's shuttle**, upon which the weft thread is wound. The weft should be in the same color as the border threads of the warp so that you can't see it around the border.

Dressing: You can make the yarn smoother and stiffer by coating it with a liquid paste made from cooked rye flour. This is particularly useful with homespun linen yarn. This "dressing" of the warp takes place after the warp threads have been drawn into the heddle. Brush the paste onto the threads while it is still warm. Remove the excess with paper towels. Separate the individual threads during the drying process. After finishing the band, the paste is then washed out with warm water.

Weaving: The steps for weaving are the same as with the belt strap. Instead of pushing with your finger, however, you will use the weaving shuttle. The pattern is created automatically through the different colors of the warp threads. Once the first weft thread is used up, a new one is put on. To do this, weave two to three rows of parallel threads (end of the first and beginning of the second). This attachment point is hardly noticeable in the finished ribbon. The overhanging ends are later pulled into the fabric with a needle.

TIPS FROM BAND WEAVER

GABRIELA MARTIN

- When threading through the rigid heddle, it is important to work starting from the middle. First pull the middle warp thread through the middle slit of the heddle. That guarantees that the heddle doesn't have more weight on one side and the weave ends up tilted.

- After each row is woven, pull the row of the weft thread tight with care. This avoids loops on the end that hang over, so you get a nice and straight woven edge.

- If you need only one piece of the finished woven fabric by the yard, you can simply cut the band. It is guaranteed not to come undone. Finish the open ends by taking out two rows of the weft with a needle and sewing this thread end through the weave twice.

- Beginners should start with a narrow band without too many warp threads.

→ Vertical Stripe Pattern p. 142

→ Rigid Heddle Instructions pp. 278, 279, 280

→ Weaving Shuttle p. 281

Gabriela Martin
Baden-Württemberg, Germany

The master weaver Gabriela Martin from Freiburg demonstrates her craft at the Black Forest Open-Air Museum Vogtsbauernhof, gives weaving courses in her textile workshop, and shows the art of her "band work" at craft markets. You can find instructions, patterns, and book tips on band weaving on her website.
www.webekamm.de

TABLET WEAVING

Four warp threads are fed through the holes in a tablet. When the tablet is turned, a four-thread cord is formed. If several of these cords are connected by a transverse weft thread, a band is formed. Tablet-woven bands are therefore particularly stable. Since only the thread that is on top during the rotation is visible, a variety of patterns are possible by changing the direction of rotation.

Strictly speaking, tablet weaving is not an endangered textile art. It has been researched for over a hundred years and is now being practiced again by a relatively large number of people. In fact, however, it is known only in certain circles, especially among Celtic and medieval reenactors. It can also be found in educational museum programs. In Norway, where *brikkeveving* used to be part of folk art, it is now on the red list of endangered craft techniques.[54]

The final products made with tablets can look very different. On one hand, this technique can be used to produce fine, highly complex fabrics, such as the braids of the Middle Ages, which were interwoven with gold thread. On the other hand, it was used to make solid, sturdy belts for rural households.

54 Norges Husflidslag Rødlista: https://husflid.no/fagsider-/rodlista/.

THE TECHNIQUE

The most common tablet weaving technique uses thin, square, four-hole tablets made of cardboard or wood. A long (warp) thread is pulled through the holes in the corners of each tablet. The ends of the warp threads are knotted together and attached to a hook, window handle, or similar. The threads are pulled taut by tying the other end of the threads to a second fixed point; for example, a belt. The tablets are combined into a stack. If you hold this stack of tablets upright in front of you, a triangular space opens up between the threads, the so-called shed. The cross or weft thread is now passed through this first shed. The entire stack is then turned a quarter turn. This opens up a new shed through which the weft thread is passed. A tablet-woven band is very stable, since each warp thread is a twist of four individual threads. Four-thread cords are connected by the weft thread. The weft thread is therefore not visible because it is tightened to such an extent that it is covered by the warp thread cords.

The tablets can move freely on the warp threads and are pushed farther and farther as the work progresses. The number of tablets and the yarn thickness influence the width of the finished band. Narrow bands can be woven with just three or four tablets. At the other extreme are examples such as the Germanic cloak from the Thorsberg moor, where the edges were made with up to 178 tablets.

Traditional patterns from northern Europe to the Middle East

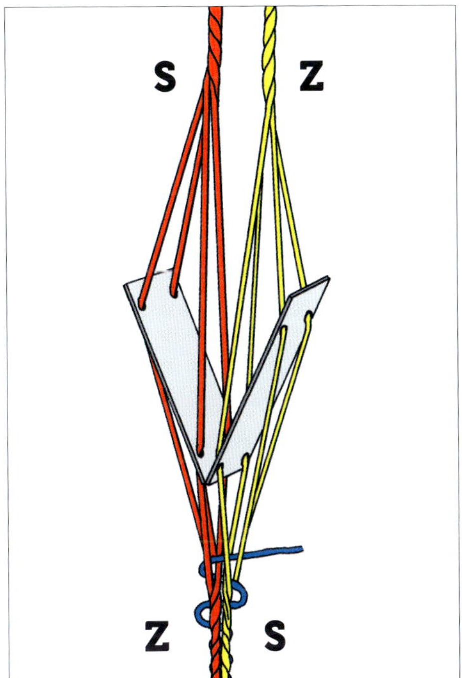

Instead of using four-hole tablets, patterned bands can also be woven using two-hole tablets. This is a time-saving way of creating a twisted textile. [Twining: p. 171] In Gujarat, India, the edges of cloth produced on the loom are stabilized and decorated with borders woven with two-hole tablets. Well-known archaeological examples of the use of two-hole tablets are the bands from the grave of the so-called Celtic prince of Hochdorf and from the burial of the Merovingian abbess Berthila of Chelles.

If all the tablets are threaded in the same direction, the finished ribbon will twist into a spiral. This can be avoided by alternating the tablets S and Z. You will be familiar with these designations from the chapter on splicing. [Splicing: p. 47] The direction in which the cords twist is also determined by the way the tablets are wound. This is called the S- or Z-twist (see drawing).

→ Twining p. 171

→ Splicing p. 47

The easiest way to create patterns is to use warp threads in different colors. The design can be varied by changing the direction of rotation. These turning points, which can be recognized by the mirror image pattern in the finished fabric, are typical of tablet fabrics. In addition, when turning in the opposite direction, the annoying twisting of the warp threads behind the tablets is eliminated, and there is no need to open the knot and untwist them by hand. In the brocade technique, a second weft thread, often made of metallic yarn, is used. This is partially visible because it is passed over only certain warp threads. Float weaving works in such a way that individual tablets are not turned. This means that the upper thread does not rotate and remains visible at the top. In the case of complicated patterns, not all the tablets are turned in one direction at the same time but are turned as individual groups of tablets or even individual tablets in the respective direction according to the pattern. In this way, picture motifs and letters can be woven. Different yarn thicknesses and different materials—for example, wool and silk—can also be combined when weaving. Even tubular fabrics are possible. Individual, particularly large and heavy tablets with three or four holes can be used to twist three- or four-strand ropes. [Rope Making with the Branch Hook: p. 72]

You can also weave and attach fringes to an edge in one go. To do this, the weft thread is guided around a wooden slat before it is inserted back into the shed. This ensures that the fringes are always the same length. This technique works in a similar way to making fringes in loop weaving. [Fringe Braid: p. 102]

THE TABLETS

The classic materials for weaving tablets are wood, flat bones (such as shoulder blades from cattle), horn, and leather (such as camel skin in Turkey). In Greenland, weaving tables were found made from whalebone; that is, from the baleen of whales killed there. It is the material from which corset stays were also cut. Parchment is also conceivable and certainly suitable as a raw material, since it is thin and stable. However, no old tablets made of this material have yet been found. Today, tablets made of wood, cardboard, or plastic are used.

The bone weaving tablets found during archaeological excavations are often decorated with a diamond pattern.

A selection of self-made weaving tablets out of paper, wood, and MDF

Decorations consisting of small circles with a dot in the middle also occur. The number of holes in the boards ranges from two to a maximum of eight. There are also various possibilities for the outer shape. Square four-hole tablets are the most common. However, there are also three-hole, six-hole, and even octagonal tablets. The edge length of the square tablets is between 1.5 and 3 inches (4–8 cm) for most of the surviving pieces but is often around 2 inches (5 cm) because this size is easy to hold by hand. The size of the holes determines which yarn can be used. The warp yarn used must fit well through the holes so that the boards can be turned easily.

Possible accessories for tablet weaving are the **weaving sword** and **weaving shuttle.** [Instructions: Weaving Shuttle: p. 281] The weft thread can be easily wound onto the weaving shuttle, and the weft is struck firmly with the weaving sword. However, neither tool is absolutely necessary.

→ Rope Making with the Branch Hook p. 72

→ Fringe Braid p. 102

→ Instructions: Weaving Shuttle p. 281

TABLET WEAVING IN ANCIENT TIMES

The band-weaving heddles described in the previous chapter are very rare archaeological finds. Weaving tablets are far more numerous, at least from the Roman period onward. Tablet weaving has been documented since the Bronze Age. The world's oldest tablet found to date was discovered under a rock shelter in the district of Göttingen in Lower Saxony. It is a square bone slab with holes in the corners and a drilled circular eye decoration. From the Iron Age, following the Bronze Age, there are various preserved tablet fabrics, such as the famous finds from Hochdorf and Hallstatt, and individual woven tablets. The four boards from the Iberian site of El Cigarralejo near Mula in the province of Murcia in southeastern Spain, dating from around 400 BCE, are made of boxwood. The two four-hole tablets from the Danish chariot find at Dejbjerg Mose from the first to the third century CE are also made of wood. A triangular ceramic tablet was found in Smolenice-Molpír in the Slovak Republic.

Only during excavations at Roman period sites do the finds of weaving tablets become more common. Most of them are triangular and made of bone.[55] The Germanic tribes and Anglo-Saxons of the Migration period used tablets to weave stable selvedges for fabrics produced on the warp-weighted loom. There are pieces of fabric that are bordered on four edges with tablet-woven bands; for example, the Thorsberg cloak from the third century CE. The tablet bands served as the start and end bands for this rectangular fabric. Lengthwise, the weft of the tablet woven edge is also the warp of the fabric. In the transverse direction, the weft was pulled through the tablet shed and then in the same working step through the shed formed on the loom.

The most famous discovery from the Viking Age is probably the set of fifty-two well-preserved boards from the Oseberg ship. Even the warp threads are still attached. The remains of a band made of gold brocade were found on the underside of a silver bowl clasp from Haithabu. In Anglo-Scandinavian York, only the warp threads of a silk ribbon have survived. The weft thread, probably made of plant fiber, has disappeared. But not all ribbons from the Early Middle Ages are precious and richly patterned. For example, the tablet-woven artifacts from the Wurt Elisenhof (eighth through eleventh centuries) are mostly single-colored, simple woolen bands. The early medieval weaving tablets were made of wood, bone, or bronze and are often decorated with circle and dot ornaments and diagonal lines. In the High Middle Ages, in addition to incredibly fine bands woven from silk, gold, and silver threads, which adorned the robes of the nobility and clergy, there were also very

55 Uwe Gross provides an overview of the finds: "Antike und mittelalterliche Webbrettchen—Quadratisch (nicht immer), praktisch, gut," *Archäologische Nachrichten aus Baden* 80–81 (2010): 26–30.

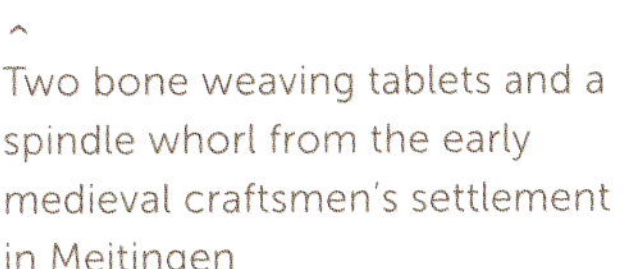

^
Two bone weaving tablets and a spindle whorl from the early medieval craftsmen's settlement in Meitingen

›
Edge of the Thorsberg cloak, rewoven by Silvia Ungerechts with 138 tablets

simple everyday and utility bands made of wool.

There are no tablet-weaving finds from the Late Middle Ages,[56] so there is a gap between the High Middle Ages and the more recent folkloristic evidence, although numerous illustrations in manuscripts show late medieval tablet weaving. In these illuminated books, the tablet weaving is always stretched between two massive vertical wooden columns.

In 1990, Heidi Stolte from the Düppel Museum Village summarized the spread of tablet weaving in the Modern Period: "As a folk art practiced on a modest scale, it can still be found today in Scandinavia, Iceland, European Russia, the Balkans, Turkey, the Caucasus, the Middle and Far East, North Africa, and now also in America, where it was probably introduced in the last century."[57] The modern products made with weaving tablets are mainly simple utility textiles: hairbands and garters, belts, reins and bridles, saddle straps, carrying straps, and tent straps.

Rediscovery

As early as 1874, the Swedish archaeologist Hjalmar Stolpe recognized a bone plate excavated in the Viking settlement of Birka as a tool for weaving. But it was folklorist Margarethe Lehmann-Filhès (1852–1911) whose publications and demonstrations in the Berlin Museum of Decorative Arts initiated a modern study of the technique. The weavers Peter Collingwood (*The Techniques of Tablet Weaving*, 1982) and Otfried Staudigel also contributed to its dissemination. Heidi Stolte did pioneering work in the field of experimental archaeology at the Düppel Museum Village in Berlin. Thanks to the medieval and Viking markets that emerged in 1980s, more and more people became acquainted with tablet weaving. Today you can easily buy ready-made tablets and the corresponding band looms. At almost every historical event, you can see costumes with tablet-woven braids, regardless of if they are being used to depict Celts, Vikings, or medieval nobles.

56 Ibid.

57 Heidi Stolte, "Technik des Brettchenwebens," in *Experimentelle Archäologie in Deutschland*, ed. Mamoun Fansa, Archäologische Mitteilungen aus Nordwestdeutschland, Beiheft 4 (Oldenburg, Germany, 1990), 434–437, here p. 437.

Round the square tablets' corners and make holes.

Thread the tablets, alternating.

In the instructions I will limit myself to simple utility bands using four-hole tablets. The turning direction always stays the same and is not important for the pattern. The examples are based on ethnological collections in different museums. If you would like to try more complicated patterns after your first attempts or other weaving techniques (brocade, float weaving, twill weave, double face, three- or six-hole boards, omitted holes), you will find them among the website and books listed in the appendix. You will also find descriptions in the literature for copying the weaves of historical bands from archaeological discoveries and church treasures. You can use the handmade tablet-woven bands in many ways, as a bookmark, key chain, bracelet, guitar strap, or suspenders. They are even strong enough to be used as dog leashes. For these, however, you should use easy-care cotton or synthetic yarn.

TRY IT!

A BAND WITH LENGTHWISE STRIPES

Materials: Scrap cardboard (cardboard box, old playing cards); yarn scraps in four colors (in my example, red, yellow, blue, and white, smooth yarn such as cotton crochet yarn works well), string/twine; belt

1 To begin, you need four small cards that you cut in a 2.5 × 2.5 in. square (6 × 6 cm, or somewhat smaller). The corners are rounded with scissors or, if available, a paper corner rounder.

Punch a hole in each corner with an office hole punch, or burn with a soldering iron.

2 Cut the yarn in 6½-foot (2 m) pieces. You need a total of sixteen threads, so 4 × 6½ ft. red, 4 × 6½ ft. yellow, 4 × 6½ ft. blue, and 4 × 6½ ft. white.

Pull the threads through the holes. Each card should have four threads of the same color. To prevent the woven ribbon from spiraling, thread the tablets alternately from the front and from the back.

3 Tie all the threads together at one end. Securely attach a stable string to the knot. Hang this string over a hook on the wall, cabinet knob, or window latch.

Keep the threads under tension and push the tablets all together along the warp threads toward the other end. Run your fingers lengthwise through the threads, arranging them and bringing them to the same tension. Make sure that the threads do not slip out of the tablets!

Connect the threads on the open end with a knot.

4 Tie this end of the warp to your belt. Stand or sit down so that the warp threads are well tensioned. Make sure you are in a comfortable position to prevent back pain.

5 Cut a weft thread, about an arm's length, of whatever color you prefer.

Arrange the tablets in an upright position. Pull the weft thread from the right to the left, allowing the thread end to protrude slightly.

6 Turn all the tablets a quarter turn toward you. If the new shed is not clearly visible, it helps to turn all the tablets along the warp threads slightly toward you and then slightly away from you again.

Pull the weft thread from the left to the right through the new shed.

7 Use your index finger to tap the weft and tighten once more. Repeat this tightening process after each additional weft.

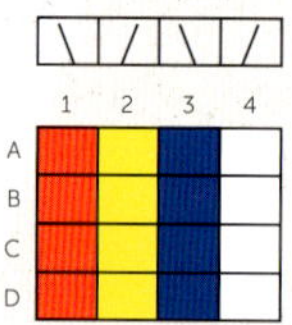

Longitudinal Stripe Pattern.
1 through 4 mark the tablets,
A through D the holes.

8 Continue weaving according to this pattern. The result is a lengthwise striped band in four colors.

9 You can see that the threads also twist into strings behind the tablets, in the opposite direction.

To break up this rotation of the warp threads, change the direction of rotation after a few turns: now turn the tablets away from you instead of toward you.

10 When the band is finished (i.e., the free space is too short to turn the tablets), cut the warp threads. If you wish, you can pull the weft thread end into the fabric with a needle.

You can let the thread ends hang down as a fringe or braid them.

If a tablet snags when turning and cannot be moved at all, check the threads. In most cases, a single thread has wrapped itself around a corner of the tablet and is holding it in place.

Order the warp threads.

Hold the warp threads under tension.

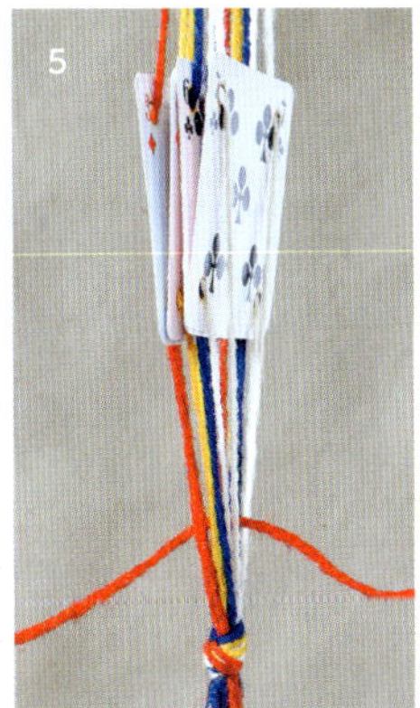

Pull the weft thread through the first shed.

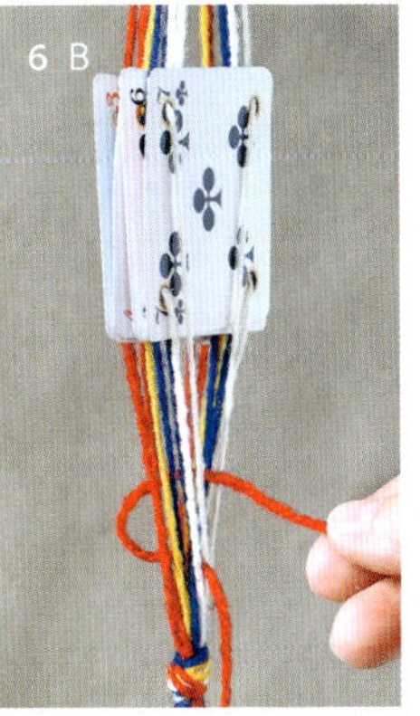

Turn all the tablets and pull the weft through.

Tap the weft with your finger.

A pattern of longitudinal stripes is created.

Change the turning direction. The turn can be easily recognized.

The completed band with braids at one end

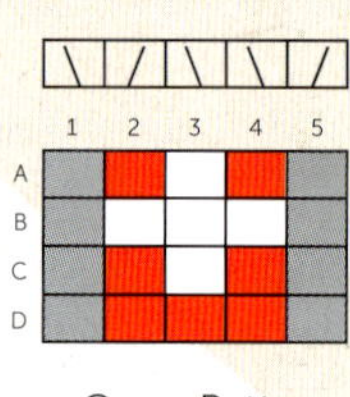

Cross Pattern

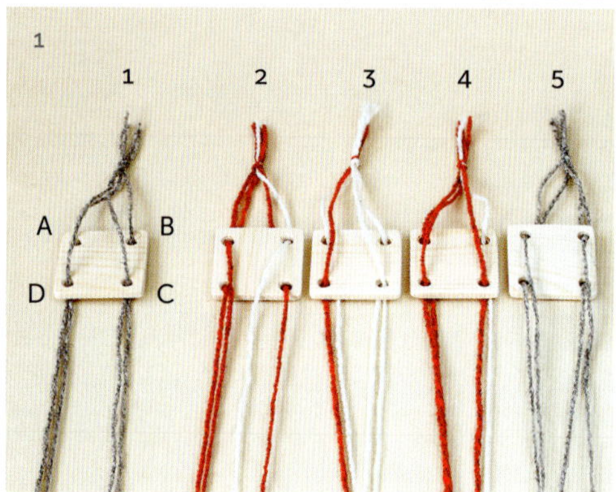

Arrange the tablets according to the pattern picture.

Stack the tablets and connect the threads.

WEAVE A PATTERNED BAND

Materials: Yarn scraps in three colors; string/twine; belt.

Tools: Five weaving tablets, one weaving shuttle, possibly a weaving sword. [Instructions for Weaving Tablets: pp. 282–283] [Instructions for Weaving Shuttle and Weaving Sword: p. 281]

Prepare the Threads

Cut about an arm's length of weft thread in the color of the edge stripe (it will almost completely disappear in the weave).

For the arrow pattern, you need eight threads in gray, five threads in white, and seven threads in red. They can be as long as you wish, but not too long for your first patterned band (somewhere between 1 yard and one arm span). If you would like to weave longer bands such as a belt, make sure you calculate enough left for the warp thread: The finished band will be somewhat shorter than the warp threads because (1) it shrinks a little during weaving, and (2) the last 8 inches (20 cm) cannot be woven anymore.

1 Sort the threads into groups of four as they should be put in the tablets. The four threads of each group should be connected at the end with a knot.

Lay the tablets next to each other on a table and arrange according to the pattern drawing: The holes in the tablets are labeled A to D, starting at the top left and going clockwise (see photo). The individual tablets are numbered consecutively.

How the threads are inserted into the holes is indicated by the diagonal stripes:

\ means move the tablet so that it hangs in this direction: \ = S. If you turn the tablet away from you, the four threads are S-twisted.

/ means move the tablet so that it hangs like this: / = Z. If you turn the tablet away from you, the four threads are Z-twisted.

The direction in which the threads in the finished band are twisted, S or Z, depends on the turning direction.

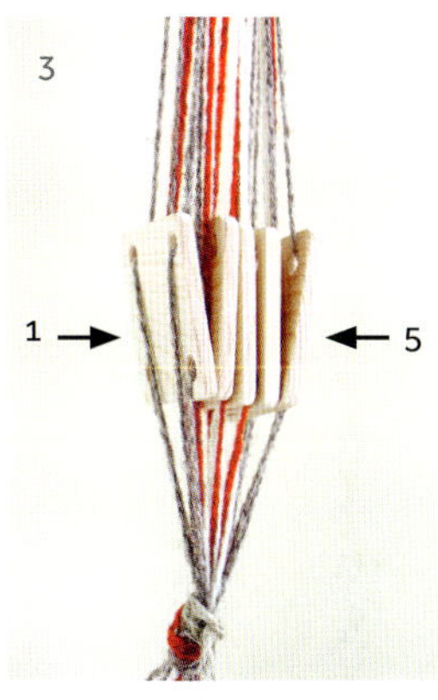

Pull the warp threads tight and align the tablets in an upright position.

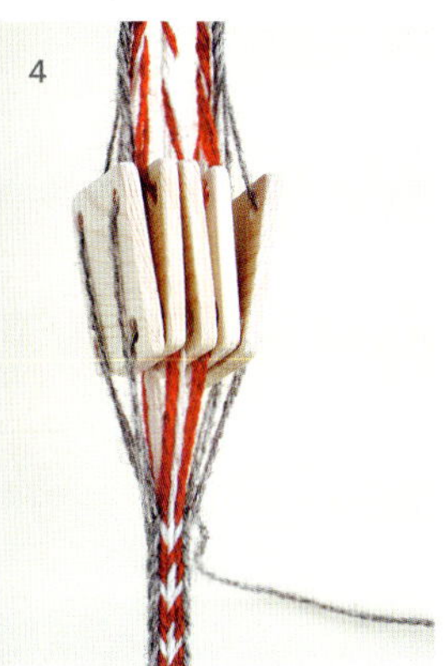

The warp threads twist above the tablets.

The turning point is recognizable in the weave.

2 Stack the tablets in order, with tablet 1 at the bottom. Hold the tablets firmly and tie all the knots together.

Hold the warp tightly between your belt and a fixed point as described on p. 153.

Align the tablets in an upright position. Before weaving, check one more time that everything is in the right spot.

3 Weave as described above. For robust straps you can use a weaving sword for pushing down the weft thread. Normally, your finger or a weaving shuttle is enough for beating.

4 Change the turning direction from time to time so that the warp threads untangle. You can also change the turning direction after a set number of rows. Then you will have a uniform pattern.

5 Once the turning direction is changed, the pattern will be mirrored.

Further Patterns

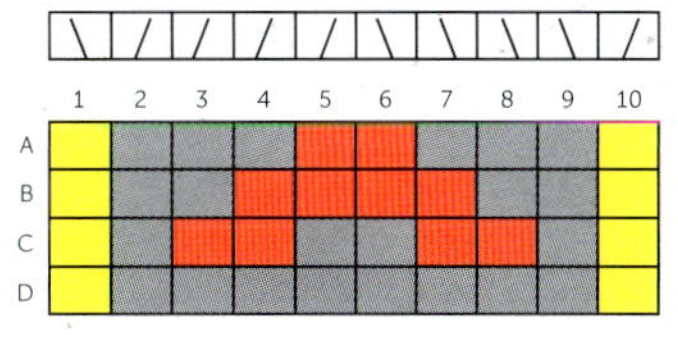

Turkey

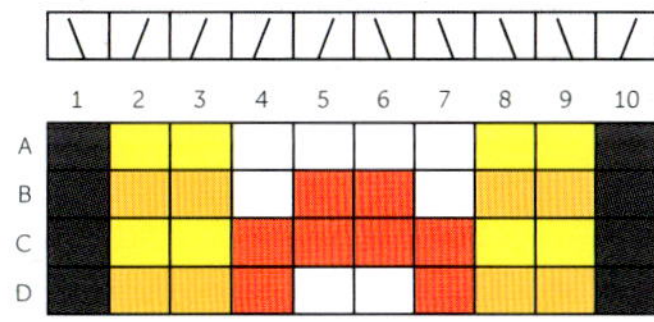

Macedonia

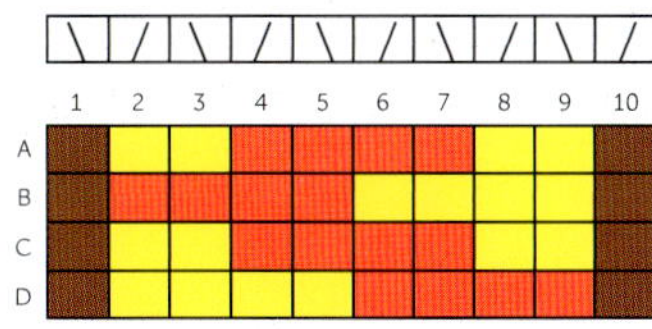

Norway

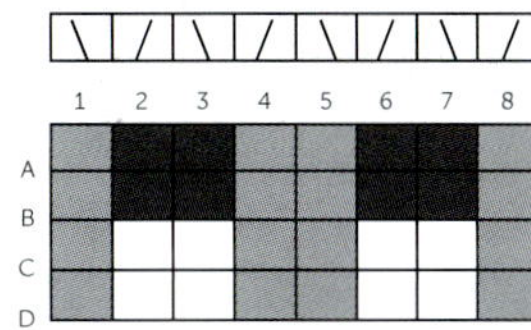

Syria

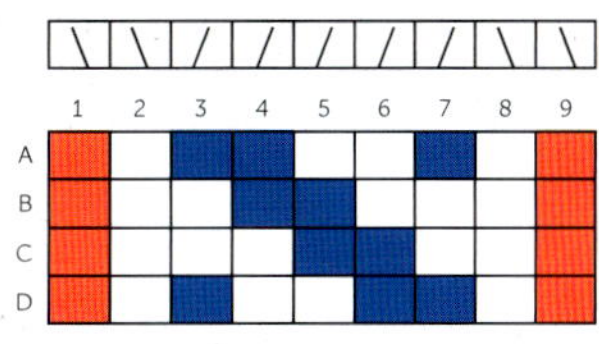

Estonia

→ Instructions: Weaving Tablets pp. 282–283

→ Instructions: Weaving Shuttle p. 281

→ Instructions: Weaving Sword p. 281

TIPS FROM TABLET WEAVER

ANDREA WAGNER-NEUMANN

- Always use plied yarn that is not too elastic. Single yarn or multi-strand not plied yarn cannot withstand the friction caused by the tablets and will unravel.

- Memorize which hole is A, B, C, and D for the first few bands and soon avoid any labels on the tablets. This disturbs you when weaving complex patterns

- A band gets shorter when weaving—even more so the thicker and stiffer the material is. Also, a part of the warp cannot be woven. It is better to plan with a warp thread that is too long than too short.

- When making patterned bands, make sure that there is enough contrast among the colors so that the patterns stand out. You can find out whether colors harmonize and contrast by twisting the threads together and looking at them from a distance.

- If three or more colors are used in a tablet, it may not be possible to change the tablet position easily. Therefore, pay attention to S and Z when threading.

- If you are using a loom, always relax the warp after weaving, to protect the threads.

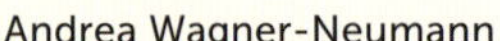

Andrea Wagner-Neumann
Rhineland-Palatinate, Germany

Andrea Wagner-Neumann is a passionate tablet weaver with a wide-ranging interest in other textile techniques, from weaving to hand spinning and sprang. She demonstrates her craft in the Celtic village on the Hunnenring, in museums, at arts and crafts markets, and at historical events. She teaches tablet weaving in courses at home and abroad in cooperation with adult education centers, museums, and associations (see www.brettchenwebershop.de). On her website wirweben.de you will find, among other things, a comprehensive list of literature on the subject of tablet weaving.

www.wirweben.de

Bands from Andrea Wagner-Neumann with patterns from Celtic to modern, in wool, cotton, and silk

CLOTHING AND ACCESSORIES

Techniques for flat textiles can be used to produce accessories and smaller garments. Here you will find ideas for bracelets and arm warmers, mittens, stockings, hats, and bags.

Perhaps you have never heard of twining or sprang. That's no wonder, because these old textile techniques became almost forgotten within the last century. Textile and needlework lessons in school were limited to crocheting and knitting, embroidery, and sewing. Traditional skills could survive only where they were passed on from elders to the younger generation, and where people continued to wear homemade clothing. Just in the nick of time, individual researchers began to look into the subject. Their documentation and descriptions are a great help in learning the old methods.

THE RIGHT TECHNIQUE FOR EVERY PURPOSE

Today, we feel most comfortable in light and stretchable clothing. The majority of our clothing is knitted jersey or tricot fabrics, such as cotton T-shirts, often with additional stretchy yarns. Clothes used to be much tougher. An example is jeans, which became softer only when they were washed and worn. That had to do first with the natural fibers used, and also with the production.

Flat garments such as shirts, dresses, and pants have been tailored from woven fabric panels for centuries. However, weaving was rarely the best choice for smaller pieces. Instead, various very special techniques were used, each of which was precisely tailored to the desired function. For example, the choice of technique can influence the direction in which a textile can be stretched. It can be made loose and permeable or tight and dense as desired. The craftsmen were aware of these special properties and used them to their advantage.

Twining is perhaps the oldest and most versatile technique. Any reasonably pliable material can be used. Depending on your requirements, you can create flexible and netlike, patterned, and very strong structures. Unlike the stitches in knitting or crochet, the loops in **nålbinding** cannot be pulled open. This means that holes in the fabric do not widen, which is practical for socks and mittens. With the **sprang** technique, you get two extremely stretchy structures in one operation. They were used to make hoods, belts, and sashes. The advantage of **slip stitch crochet** is that it is easy to learn. Instead of using five knitting needles, you need only a single wide crochet hook to make mittens or hats, for example. You can make clothing thicker and weatherproof by **fulling**. Subsequent raising (or napping) straightens the fibers, which provides good insulation and repels rain. This was particularly important for workwear for outdoor professions.

All these techniques are done with simple tools that are easy to make yourself. [Tool Workshop: p. 259] The work can be taken along—unlike, for example, a fabric started on the loom, with which you are tied to the house—and interrupted at any time. Another advantage is the possibility of using leftover yarn.

→ Tool Workshop p. 259

TWINING

Twining involves twisting threads around each other, around tightly stretched warp yarn or round rods. This technique, which is related to weaving and basket plaiting, is probably the oldest surface-forming textile process known to mankind. It has been known since the Mesolithic period at the latest.

THE TECHNIQUE

Twining is an incredibly versatile technique. Depending on the material or combination of materials used and the distance between longitudinal and transverse elements, it can be used to create a wide variety of objects. Flat, three-dimensional, or even hollow objects are possible. Anything is feasible, from very soft to really hard and firm: fine cloths, sturdy carpets,[58] flexible hammocks, perforated sieves, or solid baskets.

At first glance, twined textiles can easily be mistaken for woven textiles. However, in terms of textile systematics, there is a decisive difference. In most weaving techniques, two active elements penetrate each other; warp and weft threads run over and under each other. Twining, on the other hand, is defined as a fixed element of the structure being wrapped by at least two intersecting elements.[59]

58 For example, twined rag rugs out of colorful, sorted-out clothing pieces in the USA.
59 According to Seiler-Baldinger 1991, 80.

At least the active part—the braiding threads or the insert—must be flexible. Any material that is sufficiently flexible can be used: for example, grass, bulrush, plant bast, and all plant and animal fibers used to make clothing, but also wire and synthetic fibers. The solid or passive element is known as spokes, stakes, or chain. Any stable yarn is suitable for this, but also rigid plant parts such as straw, reed, bamboo, or heather.

Short bundles of fibers can also be attached to the warp during twining to create a soft fringed pile. In the past, this was used as additional rain protection, especially for hats, because the water runs off easily. If the individual twisted rows are pushed very close together, the entwined material is invisible. If you leave space between the rows, you get a more airy structure.

A widely used technique is the twining of sitting, sleeping, or windbreak mats. Here, the passive entry consists of solid plant stems. It is made sitting on a simple frame in the form of a notched crosspiece on two trestles. The warp threads, weighted with small weights, hang over the crossbar on both sides. The warp threads are twisted each time a new stalk is placed. The finished mat hangs down on one side. Such mats are made by the Ainu in Japan and the Zulu in South Africa, among others.

In Scotland, for example on the Orkneys and Shetland Islands, abundant heather was used to bind baskets. In the baskets, known as *cubbies*, *kishies*, or *caisies*, you can clearly see the twining technique. The fish catch, peat, and dung were transported in such heather baskets carried on the back or on a packhorse. They were also hung on the wall in the house to store various things.

Kishie basket by the artist and basket weaver Lois Walpole, tied with wild oat straw and rope scraps collected on the beach

‹
A wooden folding trestle is ideal for twining mats.

⌄
In Scotland, curly dock and rushes were used as raw material for twining.

Depending on the working direction, this is referred to as "twining the warp" or "twining the weft." Instead of looping the threads around each other by hand when twining the warp, simple weaving tablets with only two holes can be used [Weaving with Two-Hole Tablets: p. 151], which greatly speeds up the binding, or in this case, the weaving (because a shed is formed). An early example of this special technique is a band from the Celtic princely tomb at Hochdorf. In the next chapter, you will learn about a special type of twining in which the warp threads are stretched over a simple wooden mold. [Twining on a Form: p. 183]

→ Weaving with Two-Hole Tablets p. 151

→ Twining on a Form p. 183

TWINING: PREHISTORIC—WORLDWIDE

Twining is probably the oldest surface-forming textile process known to mankind. The earliest direct evidence of the technique to date comes from the Mesolithic period: a twined basket from this period was discovered in Noyen sur Seine, France.[60] However, it is conceivable that twining was already practiced by Paleolithic man, especially since no tools other than one's own hands are required.

In the Neolithic period, following the Mesolithic, twining can be described as a standard technique for the manufacture of textile products such as mats, carpets, hats, cloaks, and bags. In the lakeside settlements and pile-dwelling sites around the Alps, bags, fish traps, and hats were among the items preserved. The material for these textiles was plant fibers, especially tree basts. [Fiber Materials: p. 25] There is also Neolithic evidence of twine weaving from Syria (Tell Halula), Israel (Nahal-Hemar Cave), and various Turkish sites (Çatalhöyük and Çayönü). The five-thousand-year-old twined pieces of equipment from the ice mummy "Ötzi," from the Hauslabjoch in South Tyrol, were reproduced by the archaeotechnician and experimental archaeologist Anne Reichert. The expert in Stone Age twine binding, who died in 2022, reconstructed, for example, the dagger sheath, the inner shoe, and the hoodlike bast mat made of lime bast.[61] [Literature from Anne Reichert: p. 295]

In central Europe, the technique no longer played a major role in later history and fell into oblivion. However, mats were still twined in Iran, China, Korea, and Japan in the last century. In various Indigenous societies, twining is still used to make practical or ceremonial items. The hunting clothing of the Yupik in Alaska includes leather kayak mittens with twined inner mittens for insulation. The Choctaw in North America have rediscovered this almost-forgotten technique of twining and use it today to bind skirts made of plant fibers or bison wool. The incredibly labor-intensive ceremonial dance cloaks of the Haida and Tlingit in Alaska and Canada are also twined. It can take up to four years to make a *chilkat* blanket from strips of cedar bark.

60 See Antoinette Rast-Eicher, "Bast Before Wool: The First Textiles," in *Hallstatt Textiles. British Archaeological Reports* (2005), 117–132.

61 Anne Reichert talks about her work in an interview accessible on the internet from the *Stuttgarter Zeitung* from April 18, 2016.

^
Ceremonial *chilkat* blanket of the Tlingit in British Columbia (McCord Museum Stewart, Montreal, Canada)

›
A lime bast hat bound by archaeotechnician Wulf Hein, which is based on the find from Wangen-Hinterhorn.

→ Fiber Materials p. 25

→ Literature from Anne Reichert p. 295

TRY IT!

TWINING A SMALL MAT

If you want to understand the principle of twining, making this small mat is a good exercise. It is made up of thin rods that are connected to each other by threads. You can use the finished mat as a place mat, coaster, paintbrush case, or sushi roll mat. You can also simply tie a test piece that can be unraveled afterward.

Materials: Stable thread (twine, cotton crochet thread, string); at least ten thin sticks, each approximately 8 inches (20 cm) (wooden sticks, kebab skewers, straws, reed stalks, or similar)

Tools: Scissors or knife

Preparation: Cut three to five threads approximately an arm's length.

1 Sort the raw material: Select reed stems that have grown as straight as possible.

2 Attach the first stick to two sticks driven into the ground. (Alternatively, you can twine the mat on a table by taping the first stick to it or weighing it down to prevent it from slipping.)

3 Loop the center of the first thread. Wrap the loop around the first stick and pull both ends of the thread through the loop (cow hitch knot).

Reed stalks as a raw material

The cow hitch knot

Connect the second stick.

Push the sticks together.

Attach the first stick and distribute the threads across it.

Place the second stick between the pair of threads.

Always loop in the same direction.

Knot the thread ends to secure them.

4 Put the second stick between the threads. One thread of each yarn pair is beneath and the other one above the stick.

5 Now bind in the second stick. Cross the ends of the thread.

6 Make sure that the threads are always looped around each other in the same direction.

7 Keep the threads taut while pushing the sticks together with your thumb.

8 Knot the thread ends and remove the finished mat from the holding sticks.

A **larger mat** is worked in a very similar way. However, the material is not laid out on the ground, but instead a wooden frame is used. A simple folding trestle is ideal for this. Thin bamboo sticks, long straws, or reed stalks are suitable materials for the sticks. The warp or binding threads hang down from the frame and must be weighted down with weights. Carved wooden weights or small perforated stones from the Baltic Sea beach are practical for this. Or you can fill cloth bags with rice or sand and tie them to the threads. The procedure is the same as described above for the small mat. [Mat-Tying Frame: Photo p. 173]

→ Mat-Tying Frame Photo p. 173

VARIATIONS AND TIPS

For the instructions on the following pages:

- Instead of fiber bundles, cords that are already twined can also be used both as warp twines and as weft twines.

- A variation is created when the warp strands are divided between the twined rows so that half of the first warp is joined with half of the second warp in the following row. This creates a zigzag pattern of warp threads. In this variation, the twined rows are also fixed in position, which is particularly suitable for sieves.

- The object can be extended in any direction by simply hooking additional warp threads to the outer edge of the twined textile and twisting them with new strands of twine. The working direction can also be changed. In this way, twined textiles are created directly tailored to the desired shape.

Old handicraft techniques such as twining, pottery, and bronze casting are tested and demonstrated at the Zeiteninsel open-air museum.

Zeiteninsel (Island of Time)
Archaeological Open-Air Museum
Hesse, Germany

Zeiteninsel is a museum under construction, with five areas arranged by time period, from the Mesolithic to Roman times. Reconstructed buildings, embedded in the appropriate natural surroundings, convey a vivid impression of what it might have been like back then. School programs, guided tours, seminars, discovery days, and a challenging course program invite visitors to join in.

www.zeiteninsel.de

TWINING À LA "ÖTZI"

These instructions and tips are from Susanne Gütter and Monika Mosburger, Zeiteninsel Archaeological Open-Air Museum.

We bind vertical fiber bundles into the strands running horizontally. By turning these twined strands, the loosely hanging warp strands are fixed in position. The twined textile grows, turn by turn, with bare hands working freely on your lap. No other aids or holding devices are necessary.[62]

From the first piece you try, you can, for example, sew a small bag. The Neolithic "Ötzi" kept his flint dagger in a similar quiver. Other twined Stone Age products include bags, hats, cloaks, shoe liners, and sieves.

Materials: Raw materials such as grass and rushes are readily available and may need to be dried and remoistened so that the structure does not loosen due to drying shrinkage. Wood bast and fibers must first be prepared accordingly. Nettle fibers can be freshly harvested and stripped for twining. [Linden Bast: p. 36] [Flax: p. 39] [Nettles: pp. 34–35] An alternative is raffia or binding bast from garden or hobby stores.

We start twining, just like when plying a cord, in the middle of a thread folded in half. [Splicing and Plying with Your Fingers: p. 49]

62 If you want to work on larger pieces such as a mat or a curtain, it can be helpful to clamp the starting edge between two fixed points. This is the traditional twining technique that, for example, was used among the Choctaw and Ojibway in North America. For a twined hammock (South America, West Africa), wrap the entire warp around a wooden frame.

→ Linden Bast p. 36

→ Flax p. 39

→ Nettles pp. 34–35

→ Splicing and Plying with Your Fingers p. 49

Twined quiver

1 Insert the center of the first warp strand crosswise into the resulting < loop.

2 Now, as with cord plying, the two ends of the twine strand are spliced in an S shape away from the body and twined in the Z direction toward the body so that the first warp strand is caught and fixed with the rotation.

3 Now bend the fixed warp strand into a U shape and twist it in directly as the second warp thread in the same way, after splicing the two twine ends and turning the twine ends around each other. Now both halves of the first warp strand hang parallel to one side and are tied into the first two turns of twine at the top.

4 The next warp strand bent into a hanging U is secured in the same way with the next two twists. Continue until the desired width is reached.

5 At the end of the first twined row, after a few "empty" twists, the direction is changed, and all the hanging warp threads are twisted in again in the same way on the way back in a second twined row.

6 After twisting back the second row, a stable starting edge has been created. The warp strands can now be twisted in alternating directions in the desired row spacing.

If the fibers that serve as warp strands are turned a little around themselves between the twined rows, this increases the stability of the structure. A tight twist and close spacing result in a dense, strong textile. With soft fiber, less tight splicing and wider spacing can create softer textiles.

In this form of twining, the warp strands are fixed in their position through twining, while the twined-in rows can be easily moved against each other (if they are not pushed close together).

If a strand becomes thinner or ends completely due to the interlaced fibers running out, new fibers are simply added, overlapping and twisted in. Ideally, the thread thickness remains the same, and continuous threads are twined without knots.

At the end of the project, the ends of the warp threads that are still hanging out can be sewn, knotted, or simply twined crosswise in the finishing edge.

Insert warp strand into < loop.

Secure the warp thread.

Bend the warp thread down.

Add additional warp threads.

End of the first row

Three rows are twined.

TWINING WITH A FORM

A three-dimensional form is used to produce more complex twined textiles such as arm warmers, mittens, and hats. In Poland, the Czech Republic, and Slovakia, the tradition of twining is being revived using a wooden mold.

The technique of twining with a form is closely related to the original twining described in the previous section. However, it is much younger and was used exclusively to make thick, warm garments. The traditional material for the twisted threads is sheep's wool. Old textiles tied on the form can still be found in folklore collections in the Western Carpathians.

The binding was practiced almost exclusively by men, and the finished objects were worn only by men. People who worked in the forest in winter needed warm work mittens: woodcutters and wagon drivers who transported the trees out of the forest, charcoal burners, or vendors at the market. Experienced craftsmen needed only one to two days to make a pair of mittens.

A variety of patterns can be developed by selecting the twist direction and yarn color.

THE TECHNIQUE

When twining on a form, pairs of threads are also wound around taut warp threads. In contrast to normal twining, however, the warp threads are no longer visible in the finished textile when binding on a form. They are completely enclosed by the twined threads. Typical of this technique are the various geometric patterns formed by different-colored twisted threads.

For arm warmers, the traditional shape is a tapered round piece of wood that resembles the shape of the forearm. The wooden mitten shape looks like an oversized popsicle. The board, which is rounded at the top, replicates the shape of the palm. This board is inserted into an oval base that keeps the warp threads distanced. The thumb can either be crocheted or twined with a similar but much smaller shape.

It is then sewn into an open area in the mitten. Slippers can also be made with the mitten form. Finally, the hat form consists of a board with a rounded top that is inserted into two round boards. The circumference of the lower board corresponds approximately to the circumference of the head.

For all shapes, the warp threads are stretched back and forth over notches or wooden or metal nails. The weft or twisted threads are then placed around the warp threads. This can be done with the fingers or with the aid of wooden or metal needles. Technically speaking, this is a twining of the weft (i.e., the warp threads are passive and only the wefts are moved during the twining process). The warp threads serve only to hold the twined threads.

GEOMETRIC PATTERNS

If you want to design the pattern, you must consider the following two factors:

- Depending on the direction in which the twist goes, each crossing of the twined yarn forms either a "slash" leaning to the right or a "backslash" leaning to the left.
- When twining, a pair of threads is crossed consecutively in each row. This means that a maximum of two colors can occur in each row.

Patterns are therefore created by choosing different colors. Slashes or Vs can also be formed depending on the direction of the twining. Variations are possible if the twining direction is changed within a pattern row. Then

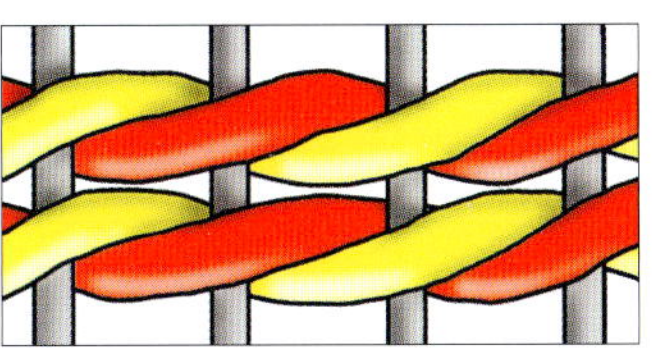

Synchronized crossing

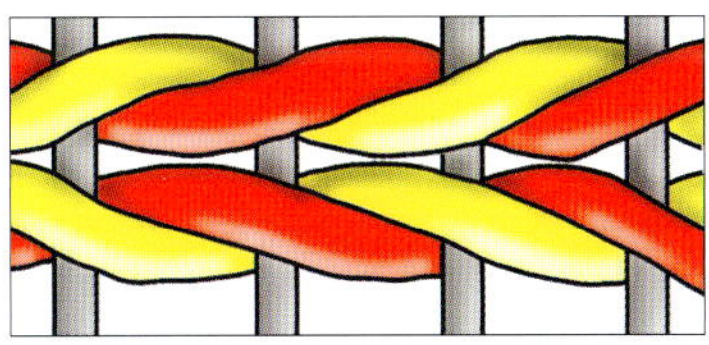

Crossing in opposite directions

the Vs can sometimes point to the left, sometimes to the right.

Many different geometric patterns are possible: horizontal, thin lines or broad stripes, vertical or diagonal stripes, box patterns, arrows and ladders. In Slovakia, where twining is a traditional textile craft, each of these patterns has its own name; for example, dice or fishtail.

Thick lining is typical of twined mittens. This is created by not cutting off the thread ends, but leaving them in place. They protrude from the surface as woolly fringes. Since the mittens are bound on the left side and then turned inside out, the fringes move to the inside.

FIRM CORD AND SOFT WOOL

The twine threads are almost always made from sheep's wool. The older mittens that have survived are made of wool in natural tones, from natural white to brown to gray and black. This was used to create patterns with strong light and dark contrasts. Later, store-bought colorful yarns were added; red and dark blue were popular. In today's crafts, a whole range of brightly colored wool yarns are used.

Shepherds used to use the wool from the sheep they herded, but of course, not everyone has this source of material available. I have found several references to the fact that thread remnants from the loom were used for mittens in the past. Spinning wool yarn was incredibly labor-intensive. It is therefore no wonder that yarn scraps were too good to throw away. These warp yarn remnants were known as "thrum" (waste wool). In addition to twining, this leftover yarn was also used for nålbinding [Nålbinding: p. 197] or crocheting mittens, for example. [Slip Stitch Crochet: p. 239]

The most important thing with the warp threads is that they are stable. The appearance doesn't matter, since the warp will no longer be visible afterward. The forms were therefore covered with flax or hemp cord, sometimes partly with cow hair. But you could just as well use tightly spun and twisted wool yarn.

Twining board with a slipper made from fabric remnants. Schanfigger Heimatmuseum in the Eggahuus, Arosa, Switzerland.

→ Nålbinding p. 197

→ Slip Stitch Crochet p. 239

WAGGONER'S MITTENS AND BEAR SLIPPERS

Twining with a form can be traced back to the beginning of the nineteenth century. It may be even older, but so far there is no evidence of this. The technique was concentrated mainly in a few regions in the Carpathian Mountains. In Poland, twining was practiced in the Western Carpathians. There, the lumberjacks made their own mittens. Because the mittens were worn by the waggoners who transported logs from the forest, they were also called waggoner's mittens. Only in the region around Nowy Sącz has this craft been preserved. In Moravian Wallachia in the east of the Czech Republic, the village of Střítež in particular specialized in binding mittens. There, "in the second half of the nineteenth century, almost every family made mittens, which were sold at the fairs in southeastern Moravia and in western Slovakia from Vizovice to Žilina. Around 1900, the number of customers declined, so that barely thirty families in the village were able to earn an additional income by making mittens. Production was discontinued in 1925."[63]

Twined arm warmers were part of the men's workwear in the mountain regions of Slovakia. They held the wide sleeves of the cuffless shirts together, protecting against injuries from branches when working in the forest, and warming the wrists. The traditional patterns were made from white and black wool, but they can also be found in colors such as green, yellow, pink, purple, and red. Today, the arm warmers are no longer used by forest workers but are worn as decorative accessories in men and women's traditional clothing.

In 1895, Louise Schinnerer described the "carpet-like production method of mittens" in her essay on the textile folk art of the Ruthenians. One illustration shows an "apparatus for weaving mittens" from "Ruthenian Galicia" in the Carpathian Mountains (now Ukraine). Twining was also used in Savoy in France in the past. The Eugenie Goldstern Collection of the Austrian Museum of Folklore contains a "mitten-weaving device." The ethnologist brought the object back from a research trip to the village of Bessans in 1914. According to the *Neuesten Illustrirten Handels- und Waaren-Lexicon* from 1875, the so-called bear slippers (Bärlatschen) were found in the Ore Mountains. Krünitz's *Oekonomische Encyklopädie* describes how these twined slippers were made from calf hair: "The hair is plaited over twine and pushed together so that it covers the twine. These shoes were often worn in winter, especially for warmth, and not only in the house but also outside it and on the journey over shoes and without shoes, soled and unsoled." In some museums in Switzerland there are old wooden forms for twined slippers made from wool or strips of material. The latter are called "Endenfinken" *(end slippers)* because of the fabric edges used.

Mitten and wooden form,
Center of Traditional Technology (CETRAT),
Příbor, Czech Republic

The only evidence for twining with a form in Germany comes from Thuringia. A wooden form for slippers is exhibited in the open-air museum of Thuringian farmhouses in Rudolstadt. Thuringian shepherds are also said to have twined mittens, called "Zipfel."[64] It could be that this craft came to the Erfurt region from the Ore Mountains.

There are efforts today to preserve the rare textile technique of twining with a form from being completely forgotten. Especially in Poland, this is attempted with imaginative ideas. After twining was presented at a "fair for dying professions" in 2018, it is now on the Polish UNESCO application list for intangible cultural heritage. Some Polish museums and textile craftsmen offer twining workshops.

63 Translation from Jitka Staňkova, *Tradični textilni techniky* (Prague, 2008), 112–114.

64 Jürgen Schönwolff reconstructed the device on the basis of the testimony of a Thuringian spinner, without knowing the technique of twining with a form. ("Schafhüters Freund oder die Kunst, Zipfel zu weben," *Das Lavendelschaf* 20 [2007]: 27.)

TRY IT!

TWINING ON CARDBOARD

From your first attempt, you can make, for example, a bracelet. If you fold it over once, you can easily sew a phone case or a small bag. Larger pieces can be turned into a bag or a backpack or sewn together in squares to create a pillowcase or a blanket.

Materials: sturdy cardboard (i.e., the back piece of a notepad); leftover cotton thread or binding thread; leftover yarn: preferably thick wool yarn in different single colors

Tools: Scissors or pinking shears

1 Cut a rectangle from sturdy cardboard. Cut notches on two edges with your scissors (this works better with special pinking shears). Lay a thread once around the cardboard and knot it, then continue winding under tension until the whole cardboard is covered. The warp thread must be wound tightly.

2 Cut two different-colored threads (in contrasting colors) about an arm's length. Knot them together or let them hang over at the beginning of the row. Twining: the threads cross over each other continuously. First one thread is on the top, then the other (see sketch on page 185). Try out different patterns in the following row.

3 You can also bind two pattern rows at the same time. For this, tie four threads together. Two threads over, two under the first warp thread. Then continuously place the two outer pattern threads on the inside or the inner ones on the outside. This creates the "V row" in a single operation. Here you work without needles, just with your fingers!

Finally, cut the warp threads in the middle on the back of the cardboard. Knot the ends, then braid them or pull them into the finished piece with a needle.

You can make chair cushions or even entire rugs from old T-shirts or bedsheets. The fabric is cut into 1-to-2-inch-wide (3–5 cm) strips. For the warp thread, use sturdy twine or strips of fabric made from a nonstretch material. A simple, homemade wooden frame or a potholder-weaving frame from the craft supplies store can be used as a twining frame.

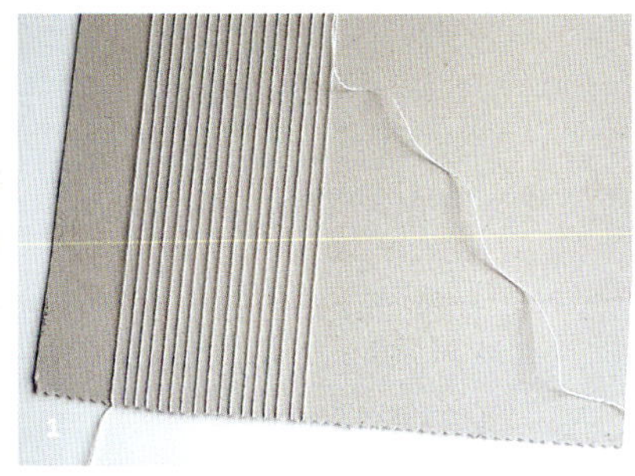

Wrap the cardboard with the thread.

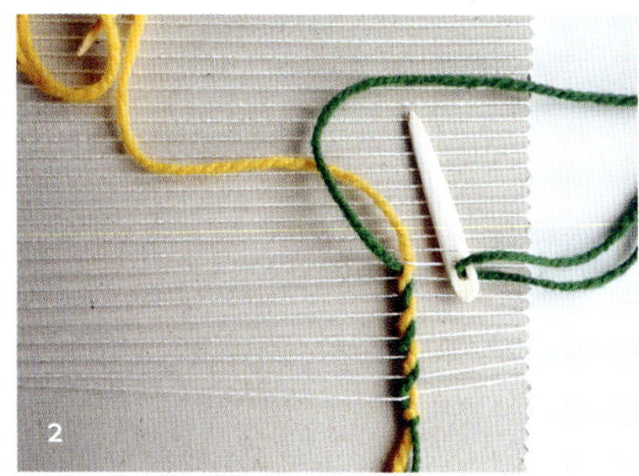

Twining with two colors

Twining with four threads
at the same time

When pushed together,
a V row is created.

You can easily make a form for twining tapered arm warmers out of a sturdy piece of cardboard that is US letter size or A4 size. Make small cuts every ⅕" (½ cm) on one of the long sides and every 0.25 inches (0.7 cm) on all other sides. Put the cardboard down horizontally in front of you. Mark the middle of the cardboard with a vertical line. Starting from this line, record your measurements for the arm warmers (measure your own arm with a tape measure—here, for example, 8 and 7 inches (21 and 18 cm) wide, 3.5 inches (9 cm) high)—and draw the shape of the arm warmer on the cardboard. Cover the cardboard with warp thread. The different distances between the incisions automatically result in slanted side edges when twining. Bind the first side of the warmer on the front of the cardboard. Do not cut the warp threads. Turn the cardboard over and bind the second side of the warmer on the back of the cardboard. Then cut the warp threads along the edges of the cardboard. A few inches must be left on the edge of the warmer for sewing! For more, see the instructions on the following pages.

BRACELET OR ARM WARMERS USING A WOODEN FORM

Materials: Linen or cotton warp yarn or sturdy linen thread; wool yarn in different colors

Tools: Wooden form for arm warmers [Instructions: Twining Form: p. 287]; two blunt darning needles or two homemade nålbinding needles [Instructions: Nålbinding Needles: p. 288]

Bracelets or arm warmers can be created either as a closed ring or as an open strip. With open strips, you work toward only one edge. The open edge can later be finished with a strip of fabric or leather or embroidered with wool. The band is closed with buttons, hooks, or short ribbons.

If you want to make a closed ring, please remember that the finished piece has to be taken off the wooden form. With a tapered form, this can be done only at the thinner end. This is why you should not work too tightly or too close to the wood. Don't worry: if necessary, you can pull the nails to remove the piece.

1 Cover the wooden form continuously with a warp thread.

2 Start binding at the narrower end of the wooden form: First, twine a single-colored row. To do this, cut a weft thread long enough for one round with an overhang of approximately 2 inches (5 cm). Hook in the weft thread. Twist the treads together in each gap between the warp threads.

Cover the wooden form with the warp.

Twining the first row

The finished and turned bracelet

3 For two-colored patterns, knot two weft threads of different colors together.

4 Push the individual rounds tightly together with your fingers or, for example, with a comb or fork.

5 Stop a few inches before the bottom end. Cut the warp threads and pull them with a needle into the inside of the textile. Or, lift the first warp thread loop next to the starting knot from the nail and pull it through (see photo). Do not pull too tightly at the edge; otherwise you will get waves. Then lift the next loop from the opposite nail, pull it through, and so on. Continue in this way until the entire warp thread has been pulled through. The thread to be pulled through becomes longer and longer. You can reuse the thread for another project or cut it as you go, which will make pulling it through quicker.

6 Release the starting knot. Lift the bracelet or the arm warmer on the thinner side over the needle row. Cut the warp threads down to a few inches in length and use the needle to weave them through into the textile. Pull off the excess ends of the colored yarn through several loops and cut off flush. Turn.

Tip: Wrap a strip of fabric around the nails to prevent the twined threads from getting caught on the nails.

Two-colored pattern row

Close the binding by pushing the rows together.

Pull the warp thread through.

If you want to make a textile with a soft lining, do not cut off the ends of the wool yarn. Attach new threads as often as possible to create a fur-like appearance. The inside is on the outside when twining, and the textile is turned right side out later. Arm warmers can also be lined with fabric sewn on the inside.

→ Instructions for Twining with a Form p. 287

→ Instructions for Nålbinding Needles p. 288

TIPS FOR TWINING WITH A FORM

FROM VÁCLAV MICHALIČKA

- The best material to use is yarn made from sheep's wool. In the past, untwisted thread was used, but it is better to work with two-ply yarn. Typically, twined products from the West Carpathians such as mittens or hats were also used for protection, which means they were made to be very thick and sturdy. Today, we use softer yarn so that the finished product also turns out softer. It will still be durable enough.

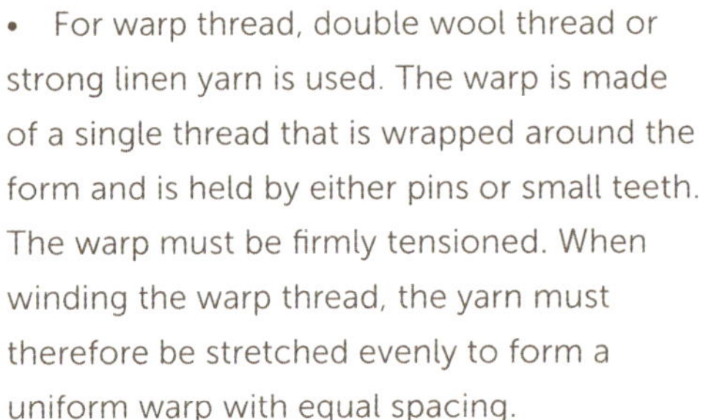

- For warp thread, double wool thread or strong linen yarn is used. The warp is made of a single thread that is wrapped around the form and is held by either pins or small teeth. The warp must be firmly tensioned. When winding the warp thread, the yarn must therefore be stretched evenly to form a uniform warp with equal spacing.

- It is best if you begin with a bracelet or a simple bag. A hat is more complicated. Mittens belong to the most challenging projects. It is not very easy to create the thumb.

- The weft is made of short threads anywhere from 4 to 12 inches (10–30 cm) long. For a warm lining, the ends of the threads are not cut off but are kept on the inside of the textile.

- The basic principle is to simultaneously weave two weft threads around the warp threads in a row. The two weft threads are wrapped around each other behind the warp thread. This can also create interesting patterns.

- The edges of the completed textile can be finished by binding the warp threads together. Or you can place the warp threads around the edge of the weft threads and pull them between the weft threads with a crochet hook.

Václav Michalička

Moravkoslezský kraj, Czech Republic

Václav Michalička is the head of the Center for Traditional Technologies in Příbor (CETRAT), a branch of the Museum of the Region Novojičín in Moravia, in the eastern Czech Republic.

In addition to its scientific activities, CETRAT also documents, reconstructs, presents, and teaches traditional craft techniques for processing natural materials. As a professional experimental workshop for the preservation of old craft techniques, CETRAT offers workshops on craft topics such as archaic technologies with materials such as flint, bone, and leather.

www.muzeumnj.cz/pribor

Book Tip

Václav Michalička, *Die Brennnessel: Kleidendes Unkraut* (Klagenfurt, Austria: Wieser Verlag, 2021).

NÅLBINDING

Through the revival of interest in medieval living history, nålbinding was discovered once again. With a thick needle and short threads, you can sew textiles that look like they were crocheted. They are sturdier than knitting or crocheting because there are no dropped stitches and holes cannot expand.

Textiles done with nålbinding can be found practically worldwide. The most well known are surely the socks from the time of the Vikings, mittens from northern Europe, and the Coptic socks from Egypt. Bags created with nålbinding can be found in South America and Papua New Guinea, and full-body masks can be found in Africa for ritual dancing. Scandinavian milk and beer sieves made from cow tail hair are more of a niche product. Another very special but practical application for nålbinding is Arabian sand socks and camel muzzles.

THE TECHNIQUE

Unlike knitting and crocheting, you don't work with a virtually endless thread from the ball of yarn, but with individual pieces of thread that are not too long. Because of this, this technique is great for using up remnants. In the past, for example, cutoff remnants of warp yarn from the loom were used. Leftover hemp yarn from straw bale binding was also used to make robust work mittens.

Nålbinding produces a sewn fabric with a looped structure. According to Annemarie Seiler-Baldinger's textile systematics, the simplest production technique for sewn looped fabrics is the so-called "einfache Verschlingen" (simple looping).[65] Examples of this are carrier bags sewn from spruce shavings or rope boat fenders. [Instructions for Simple Looping: p. 208] Real nålbinding works in a similar way to "simple looping." Here too, new loops are hooked into those of the previous row. However, they are also joined laterally to the neighboring loops.

With nålbinding, there are countless ways to connect the new loops with the previous ones. The needle is guided over and under a certain number of loops. These stitches are usually named after the region where they were or are used (e.g., "Finnish stitch") or after the place from which a known find originates (e.g., "York stitch," after the so-called Coppergate sock from York during the Viking Age in England). A popular beginner's stitch is the "Oslo stitch." Because the description of creating the loops is hard to do with words, a simple depiction of the method was looked for. The most popular is Hansen's notation, which was developed in 1987 by the Dane Egon Hansen.

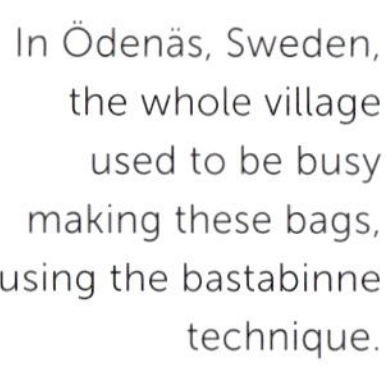

In Ödenäs, Sweden, the whole village used to be busy making these bags, using the bastabinne technique.

65 Book by Annemarie Seiler-Baldinger (1991): see Reading Tips at the end of this book.

The thread course is described in the clockwise direction and labeled with capital letters. O stands for *over* and U stands for *under* the thread of the starting loop. The turning point is marked with a slash.

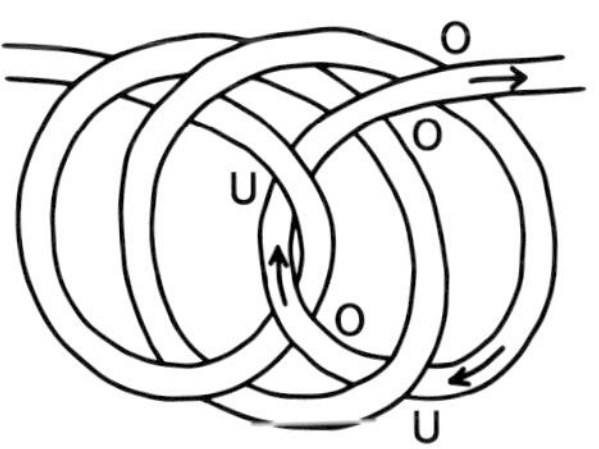

The thread course is described using arrows and letters.

Very clear drawing and photos of various Danish and Swedish engravings can be found in Margrethe Hald's book *Ancient Danish Textiles from Bogs and Burials*, which can be downloaded as a PDF from the Danish National Museum's website.

Some principles of nålbinding:

- Before you start, you must decide if you are going to work freehand or if you will put the loops over your thumb. When using your thumb, the loops will be uniform in size, and you will be able to progress faster. With the freehand method, it is easier to see the course of the threads.
- If a tubelike object such as a mitten or a sock is to be created, you will work in rounds (not in alternating rows). For a hat, you start in the middle and work in spirals to the edges.
- Usually, nålbinding is done from left to right, so the opposite of crocheting and knitting. But it works just as well in the other direction.
- You work on the right side of the textile, meaning the side that will be showing outside. If you end up liking the structure of the back better, of course you can turn the piece once it's done.

Mittens can be started either at the tip (Finnish technique) or from the bottom. With socks, you have different options for nålbinding the heel—the transition between the foot and leg parts. As model, you can use the famous Coppergate sock. Further variations can be found in the specialist literature and on the internet. [Reading Tips: p. 297]

→ Instructions for Simple Looping p. 208

→ Reading Tips p. 297

Because you are working with relatively short threads, you have to add yarn often. There are many ways to do this. The thread can be felted, spliced, or joined by overlapping, and the excess threads are simply cut off at the end. When felting, loosen the end of the old thread and the beginning of the new thread slightly with the nålbinding needle. Then place the beginning and end on top of each other, with an overlap of approximately an inch (3 cm). The connection is made by rubbing vigorously between the hands or on the thigh. The wool should not be moistened, either with saliva or water, since this will make it snag and difficult to pull through. If you can still see fuzzy areas at the ends in the finished piece, you can place a sponge underneath and push the ends inward with a felting needle.[66]

Mittens done with nålbinding were often fulled to make them thicker. This was particularly important for forest workers or sailors. The mittens were made a few sizes too large for this purpose, since they shrank during fulling. [Fulling: p. 253]

Nålbinding is a slow, time-intensive textile technique. That is probably a reason why it was overtaken by knitting and crocheting, which are much faster. Those who use nålbinding today can enjoy the calming effect of the continuously repeating loop formation.

THE TOOLS

Nålbinding needles were traditionally made from bone, such as from the fibula of a pig or a sheep. You can just as easily use metatarsal bones from cattle. Needles made from the bones of the mountain hare have also been preserved. Antlers (elk or reindeer) and wood are also suitable. [Instructions: Nålbinding Needle: p. 288] If you would like to try out the technique, a thick darning needle with a blunt tip is sufficient to start with.

THE MATERIAL

Nålbinding works with all different kinds of yarn. If the structure of the loops should stay clearly visible, you should choose a more stable material that will not change with use. If there should be a dense surface, and the finished object will be fulled, pure sheep's wool (e.g., common felting wool) is best suited. In earlier times, different raw materials were chosen depending on the use of the textile. For warm clothing, sheep's wool was used; for durable mitts and socks, cow or horsehair. Even for milk sieves, animal hair was the material of choice, but fibers from plant bast were also used. [Bast Fibers: p. 25]

Almost all nålbinding-created textiles that are stored in museums have in common that the manufacturing technique was misinterpreted. They were often labeled as knitted or braided. It was actually the Viennese needlework teacher Louise Schinnerer who deciphered the "stocking sewing" of the "ancient Egyptians" as early as 1900.[67] However, it was not until Margrethe Hald's research from the 1950s onward that nålbinding became better known. It was now possible to assign the interlacing to the correct technique. In Scandinavia, nålbinding became fashionable again as a handicraft technique from the 1960s onward.[68] In Germany, it took a little longer for the Viking- and medieval-period-oriented living history groups to discover it for themselves.

→ Fulling p. 253

→ Instructions: Nålbinding Needle p. 288

→ Bast Fibers p. 25

66 Nålbinding felting tips from Silvia Schnell from the "Viking Hoard" in Oberhausen.

67 Luise Schinnerer, *Antike Handarbeiten* (Vienna, no year, but after 1893).

68 Sanna-Mari Pihlajapiha cites on www.neulakintaat.fi the Finnish ethnologist and textile researcher Toini-Inkeri Kaukonen, who already recognized that "in the past years, nålbinding has become a 'fashionable' hobby."

^
Woolen mitten done with nålbinding from Sorunda, Sweden, embroidered in chain stitch

›
Coptic sock, replica based on Nr. EA53913 from the British Museum

Prehistory and Early History: Nets Made from Bast Fibers

The history of nålbinding goes back to the Stone Age. Together with the twining described in the previous chapter, it is the first method that allowed man to create flat textiles out of threads and yarn. With twining, relatively rigid structures could be made first and foremost, such as mats or blankets. [Twining: p. 171] Nålbinding allowed for netlike and flexible structures to be made when needed.

The oldest proof of interlacing worldwide is the multiple fragments from the cave of Nahal Hemar in Israel. The finds are dated to about 8000 BCE and are made from plant fibers and hair. The textiles from the Middle Stone Age settlement of Friesack in Havelland district are also made of plant-based yarn. Fragments of net—the oldest nets found in the world to date—were found in the damp soil, including a net fragment made from nålbinding. Several nålbinding pieces have been preserved from the Neolithic period. One example is the discovery from Tybrind Vig in Denmark. The discoveries from Sos Höyük, Turkey; Chobareti, Georgia; and Altküla, Estonia, are dated to the Bronze Age. These are not preserved textiles, but their impressions in soft clay, which have been preserved in ceramic vessels. A very special piece is the approximately three-thousand-year-old cap of one of the Ürümchi mummies from China. The so-called Tarim beret is made of brown wool and is completely preserved.

The finds from which nålbinding was first studied date from the first centuries CE: the Coptic socks from Egypt from the Roman period. Many of them stand out due to the division into two parts for the toes, which was necessary for wearing the sandals that were common at the time. The stitch that was most frequently used for these woolen socks is "cross-knit looping." It looks like stitches knitted through the back loop (k tbl, which creates a twisted stitch). Such socks were worn not only in Egypt, but also in Roman Britain and in the Netherlands.[69] Similar old nålbound textiles have also been found on the American continent, in Peru, and in Arizona. A really old nålbound textile with a needle still attached has not yet been discovered.

Middle Ages: Clothing for Workers and Noblemen

Around 970 CE, a Viking in precious clothing was buried in the wooden chamber grave of a burial mound. The mound lies between the towns of Mammen and Bjerring, north of the Danish Silkeborg. While the so-called Mammen Grave was being excavated, two silk pieces about 8 inches (20 cm) in length with nålbound insets of golden thread were found along

69 In a surviving letter from the Roman period in Vindolanda, along Hadrian's Wall, someone writes, "I have sent you socks, sandals, and underpants from Sattua." In a Roman burial mound in Esch in the Dutch North Brabant, small remains of a nålbound textile were discovered. Adhering organic remains, probably leather, and a round fastener could point to a sandal.

→ Twining p. 171

with other textile fragments. The well-known Coppergate sock of about the same age from Viking-era York doesn't look especially impressive compared to the Mammen find. It must have been worth a lot to its owner (and creator?), however, because it was patched at least twice. I will not individually list the multiple other preserved clothing pieces (socks, mitts, and hats) as examples of medieval nålbinding; they can be found in the nålbinding book from Ulrike Claßen-Büttner.[70]

Modern Age: Mittens, Snow Socks . . .

Since the fifteenth century, nålbinding was overtaken by knitting and was practiced only in certain regions starting in the seventeenth century. Evidence has been found from more-recent times in northern Germany,[71] Scandinavia, the Baltics, and Russia. Nålbinding was limited to creating practical pieces for which other kinds of textile techniques are not really well suited. As far as clothing pieces go, mittens, socks, and hats especially were created with nålbinding. The mittens were often colorfully embroidered. In Finland, nålbinding was practiced in some regions up through the 1950s. Simple work mittens and socks for fishermen were created from horsehair from the mane or tail or from cow hair instead of from sheep's wool, because they don't absorb water. The final fulling of the mittens was not practiced by everyone. It was said that they would felt anyway once they were used.[72] [Fulling: p. 253]

A Scandinavian specialty is shoe socks. They went over socks as an additional layer of insulation in the shoe. Incidentally, "Ötzi" wore similar socks when he was walking in the Alps in the Neolithic period. However, his net socks, made of lime bast, were twined [Twining: p. 174]. In northern Europe, people also made snow socks that covered only the front of their shoes, to protect them from slipping on snow and black ice.

. . . Milk Sieves, and Muzzles

In areas with dairy farming and cheese dairies, special sieves were part of the equipment. They consisted of a wooden funnel into which a permeable material was placed as the actual sieve. This was used to remove straw, flies, or cow hair from the milk. In Sweden, Norway, and Iceland, these sieves were nålbound from cow tail or goat hair. They also were used as a pot cleaner when doing dishes.[73] Similar sieves were used, at least in Norway, to brew beer as a way to filter the hops. Nålbound sieves from the more southern regions are not known to me. However, there are references to braided or knitted sieves from the folk literature in Alpine regions. In Austria, they were known as "Seihfleck" or "Seihriedel" and were made from roots or spun cow tail hair. However, these circular or oval sieves

70 See Reading Tips at the end of this book.

71 A documentary film from 1973 shows a nålbinder from Schleswig: Arnold Lühnig, *Anfertigung eines Handschuhs in Schlingennähtechnik* (1973), *Encyclopaedia Cinematographica*, D 1889 / 1995. IWF-Film (Göttingen, Germany, 1995). Online on the TIB AV-Portal: https://av.tib.eu/media/11151.

72 Information from the Finnish website www.neulakintaat.fi.

73 "Odd Nordland: Primitive Scandinavian Textiles in Knotless Netting" (Oslo, 1961).

^
Making a milk sieve,
Norway 1943

›
A nålbound milk sieve
from horsehair, 8 inches (20
cm) in diameter

→ Fulling
p. 253

→ Twining
p. 174

Camel with a nålbound muzzle, Dubai

cannot be easily created by braiding or knitting, which indicates that the reporters did not know the nålbinding technique and therefore could not identify it.

Modern examples other than the archaeological finds mentioned above show that nålbinding was not limited to Europe. For example, in Iran, nålbound shoes (called giveh in Kurdish Kalash) are still worn. In Papua New Guinea, bags called bilum are made. Traditionally, they were nålbound with bast fibers and dyed with plants such as turmeric. More recently, the nålbinders are switching to cotton or synthetic yarn, especially for bags that are made to be sold to tourists. Another modern example of nålbinding is the very sturdy toothbrush rugs in the US. They are made with a wooden toothbrush that is made into a needle and are nålbound with a simple stitch. Colorful fabric remnants torn in strips are used for material. The last two examples come from the Arabian Peninsula: nålbound sand socks and camel muzzles! They used to be made using handspun yarn. Nowadays, the muzzles have very becoming colors.[74]

74 Here I would like to thank Anne Marie Decker, on whose website, www.nalbound.com, I first discovered these muzzles.

TRY IT!

SIMPLE LOOPING

If you have never done nålbinding, you should definitely start with this preliminary exercise. Due to the stable yarn, the loops have a certain durability, and you can easily follow the path of the thread. Additionally, the wooden roll provides support, which is easier than holding the textile in the air while working. As with nålbinding in general, the following also applies here: You shouldn't be in a rush. If you notice that you're stressed, put the work down and take a break.

This simple nålbinding stitch was already used in prehistoric times; for example, for the woolen hat of the Trindhøj Man from Denmark in the Bronze Age. It can be used to stitch in objects to cushion them or to hold a loose filling together. Small, spherical wooden buttons to large ship finders were stitched around in this way. In Sweden, sturdy bags were nålbound within a netlike structure. [Bastabinne Bags: p. 198] It even appears when making fine needle lace. Maybe you already know "simple looping": It is nothing more than the buttonhole or festoon stitch used in sewing.

Materials: String, a strong darning or sewing needle, and a round object to sew around. I used an old rolling pin, but it also works well with a glass bottle.

1 Cut a string about an arm's length (measure from hand to hand with arms outstretched sideways). Lay the string around the roll, but not too tight, and tie it securely.

2 **First row:** Thread the needle. For the first stitch, push the needle from the bottom through the taut beginning thread. Pull the needle out through the top. The thread loop lies behind the needle.

3 Pull the loop only tight enough to leave a small bow over the starting thread.

4 Work the next and all subsequent stitches in the same way. Work from left to right. Try to make the stitches approximately the same size. If the working thread curls too much, let it occasionally hang down with the needle until it untwists.

5 Place further stitches in the starting thread until you have worked once around the roll. For the second row, slide the needle under the arch of the stitch of the previous row. The stitch is the same as described above.

Keep working this way until the first thread is used up. Tie on the new threads. If the connection point should not be noticeable, "whipping" is available: Put the thread ends parallel to each other and wrap tightly in twine with a matching color. Allow the twisted ends to disappear in the twine and cut short. It is nice, but difficult, to attach the new thread by "marine rope splicing."

Tie the thread around the roll.

Push the needle through the bottom.

Pull the loop loosely.

Work the subsequent stitches in the same way.

Put the stitches of the next row through the loops of the previous row.

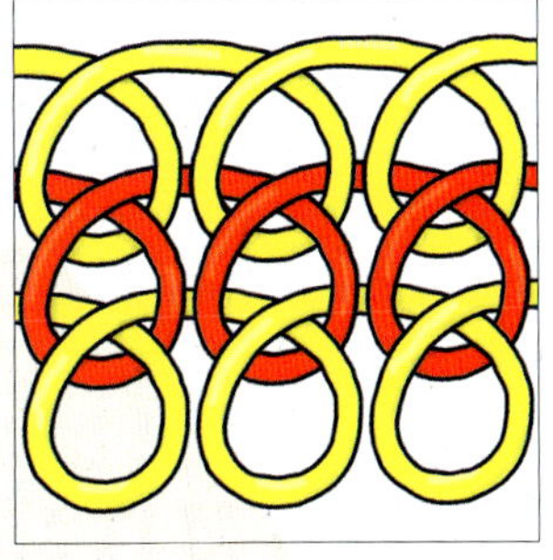

Instead of working from left to right as shown here, you can also work from right to left. The starting thread must be on top, and the textile will expand downward. The needle is inserted through the top, downward through the starting thread.

→ Bastabinne Bags p. 198

TIPS FROM NALBINDER

BERNHARD DANKBAR

- **What differentiates nålbinding from other textile techniques that use a needle?** The difference between knitting, crocheting, and nålbinding can already be seen in the tools that are used. For knitting, normally two knitting needles are used; for crocheting, a crochet hook; and for nålbinding, a sewing needle. In knitting, your starting row of stitches is created on a knitting needle; in crocheting, it's a row of chain stitches. If you pull on one end, all the stitches will unravel. When nålbinding, however, you form a loop, and in this loop, a new loop will be sewed again and again. A loop is a stitch arch with a loop on the end, so more or less a knot that's been left open. The fact that a new loop is made in each loop during nålbinding means that the textile formed in this way can be cut at any point and does not unravel.

- If a uniform loop width is required, you should work with **thumb loops**. When working freehand, it is difficult to form loops of the same size.

- **Which yarn should be used?**
In the past, yarn made from sheep's wool was almost exclusively used. This allowed the individual threads to be pieced together by splicing and felting and then became one continuous thread in the finished piece.

To start, it is advisable to use light-colored, feltable wool roving yarn for needle sizes 3 to 5. Other twisted and feltable yarns are also suitable.

- **Which needle should be used?**
Originally, the needles were made of natural materials such as wood, bone, and horn materials, later out of metal, and today even from plastic. The size of the needle is variable, depending on the material, from 2 to 5 inches in length (5–12 cm), from 2 to 12 millimeters in width, and from 1 to 5 millimeters in thickness. The shape should be flat, rounded on the bottom end, and tapering to a rounded tip, as commonly seen in wool needles. Round needles were not commonly used for nålbinding, although older Finnish needles made of juniper wood had a rounded tip.

- **Fulling:** If you would like to have your nålbound textile fulled, a test piece should be made in order to better gauge the shrinkage. [Fulling Instructions: p. 256] No specific percent values can be given for shrinkage while fulling, because it is dependent on the wool, the kind of sheep, and the length of the fulling procedure. If it should be done quickly,

You can full in a dryer with added tennis balls. Stop it now and then and try it on. Stop when it fits.

Bernhard Dankbar
North Rhine-Westphalia, Germany

Bernhard Dankbar discovered nålbinding for himself over twenty years ago and coined the German term for nålbinding, "Nadelbinden." He is involved with the international nålbinding scene. At the Krefeld Flax Market, for example, visitors see him demonstrating nålbinding. In courses and weekend seminars, he teaches nålbinding, using the thumb-catching method.
www.nadelbinden.nalbinding.de

DANISH STITCH

Here, I will demonstrate a stitch that is well suited for beginners, the "la" stitch, according to Margrethe Hald, but also known as the "Danish stitch" in the freehand technique. Hansen's notation labels it as O/UO because it first goes over and then under and back over the thread of the previous loop. When worked freehand, the sequence of the stitch and the course of the thread are easy to follow. Advanced nålbinders are better off using the thumb loop method.
[Reading Tips for Nålbinding: p. 297]

The Danish stitch is similar to the "simple looping" from the previous chapter. However, it is a real nålbinding stitch because each loop is laterally connected to the neighboring loops ("interlocked interlacing").

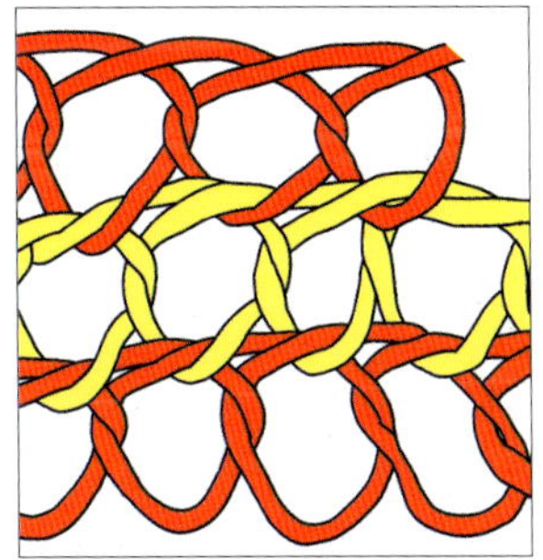

All you need is a scrap of yarn and a darning needle. The yarn should be as light as possible so that you can easily see the individual stitches. For your first attempts, it does not necessarily have to be a feltable wool yarn. Just use what you have at home. However, it should not be too thin a yarn or one that splits into individual threads while being worked. You can find the instructions for a homemade nålbinding needle in the Tool Workshop. [Instructions: Nålbinding Needle: p. 288]

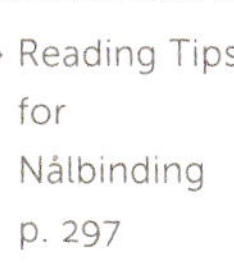

→ Reading Tips for Nålbinding p. 297

→ Nålbinding Needle Instructions p. 288

→ Fulling Instructions p. 256

1 Cut a thread about an arm's length (hand to hand with outstretched arms) and thread through the needle. For the first row, make a chain of stitches (I call it a "pretzel chain"). For the first loop, lay the thread ends on top of each other so that the arch is faced downward, the short end to the left and the long working thread with the needle on it to the right.

2 Insert the needle from above into the first loop; with the point facing away from your body, guide it under the thread to the right of the crossing point and pull the needle out.

3 Tighten the thread carefully so that both loops are the same size. Work loosely; the loops must not be too small. (For a uniform size, the loop can be placed around the index finger for measuring.)

4 For the third loop, insert the needle again from above, pull through, and tighten the thread.

5 Continue this until you have created approx. twenty-five loops. Lay the chain to form the ring. The beginning of the chain should be on the right, the end with the working thread and needle on the left.

6 From the **second row** onward, the upper curve of the loop from the previous row is taken onto the needle for each new loop. The next stitch therefore goes through the upper arch of the first pretzel of the first row and then continues directly as usual; from above through the previous loop, tighten the thread. Instead of just going through the arch, you can go through the intersection of the arches of the previous row, as shown in the sketch above. Working direction **from left to right!**

7 Continue working in this way until the thread is used up. Attach the next thread as explained above, under "Technique." [Adding Thread: p. 200]

8 Finish the work after a few rounds and sew up the thread ends. You can use your practice piece as a napkin ring or bracelet, depending on how large it has become.

In the example described here, a tube-shaped textile is created. Mitts and socks can be needled in this way if you start at the edge. Hats are usually started in the middle. To do this, first make a thread ring into which the first round of stitches is hooked. In the following rounds, the number of stitches is gradually increased to create a plate-shaped piece. Once you have tried out and understood the principle, you can move on to other stitches. I recommend the Oslo stitch next. You can find explanatory videos on the internet.

The first loop is created by crossing the ends of the threads.

Insert the needle moving away from your body from above.

Form the second loop by pulling the thread.

Form the third loop.

Close the chain to form a ring.

Close the ring with the first stitch of the second row.

The first stitches in the new row

Use soft yarn for clothing.

→ Adding Thread p. 200

SPRANG

For sprang, parallel threads are twisted together to create a netlike, stretchable textile. The practical thing about this technique is that you have to work on only one-half of the workpiece. The other part is formed automatically. Examples of sprang range from the Bronze Age and Coptic hats to Prussian officers' sashes.

THE TECHNIQUE

The term *sprang* originates from the Norwegian. During the sprang process, a flat textile is created by intertwining longitudinally stretched threads. In terms of textile systematics, these warp threads would therefore be described as an active system: All longitudinal threads are involved and are moved. There is no transverse thread as in weaving, for example, except for one thread that is needed for securing at the very end of the work. The result is a stretchy fabric that is not very stretchable lengthwise, but very stretchable horizontally.

The continuous warp thread is put up lengthwise between two horizontal crosspieces or between tightly stretched holding threads in a frame. In Finland and Russia, wooden sticks were used, which were inserted into the joints of the wooden house wall (hence the Russian term "weaving on the wall"). Over the course of the project, the warp threads shorten due to the ongoing twisting. The thread tension must be adjusted gradually. In the frame, this is done by moving the crosspieces, while on the wall, it's done by repositioning the small pieces of wood. In Canada,

In this hammock from Yucatán, the thread course under two / over two is clearly visible.

one end is tied to a tree and the other end to a peg driven into the ground. Here too, the tension can be reduced by moving the peg. In Romania, the sprang work was hung from a ceiling beam. While working, you could sit comfortably in front of it and regulate the thread tension by placing your feet on the crosspiece hanging below.

Start crossing the threads at the top edge. The same pattern is automatically created on the opposite side of the work—but in mirror image. Sprang is therefore a time-saving technique: you have to work only one row to get two rows. In the middle, where the two halves meet, a cross thread is pulled through or crocheted in. This protects the workpiece from untwisting. If the center is not closed, but divided, you get two identical pieces that can be sewn together to make a garment with the same front and back, for example. It is also possible to wrap the warp threads in a circle around a frame instead of back and forth. In this case, the pattern is formed starting from the center in both directions. Patterns are created either by using different-colored threads or by incorporating holes. If white, fine yarn is used for sprang with hole patterns, the textile looks like bobbin lace at first glance.

It is typical for sprang that the textile curls or spirals as soon as it's released from the frame. If it is stretched again—for example, by using it as a belt, it straightens out again.

Peter Collingwood, who wrote a fundamental book on sprang, distinguishes between three types of sprang: **interlinking**, **interlacing**, and **intertwining**. In *interlinked sprang*, the threads are twisted together. [Interlinked-Sprang Instructions: p. 226] This technique is the most well known and can also be used to create complicated hole patterns. It produces a very stretchy textile. The result of *interlaced sprang* is similar to a plain weave, but the threads run diagonally to the edge. [Interlaced-Sprang Instructions: p. 234] It is less flexible than interlinked sprang. *Intertwined sprang* is worked with pairs of threads that are twisted around each other at cross points. These three techniques can also be combined with each other, which expands possible patterns. The combination of interlinked and interlaced sprang was sometimes used in modern miser's or stocking purses. [Sprang Purse: p. 222] This combination can also be found on the hairband of the Iron Age bog body from Windeby.[76]

Interlinked sprang stretched out

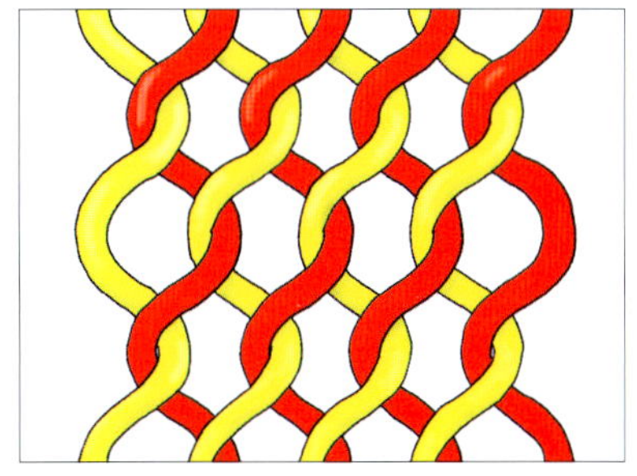

The same band but pulled apart

→ Interlinked-Sprang Instructions p. 226

→ Interlaced-Sprang Instructions p. 234

76 Penelope Walton, in *Textiles, Cordage and Raw Fibre from 16–22 Coppergate* (York, UK, 1989), 359), refers to the description in Karl Schlabow, *Textilfunde der Eisenzeit,* Göttinger Schriften zur Vor- und Frühgeschichte 15 (Neumünster, Germany, 1976), p. 94, fig. 242–4.

A wire-mesh fence is also a kind of sprang. During production, however, the new wire is prebent and then pushed through the last row of wire in a screwing motion. In other words, it is not laid around each other, as in the case of sprang with threads. A similar technique is used to make the Yucatecan hammocks in Mexico. The warp is stretched between two vertical posts. The continuous thread is looped into the front row with a kind of netting needle.

Sprang is not difficult, but it does require a lot of concentration. More than with other textile handicrafts, you have to get used to the workpiece and the technique. If you are not careful, the twists can quickly unravel. Perhaps this is the reason for the special significance that sprang textiles had in many countries. Especially the red-colored sprang belts, which were worn in Greece and in other places, were believed to be charged with power. [Sprang Belt Zostra: p. 224] These belts were supposed to protect against illness and evil influences. The soldiers of the eighteenth century probably also relied on the good wishes worked in their sashes. [Sprang Sashes: p. 222]

A modern sprang piece from the Czech textile artist Sylva Antony Čekalová

→ Sprang Bag p. 222

→ Sprang Belt Zostra p. 224

→ Sprang Sashes p. 222

SPRANG TEXTILES SINCE THE BRONZE AGE

Prehistoric Times Through the Middle Ages: Hair nets and leggings

The oldest proof of the sprang technique is textile imprints on fired clay. In Rietzmeck, a district of the town of Dessau-Roßlau in Saxony-Anhalt, **Neolithic** pottery vessels with such imprints were excavated. When they were made over four thousand years ago, the textile structure was deliberately pressed into the still-damp vessels and was preserved by firing the pottery. Similar impressions were also found on Bronze Age pottery from the Bruszczewo site in Poland.

Several preserved Bronze and Iron Age hairnets made of wool are definitive proof of sprang. The hairnet from Borum Eshøj is the most famous sprang discovery from the **Bronze Age**. It belonged to a female burial with completely preserved clothing in an oak coffin in the Borum Eshøj burial mound, Sabro, northwest of Aarhus, Denmark. The wool fibers were preserved by humic acids and tanning agents.[77] The Celts of the **Iron Age,** following the Bronze Age, were also familiar with sprang, as shown by a textile remnant on a sword chape from Glauberg in Hesse from the early La Tène period. Sprang was used not only in prehistoric Europe, but also on other continents. During an excavation in Turfan, China, an exceptionally well-preserved three-thousand-year-old burial of a horseman was discovered. The ribbons that held his clothing together were done with sprang.[78]

Many of the references to the occurrence of the sprang technique in **antiquity** are only indirect; for example, depictions of women with sprang frames in their hands on Greek vases or a Roman woman's head made of bronze with a very detailed depiction of a sprang hairnet.[79] There is no clear evidence to date for the appealing hypothesis that the Scythians, Persians, and Amazons, who were fought over by the Hellenes from the fifth century BCE onward, wore sprang leggings with zigzag patterns.[80] From the Roman legionary camp of Vindonissa, Switzerland, from the first century CE, there is a fragment of a sprang textile, which is probably the remnants of a hairnet. After the **Coptic** sprang textiles, which were produced by Greeks living in Egypt from the third century CE, sprang was initially also referred to as "Egyptian braiding."[81]

Some finds have been preserved due to them being stored in bogs. For example, the belt of the bog body Meisje van Yde ("Girl from Yde") from the Netherlands got in the bog around the time of Christ's birth. The sixteen-year-old girl was strangled, and the belt, originally probably around 6½ feet long (2 m) and made of thirty-seven warp threads, lay around her neck. Well-preserved textiles have also been found in Norwegian bogs during peat cutting. The finds from the province of Rogaland were probably deliberately deposited in the bog during the **Migration period.** A sack with wool remnants was discovered in Time,

Norway.[82] The sack also contained a woolen legging with a sprang pattern of rows of small triangles. The upper and lower edges of the legging are tablet-woven.

From a bog in Tegle, Norway, comes a tube-shaped spranged textile with a tablet-woven edge, which may also be a legging or perhaps a sleeve. Unfortunately, the dating of a woolen leg warmer with a striped pattern from York, Great Britain, that was excavated in 1838 is unclear. It may belong to the sixth century. Several textile finds prove that the **Vikings** were familiar with the sprang technique. They even used precious silk yarn as a material, as shown by a hairnet excavated in Waterford, Ireland. Other sprang fragments come from Birka in Sweden. In the famous Oseberg ship, which dates back to around 850 CE, a wooden frame was found that may have been used as a sprang frame.

Rare finds from the **High Middle Ages** include two ribbons excavated in Poland, one of which is made of silk thread wrapped in silver,[83] and the other a cord used by a Nubian bishop to tie his trousers in the fourteenth century.[84] There are several illustrations from the **late Middle Ages** showing women working on narrow, vertical frames. Obviously spranged hairnets can be seen in paintings and images from the fifteenth and sixteenth centuries.[85] An archaeological find that caused quite a stir is the late medieval textiles from the fifteenth century from Lengberg Castle, Tyrol. A textile that was initially thought to be a brassiere with a spranged hole pattern insert made of 120 warp threads turned out to be a headdress upon closer examination.[86]

Ethnology and Modern Times: Purses and sashes

In central Europe, sprang was still widespread until the nineteenth century. Unfortunately, we do not know all the earlier names for the sprang technique, which makes it difficult to find written evidence of it. In **Germany**, gloves, purses, and shawls were *rahmengestrickt* (frame-knitted) or, as it was called in **Switzerland**, *greifgestrickt*. In Württemberg, the

77 Karina Grömer, "Textilien der Bronzezeit in Mitteleuropa," *Archaeologia Austriaca* 90 (2006): 31–72.

78 Moa Hallgren, Ulrike Beck, and Mayke Wagner, "Silk Road Fashion: Textile Flächenbildung und Verschlusstechniken," e-Forschungsberichte des DAI, 2016, Faszikel 3, 36–47.

79 The Art Museum, Princeton University, from Chiavenna, Italy.

80 Dagmar Drinkler assumes such leggings existed in the Renaissance as well; see Dagmar Drinkler, "Eng anliegende Bekleidung in Antike und Renaissance," *Zeitschrift für Kunsttechnologie und Konservierung* 24.1 (2010): 5–35, a presentation online at https://docplayer.org/4475407-Die-rekonstruktion-eng-anliegender-bekleidung-aus-antike-und-renaissance-dagmar-drinklerbayerisches-nationalmuseum-muenchen.html. According to Beatrix Nutz, there is no proof for this time period because no originals exist. Beatrix Nutz, "Linen Sprang from Lengberg Castle," in *Ancient Textiles Modern Science II*, ed. Heather Hopkins and Katrin Kania, Ancient Textiles Series 34 (Oxford, 2019), 60–72.

81 See, for example the exhibition catalog of the Textilmuseum Krefeld: Annette Paetz gen. Schieck, *Aus Gräbern geborgen—koptische Textilien* (Krefeld, Germany, 2003).

82 Time, Jæren, Rogaland, Norway (near Stavanger). Norsk Folkemuseum, NF.08455-027.

83 Junkrowy, Poland, eighth–eleventh centuries, and Gdańsk, Poland, twelfth century.

84 Kania 2010, 63.

85 Nutz 2019.

86 Ibid.

technique is said to have been called *krabbeln*.[87]

Purses spranged from silk thread made their way from Europe to **North America** in the seventeenth and eighteenth centuries, as surviving examples in the Colonial Williamsburg Museum and elsewhere show. Snuff was kept in similar pouches in the Dutch province of Groningen until the nineteenth century. The opening for removing the tobacco (or coins) was closed with sliding metal rings.[88] The threads at one end were tied together to form a decorative tassel. The actual pouch area of the surviving pouches is made using a more tightly woven technique, so that the small change could not slip through the larger openings of the net structure.

From the seventeenth century to the beginning of the nineteenth century, officers in many European countries wore woven and sprang sashes as part of their uniform. These military insignia ended in pompous tassels with long fringes. The color scheme depended on the respective national flag. In Prussia, for example, they were made of silver thread with horizontal strips of black silk thread. These sashes were up to 10 feet long (3 m), since they were wrapped around the body twice or worn folded over.[89] These "net-shaped sashes of the officers"[90] were made by craftsmen specialized in passementerie and braid. The sashes of the marksmen's guilds from the eighteenth century, which can be admired in **Dutch** museums, have particularly beautiful hole patterns with ships, mermaids, or tree-of-life designs. It is assumed that these marksmen's sashes developed from military sashes.[91]

In **Romania**, the **Czech Republic**, and **Slovakia**, sprang used for belts and women's hoods belong to the traditional textile techniques. In **Ukraine,** too, hoods with sprang inserts and sprang belts or sashes were known. Since the middle of the twentieth century, however, these belts were no longer worn as everyday clothing. As a result, knowledge of how they were made almost disappeared. More recently, however, more craftsmen are working with them again, and the belts are now worn on special occasions.[92] In **Belarus**, sprang belts were also part of the traditional clothing of women and men. They had a high symbolic and ritual significance.

Sprang was also known in the Baltic states and Scandinavia. In **Estonia**, men's sprang sashes were called "net belts" (*võrkvöö*). In **Lithuania**, there were spranged women's hoods, as well as colorful ribbons in a checkered tartan pattern, which were not made with real sprang, but with loosely hanging thread ends. In **Sweden**,

87 Th. Dohrenburg, "Sprang—eine dreitausendjährige Handarbeit," *Frauen-Kultur* 9, booklet (Sept. 1936), issue A, cited according to Peter Collingwood, *The Techniques of Sprang: Plaiting on Stretched Threads* (London, 1974), 42.

88 Info from www.denblauwenswaen.nl/ambachten/sprang.

89 See Martin Kloeffler, *Versuch einer Typologie preußischer Offiziersschärpen* (Düsseldorf, Germany, 2008).

90 Johann Beckmann, *Beytrage zur Geschichte der Erfindungen*, vol. 5, *Stricken* (Leipzig, 1805), 164.

91 Johan M. Oomen and E. A. G. Reker, *Vlechtwerksjerpen van de Noordbrabantse Schuttersgilden* (Eindhoven, Germany, 1991).

92 Olena Kozakevych, *Tradition of Woven Sprang Belts* (Lviv, Ukraine, 2020).

^
Swedish parade sash
ca. 1820

›
Sprang garters from
Rendalen, Norway

Sprang children's clothes made by Sylva Antony Čekalová, Prague

ribbons with a diagonal plaid pattern were also woven not only with a fingerweaving technique [Fingerweaving: p. 129], but also in real sprang (i.e., with a warp attached on both sides).[93] In **Norway**, sprang was even used through the twentieth century. In the meantime, however, it is on the red list of endangered craft techniques. In the past, it was used for curtains, decorative towel borders, church textiles, tablecloths, and cushions, and for gloves, hats, and sweaters. *Muddband* or *pelsskjerf* was the name given to the several-yard-long, often red-colored ribbons used to tie the buttonless fur coats of men and women. They were made on a long wooden bar, the 3-to-5-yard-long *bandstanga* ("band pole). These sprang tools were also known in northern Sweden, where they were called *bandslå* and were used to sprang garters. [Instructions: Pin Band: p. 226]

The women's belts known as *zostra* or *zonari* in **Greece** used to be an important part of womenswear. We find another special meaning here: the belts were supposed to be a magic remedy during childbirth and for back pain. The red coloring was a symbol of life and fertility, and the beauty of the textile should draw the evil eye from the beauty of the woman.

Outside Europe, sprang is still done in **Pakistan** and in Indian **Punjab** (thin bands and drawstrings for clothes) as well as in **Central** and **South America** in Peru, Guatemala, Mexico, and Colombia (hammocks and bags).

Rediscovery

The sprang technique, which was virtually forgotten at the time, was deciphered independently by a Danish woman and an Austrian woman shortly before 1900. In both cases, this was triggered by the study of prehistoric textile finds: In Copenhagen, the items of clothing found in the Borum Eshøj burial mound, excavated in 1871, were examined with a microscope. The use of scientific methods was not yet a given in archaeology at that time. Since it was not known what technique had been used to make the hairnet, an art student was commissioned to examine the material. Petra Godskesen noticed flaws in the textile that were repeated symmetrically and at the same distance from the center. She recognized a textile technique that had not yet been completely forgotten in Scandinavia. However, a name for this Bronze Age braiding technique is not mentioned in the 1891 publication. A sprang copy of the headdress made by Mrs. Godskesen was on display in the archaeological section of the Paris World Exhibition in 1889. The Viennese needlework teacher Louise Schinnerer was able to solve the mystery of the Coptic bags and hairnets around 1895.[94] Austrian textile experts who had previously examined these textiles from Egypt (400–700 CE) were initially uncertain about the manufacturing technique. Louise Schinnerer realized that the "Ruthenian weaving method," which she had learned in Podolia (today Ukraine) could be used to precisely re-create Egyptian textiles. With this knowledge, other textile stored in museums could now also be reinterpreted.

In 1935, H. C. Broholm and Margrethe Hald described sprang on the basis of Bronze Age hairnets from Denmark.[95] The sprang technique was not systematically studied and published again until 1974, by the British weaver and textile expert Peter Collingwood (1922–2008), together with the Swiss textile artist Noémi Speiser. Today, sprang is used by some craftsmen for modern garments. The Canadian Carol James, who came to sprang in the 1990s through her interest in the fingerwoven North American sashes, is currently probably the most renowned sprang expert in the world. [Canadian Sashes: p. 120]

93 Maria Collin, "Gammalskånska band," in *Fataburen* (1915): 14–31.
94 Schinnerer, n.d.
95 H. C. Broholm and Margrethe Hald, "To sprangede Textilarbejder i danske Oldfund," *Aarbøger for Nordisk Ødkyndighed og Historie*, Jan. 1935, 29–46.

→ Finger Weaving p. 129
→ Instructions: Pin Band p. 226
→ Canadian Sashes 120

TRY IT!

BRAID OF THREE

1 Wrap a thread (the material doesn't matter) around a book or picture frame three times. Tape down or knot the beginning and end.

2 Arrange the book or frame in front of you so that the threads run vertically to the table edge.

3 Make a braid from three threads, just like braiding hair. Always put the outer threads in the middle, alternating from right to left. You will easily be able to see how the same braid forms are mirrored on the other end of the wrap.

SIMPLE INTERLINKED SPRANG

The Swedish pin band, which is introduced here as the first project, actually belongs as a thin object to the chapter "Bands and Braids." But since the working steps of bands in sprang are the same as using sprang with wider pieces, I will describe this band here in the "Clothing and Accessories" chapter. Pin bands were spranged in pairs on long wooden slats and were used to fasten stockings.

HORIZONTALLY STRIPED PIN BAND

Tools: Long wooden slat with three nails [Building Instructions for Sprang Board: p. 290]; four wooden sticks (kebab skewers, long fireplace matches, or reed stalks—like in India); scissors

Materials: Thin cotton or wool yarn in two colors (e.g., red and green).

During sprang, it's best to sit in a chair with armrests, upon which you can lay the wooden plank comfortably.

Preparation

1 Secure the first thread with a knot on a single nail. From there, wrap in rounds, always from the individual around the outermost nail and back to the individual. Wind with medium tension; the yarn must not be pulled too tightly. Cut the yarn after six rounds. Knot on the second color. Wrap six rounds again. Then cut the thread and knot the end to the individual nail.

The threads are tensed.

The threads are separated.

Separate the threads into upper and lower threads.

Always bring one green thread upward and one red thread downward.

Insert a wooden stick in the shed.

Open the shed to the other end.

2 To form the pattern, lift the six red threads from the left over the second nail to the right side. Lift the six green threads from the right to the left.

3 Place your left index finger in the middle between the two colors. There are twelve red upper threads on the finger and twelve green lower threads behind the finger.

4 Starting on the right with the right index finger, alternately take one green thread upward and push the next red thread downward.

5 Secure this arrangement by inserting a wooden stick.

6 Run your finger through the resulting shed to the other end of the wooden slat. Insert a wooden stick here too.

→ Building Instructions for Sprang Board p. 290

Row 1: First two to the top, one to the bottom. Then continue with one to the top, one to the bottom.

Push together and insert wooden stick.

Row 2: Always one to the top, one to the bottom

Push together and insert stick.

Sprang

7 * First row, work from right to left: Bring the outer two red lower threads up, place the first green upper thread down, then the next lower thread up again, and so on. Bring the last two upper threads to the bottom. All the red threads are now on top.

8 Push the threads down with your finger and insert the third wooden stick.

Run your finger through the shed to the other end of the stick, push, and insert the fourth wooden stick.

9 Second row, again from right to left. Bring the outermost green lower thread up, place the first red upper thread down, then the next lower thread up again, and so on until all the green threads are up.

10 Push with your finger; take the first wooden stick out of its place and put it in the new shed.

Run your finger to the other end and push, take the second wooden stick out of its place, and put it in the new shed. *

Continue working the steps between * and *.

Cutting the warp threads

Control: A pattern of horizontal stripes should be created. At the end of a row, all the threads of one color are always at the bottom, and all the threads of the other color are at the top. When the textile is pulled out in width, it must be connected and have a net structure. [Sprang Diagram: p. 217] It must not split into individual longitudinal threads. If the warp threads are under too much tension while working, they are tied together with a sturdy cord on the side with the single nail. They can now be lifted off the nail and tied back on again, shortened, using the cord. Later, the cord loop can be adjusted as often as necessary.

Finishing: At some point, you will no longer be able to get your finger into the gap between the two split halves. Then cut the warp threads and secure both ends by wrapping a thread around them. If you like, iron the finished bands so that they don't curl too much.

→ Sprang Diagram p. 217

SPRANG BAG

Tools: Sprang frame [Building Instructions: Sprang Frame: p. 290], scissors, crochet hook

Materials: Cotton, linen, or wool yarn in one or multiple colors

Preparation: The warp is wound in the frame either around two cross-tensioned threads or around two crosspieces of wood. When using wood, it is easier to tension the thread evenly because nothing bends. As the stretched textile shortens in the course of the work, there must be a way to gradually reduce the warp tension. This is easy to do if the crossbeams are tied: Undo both knots, move the wood slightly toward the center, and tie it down again on both sides.

The warp consists of a single thread. It is wrapped in a figure-eight form around both of the crosspieces of wood: Knot the thread at the bottom and wrap from front to back over the top piece, from front to back over the lower piece, and so on. You will end at the bottom. This gives you the same number of upper and lower threads, or pairs of threads. For a small bag, you need about thirty pairs of threads. If you want to use sprang to make a multicolored bag, change the color after a certain number of wraps. Knot the new yarn at the bottom and continue wrapping as usual.

The bag works in the same way as described above for the pin band, except that you now work with more threads.
[Pin Band Instructions: p. 226]

Sprang

1 The threads are divided into upper and lower threads by the crosspieces (in weaving, the space in between is called the shed). Every second thread is on top. The left hand reaches into the shed and holds the upper threads.

2 * **Row 1**: Pick up the first **lower two threads** with your right hand and release one upper thread / push it back. Then continually one lower thread up / one upper thread down. At the end of the row, there should still be two upper threads in your hand, which you now also push to the back.

3 Push the threads up and down to get them close together. Secure a wooden rod (or knitting needle or similar), or the securing thread is led though the newly created shed.

4 **Row 2**: Start from the right once again. This time, take only one lower thread with your right hand and release an upper thread. Continue through the end of the row. Then secure (see above, on page 229).*

Continue working the steps between * and *.

Row 1: First two to the top, one to the bottom. Then always one to the top, one to the bottom.

At the end of the row, two threads to the bottom

→ Building Instructions Sprang Frame p. 290

→ Pin Band Instructions p. 226

Push together and secure.

Row 2: Always one to the top, and one to the bottom

Use the crochet hook as help.

Pull the thread through to secure it.

5 If the space in the middle is so small that you can no longer get your hand in, use a crochet hook to help. It replaces the fingers of the right hand.

6 Where the two halves meet, the sprang work must be secured so that the twists do not come loose again. To do this, take a new thread doubled and pull it through. You can also secure it by pulling one loop through the next with the crochet hook. You can find instructions for this at www.krosienky-sprang.cz, by Sylva Antony Čekalová.

Forming the Bag

7 Take the sprang project from the frame. Don't worry; the start and end loops won't open by themselves. A cord is pulled through the loops later.

8 Fold both halves together at the center dividing line and sew both edges together.

9 Finally, pull a cord through the open edge. You can either crochet the cord [Chain Stitches: p. 246], knit it with a lucet, whipcord it [Whipcording: p. 87], or make a fingerloop braid [Fingerloop Braiding: p. 101].

Take off the sprang project.

Sew the bag together.

How to sprang hole patterns is well explained in *Sprang, eine uralte Flechttechnik* by Bertha Schwetter, available as a PDF at www.krosienkysprang.cz.

→ Chain Stitches p. 246

→ Whipcording p. 87

→ Fingerloop Braiding p. 101

BAND IN INTERLACED SPRANG

This band can be made either with sprang or fingerweaving. [Fingerweaving Checked Pattern: p. 129] If you want, you can try both techniques to see which one you like more. Here are the instructions for interlaced sprang:

Materials: Eight threads approximately 5 feet in length (1.5 m) in three colors; for example, four gray, two yellow, two purple. The finished band will be approximately 28 inches (70 cm) long.

Preparation: Traditionally, the threads in these ribbons are not tensioned, but the ends hang down open. However, you can also use a sprang frame. If both ends are fixed, braiding is twice as fast. Fold the threads in half and wrap them around a thin stick (pencil, knitting needle, chopstick). Distribute the colors symmetrically from the middle. Work alternately from the right to the left and from the left to the right.

1 **Starting row:** Starting from the right, bring the first thread from the top to the bottom and the second thread from the bottom to the top. Continue bringing one to the bottom, one to the top until the end of the row.

2 **Start the first row from the left:** Bring the first thread from the bottom to the top, the second from the top to the bottom. * One to the top, one to the bottom. * Continue from * to * until the end of the row (results in an S crossing).

3 **Start the second row from the right:** The first on the bottom stays on the bottom! The second, from the bottom to the top. * One to the bottom, one to the top. * Continue from * to * until the end of the row (results in a Z crossing).

4 Always alternate between row 1 and row 2.

5 **Tip:** If you don't know whether to continue to the right or left: If you lay the ribbon in front of you, the threads at the open end will form an inverted V. If the top layer of the V points to the left, it continues to the right. If the top layer points to the right, it continues to the left.

The ends of the threads will wrap around each other. They need to be untangled from time to time. This is very easy if only one thread is pulled out upward at a time.

From the right: one to the bottom, one to the top

From the left: one to the top, one to the bottom

From the right: one stays on the bottom, and the second one comes to the top.

Back from the left: one to the top, one to the bottom

Continue from the right.

Continue from the left.

→ Fingerweaving Checked Pattern p. 129

TIPS FROM SPRANG EXPERT

SYLVA ANTONY ČEKALOVÁ

- If you are a beginner, use a strong cotton yarn, light in color. Don't use wool. It tends to felt, and in the beginning the smooth yarn is better.

- Start with a small item, such as a small bag or a belt, for which twenty pairs of threads are sufficient.

- Don't worry about mistakes. Make mistakes! That is the best way to learn.

- You don't need any special frame to begin with the sprang. Use what you find at home. You can stretch the leading cords for the sprang warp between, for example, legs of a table or a chair, on a photo frame, or on a stepladder.

- Don't worry about the edges; in the beginning you can make mistakes with the starts and the ends of the rows. Just continue and focus on the middle of the work. Correctly made edges will come with time, when your eyes start to see and understand the sprang structure.

- With the basic flexible sprang technique—interlinking—you can use a simple rule to control if you do it right: One back thread always goes behind two front threads. If it goes behind three front threads, you are creating another pattern; if it goes under just one thread, you don't create sprang structure at all.

- If you create, for example, a small bag, leave the first and the last thread of the warp longer. Later you can use them for sewing the edges together.

- When you get near the center of the sprang fabric and there is not much space for your fingers anymore, use a tool—needlehook (knook), knitting needles, or a crochet hook.

ADVANCED TIPS

- When working on a wide warp, work in sections—hold just a few threads in your hand, secure them after braiding, using a safety cord, and continue with another bunch of the threads. This way, you don't need to have your hand in the whole warp all the time, and you can make a really wide item such as a blanket or a hammock.

- You can even create big sprang pieces such as clothes on a small portable frame by using different types of warping or connecting together smaller sprang pieces. Feel free to experiment.

- Various sprang techniques have different features. You can use them for shaping the sprang fabric.

- You can also shape the sprang fabric by adding additional threads to the warp or starting to braid with twisted yarn, which you later divide into individual threads.

Sprang is a fantastic ancient technique, one that offers much more than just traditional patterns. I believe there is still much to explore. Allow yourself to experiment with different materials, combinations of various sprang techniques, creating your own patterns, and finding your own finger movements. Everything that leads you to your desired result is allowed. Enjoy!

Sylva Antony Čekalová

Prague, Czech Republic

Sylva Antony Čekalová is a trained tiled-stove restorer. She has been working intensively with the sprang technique for more than fifteen years. She designs and creates sprang garments, usually on small portable frames, and looks for contemporary ways to apply this ancient technique. She passes on her enthusiasm for sprang in the Czech Republic and abroad, including at exhibitions, courses, and conferences in Norway, Croatia, and Austria.

You can find many sprang tips on her website.

www.krosienky-sprang.cz

SLIP STITCH CROCHET

On the North Sea and Baltic coasts, including in the Netherlands and the Baltic states, fishermen and shepherds crocheted extra-warm mitts with thick sheep's wool yarn and a special needle. The technique was rediscovered in East Frisia.

At first glance, crocheting doesn't seem to be anything special. Instructions for modern beanie hats or amigurumi figures are easy to find. You may also remember crocheting potholders in needlework lessons. However, slip stitch crochet is the predecessor of modern crochet. A very special crochet hook is used for this, which differs from today's crochet hooks. Another typical feature is the diagonal patterns with jagged edges that are created when crocheting with different colors. This original crochet technique is largely unknown today. Sometimes slip stitch crochet is also referred to as Tunisian crochet. In Tunisian crochet, however, all the stitches in a row are on a special, very long crochet hook and are crocheted off one by one. It is therefore definitely a different method.

THE TECHNIQUE

Slip stitch crochet is a crochet technique that uses the slip stitch as the only stitch. Nevertheless, a wide variety of patterns are possible by inserting stitches into the front or back of the stitches in the previous round. If you stitch in at the front, rows of loops are formed running crosswise. Clearly defined motifs are possible with different-colored yarns. In Scandinavia, this stitch is used mainly for colorful patterned mitten cuffs. If, on the other hand, you stitch in the back, a structure of almost vertical threads is created. Seen from a distance, they form diagonal rows. If you alternate the colors when crocheting, stripes or diagonal geometric patterns such as crosses, rhombuses, or triangles can be incorporated. The yarn of the unused color is carried along on the reverse side, as when knitting Norwegian patterns. The frayed or dashed edges on the slanted sides of the motifs are striking. They appear only when the slip stitches are inserted at the front. This is because each of these stitches appears in the stitch pattern as a combination of two offset loops. If you know what this looks like, you can easily identify slip-stitch-crocheted textiles.

Slip stitch crochet is easy to learn, especially when crocheting roughly and with large stitches. It works even with unspun, slightly twisted sheep's wool. On the other hand, you can also crochet very finely, with lots of stitches and fine yarn. In both cases, the result is a dense textile. The finished work can be stretched very much vertically, but only slightly horizontally.

It is always worked in continuous rounds on the front side. The technique is therefore particularly suitable for tubular objects: stockings, bags, mittens, and gloves. In appearance, slip-stitch-crocheted pieces are similar to those in nålbinding. [Nålbinding: p. 197] However, unlike needle binding, the thread does not have to be pulled all the way through. The new stitch is pulled from a thread loop directly next to the last stitch formed. You can therefore work with a continuous thread from the ball of yarn.

You can also achieve the same structure using the nålbinding technique, but it is much quicker with a crochet hook. Nålbinding is usually worked from left to right, while slip stitch crochet is worked from right to left. In nålbinding, the entire end of the thread is pulled through, whereas in crochet only one loop is pulled through. The similarity in appearance is certainly the reason why slip-stitch-crocheted textiles are sometimes

→ Nålbinding p. 197

Slip-stitch-crocheted *jurab* socks from Tajikistan

mistaken for nålbinding textiles. Examples of misinterpretation can be found in some collections and museums. In some regions there is actually a tradition of both techniques; for example, in Cameroon and Guatemala. In most cases, however, only one or the other is known.

It is interesting to note that slip stitch crochet, at least in northern Europe, was a typically male craft. The warm, robust mitts were popular with fishermen, shepherds, forest workers, and coachmen, and generally with anyone who had to work outside in cold weather. The mitts became even warmer if they were made a few sizes larger and then compacted by fulling after crocheting.

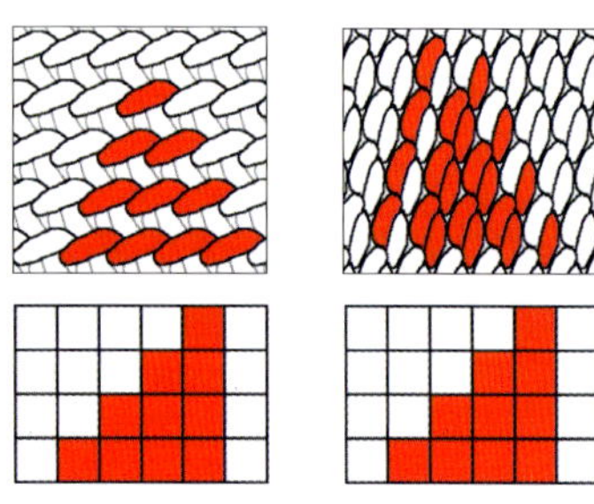

The same pattern,
stitched into the back (*left picture*)
and stitched in the front (*right picture*)

THE CROCHET HOOK

When slip stitch crochet, you work with a special flat needle that gets wider toward the handle. Each new loop of yarn is pulled onto the handle, and a very wide stitch is automatically created. The surface of these crochet hooks must be as smooth as possible so that the yarn does not catch on them. Traditional materials for this are therefore polishable wood or bone. In former East Prussia, a special bone from the horse's leg was used for this purpose. This so-called stylus bone naturally has almost the right shape of an elongated triangle that narrows at the tip. Metal is also well suited for crochet hooks. In Tajikistan, for example, reworked old silver spoons are used. Spoon handles as a basic material are also found in Germany around 1800 in the Leipzig region.
[Instructions for Crochet Hooks: p. 291]

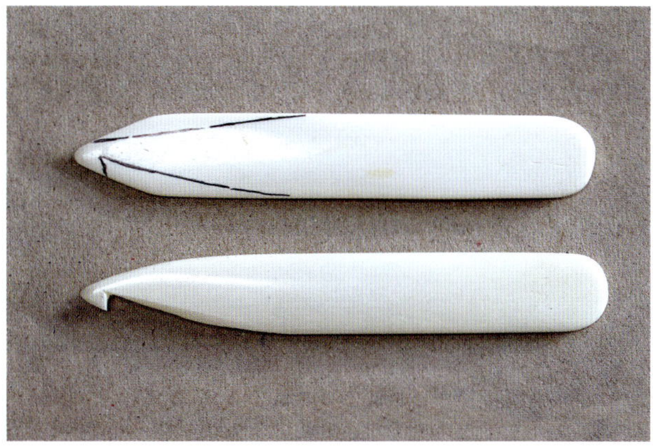

Bone folders from the craft store are well suited for creating crochet hooks.

Dutch mittens crocheted from wool remnants in the 1940s

→ Instructions for Crochet Hooks: p. 291

EUROPE'S FIRST CROCHET STITCHES

Slip stitch crocheting is the first crochet technique that spread in Europe. No one knows just how old it is. The first reports of it are from the time just before 1800. At that point, crocheting was known as "knitting with a hook." The term *crocheting*, which was derived from the French word for hook, *crochet*, was known only later. In 1785, an illustration of tricot au clou (nail knitting) in a French book shows both a nail-like crochet hook and the typical wide (in this case, triangular-shaped) crochet hook.[96] In 1792, it is said that "a foreign workman" had made the method of "hooking" men's mitts known in Schleswig-Holstein. In 1800, a knitting book introduces "hook knitting" and reports that woolen shoes were made with it in Leipzig. A pair of children's shoes, *baby's bootees*, made of red wool with leather soles, which can be found in the Scottish National Museum, give an idea of the appearance of such shoes.[97] A household instruction book from 1801 recommends "hook knitting" for purses and stockings. In Scotland in 1812, the wife of an old sea captain crocheted nightcaps, long underpants, and vests for her husband "in a stitch she called shepherd's knitting" from wool she had spun herself. She made the crochet hook herself from a tortoiseshell comb. Since the 1820s, work with the hook needle has been known in Germany as *häckeln*, or *hekelen* in the Netherlands. In 1835, a book appeared in Ireland with handcraft instructions in which *scotch knitting* was explained—including instructions for a nightcap with a miniature cap taped in the book! Starting around the **middle of the eighteenth century**, the originally French term "crochet" was adopted into English. In 1897, the textile instructor Louise Schinnerer introduced the term "Bosnian crochet." She explained it by using a crocheted cap and stocking from Bosnia and Herzegovina. In Lavia and former Eastern Prussia, crocheted woolen mitts with slip stitches were also made. In the Slovakian Carpathians, plain slip-stitch-crocheted mitts from coarse, handspun woolen yarn were worn as working gloves. These were still known in the 1950s in Scotland as cleekit gloves. The technique must have also been known in the Netherlands through the middle of the last century, because in 1954 the herdersteek, the "shepherd's stitch," was introduced as a crochet idea for warm mittens.

Stickbreyen, which translates as "stick knitting," is being practiced again in East Frisia **today**. A few years ago, the Dörpmuseum in Münkeboe revived the old method used by North Sea fishermen to crochet their work mitts and now teaches it in courses. [Tips from Münkeboe: p. 251] In Scandinavia, slip stitch crochet is still relatively widespread. Other than in the Finnish regions of Karelia and Ostrobothnia, it is still known in Norway, Sweden, and Denmark. The special thing about Scandinavian mitts and arm warmers is that the patterns are made from colorful wool. Whether there is a connection to the richly patterned, colorful socks, *jurab*, made in the Pamir Mountains in Tajikistan, using the exact same technique, is unknown. There are similar socks in Turkey. Bags are crocheted in India, stockings in Afghanistan, and hats in Palestine, Morocco, and Cameroon. Perhaps it will be discovered in even more regions in the world?

Slip Stitch Pieces in Collections

Some examples of nineteenth-century slip stitch crocheted mitts can be found in Swedish, Norwegian, and Finnish museums, among others. The Estonian National Museum also has several pairs of mitts crocheted using this technique, all of which were made between 1821 and 1907.[98]

The miraculous hair shirt of Saint Nilus of Sora or Nil Sorky (1433–1508) is crocheted using slip stitch crochet,[99] as is a cotton nightcap in the Museum Admiralty House Dokkum, Netherlands. The cap is not dated, but on the basis of the material used, it is estimated to be from the eighteenth or nineteenth century.[100]

A recent example of preserved slip-stitch-crocheted textiles is two mitts in the Dutch Textile Museum in Leiden. They were made during the Second World War. They were probably made from leftover wool due to the scarcity of materials at the time. To make mitts look more fashionable and less rustic, small flowers were applied from pastel-colored yarn.[101]

96 The references for this and the following citations can be found on my website, www.ausgraeberei.de.

97 Museum number: H.TWG 4.2; dated around 1780.

98 Sigrid Talviste, *Bosnia tehnikas heegeldatud kindad Eesti Rahva Muuseumi kogus* (Viljandi, Estonia, 2014).

99 Anne Marie Decker explains on her website, www.nalbound.com, her analysis of the hair shirt.

100 Gudrun Böttcher, who analyzed the structure of the cap, believes it is done with nålbinding: "'Nightcap' in Dokkum," in *Experimentelle Archaologie: Bilanz 1998*, Archäologische Mitteilungen aus Nordwestdeutschland, Beiheft 24 (Oldenburg, Germany, 1998), 125–136.

101 Exhibit: *Textile Tales from the Second World War*, TRC Leiden, Netherlands, object nr. 2016.2335a-b and 2016.2337a-b.

→ Tips from Münkeboe p. 251

TRY IT!

SLIP STITCH TUBE

For the first try, a normal crochet hook is suitable (two number sizes larger than the yarn recommendation) and remnant yarn (if possible, not too fluffy; it's easier to see the stitches with smooth yarn). I will describe the steps that match the photos for right-handed people. If you work with your left hand, consider everything mirrored.

st = stitch, **ss** = slip stitch,
ch = chain stitch

1 Form a loop from the start of the thread.

2 Place the upper thread behind the loop and pull the back thread through to the front with the crochet hook.

3 Tighten the loop to create the starting stitch. The size can be adjusted by pulling the short end of the thread.

4 Wrap the working thread around the finger of your left hand. That is how the thread is held taut.

5 The hook is still in the starting stitch. Pull the working thread through with the hook = 1st ch.

6 Crochet a short row of ch; for example, 30 ch. Try to keep the crocheting loose. This should result in large loops; the hook should have a lot of space in the loop.

7 Close the ch row with a ss to form a circle: Grab the working thread with the hook and pull it through both loops at once. The **first slip stitch** has been formed.

8 The work is done from right to left. A ss in each ch: The hook is inserted in the first ch; the thread is grabbed and then pulled through the loop onto the hook.

Work the next and all other ss in the same way. At the end of each round, simply continue crocheting. You have the choice of inserting into the upper or back loop (yellow arrow) or . . .

9 . . . into the lower or front loop of the stitch (red arrow). A different stitch pattern is created in each case.

10 Work your way up in a spiral. A tube is created.

You can turn your initial piece into a bracelet or an arm warmer, for example. When the piece is long enough, cut the working thread and pull it through the last st. Sew the beginning and end threads on the inside.

1 Loop the starting yarn.

2 Put the upper thread behind the loop and pull the loop through.

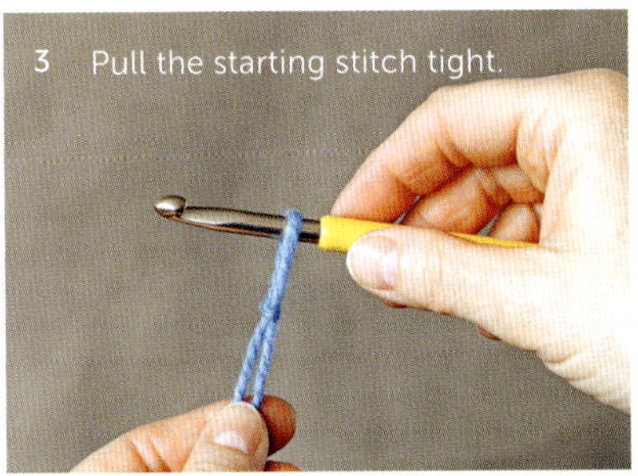
3 Pull the starting stitch tight.

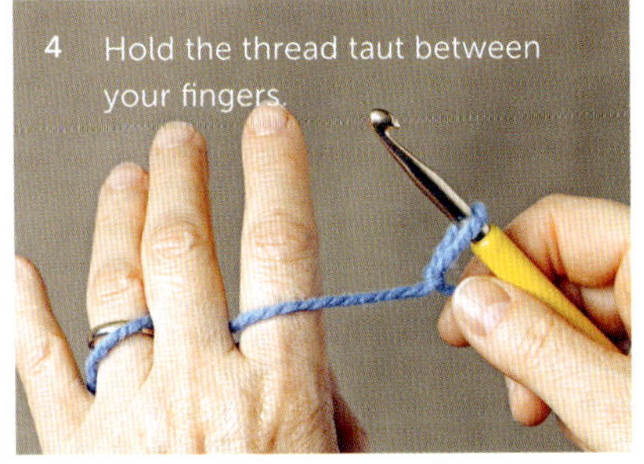
4 Hold the thread taut between your fingers.

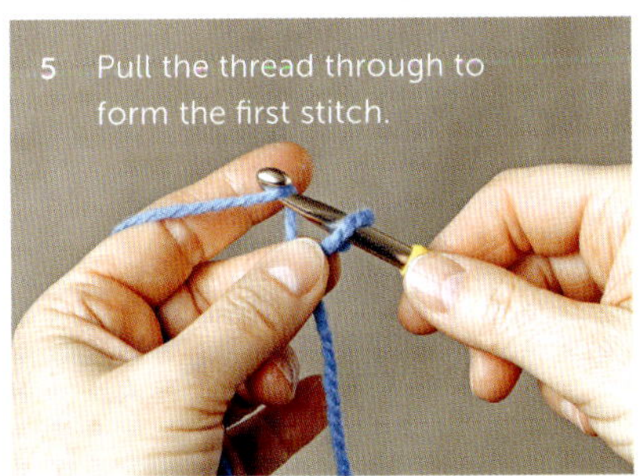
5 Pull the thread through to form the first stitch.

6 Crochet the row of chain stitches.

7 Use a slip stitch to form a circle from the chain stitch row.

8 Insert either always from behind (yellow arrow) . . .

9 . . . or from the front (red arrow).

10 The nearly finished bracelet

MITTENS

The Crochet Hook

As described above, you can work with an everyday crochet hook. It works easier, however, with a special crochet hook. Where would you find this tool? Sometimes these flat crochet hooks are offered in online shops; for example, on Etsy. You can sometimes also find them in some Scandinavian craft stores. In the USA, the company Lacis offers "pjoning hooks for Bosnian crochet." You can also easily create one of these crochet hooks yourself—instructions can be found in the Tool Workshop. [Building Instructions for Crochet Hook: p. 291]

The Yarn

In principle, any kind of knitting or crochet yarn will work. Traditionally, sheep's wool was used. Shepherds used to process the row, unspun, or only slightly twisted wool. If the ends of these short threads are not sewn but left hanging loosely on the inside, you automatically get a soft lining.

The closest you can get to the look of these shepherd's mittens is to use wool roving or so-called felting wool, i.e., single-ply, lightly twisted wool without a superwash finish. You can get particularly thick mittens by working them approximately 30 percent larger than the actual size and then fulling them by hand or in the washing machine. [Fulling Instructions: p. 256]

The Pattern

The mittens presented here are crocheted in a single color. If you enjoy experimenting, try out different-colored patterns. A special feature of slip stitches is that stripes that are vertical in the pattern drawing appear slanted to the left in the finished textile. Examples can be seen on the following pages. Templates for designing your own patterns can be found on my website, www.ausgraeberei.de.

st = stitch, **ss** = slip stitch,
ch = chain stitch

Close the chain-stitch row with a slip stitch.

Stitch from the back of the loops to create the cuff.

Starting now, the stitches continue from the front of the loops.

Leave an opening for the thumb.

1 Crochet a row of chain stitches (see above) a few centimeters more than you will need afterward, because the work contracts considerably in the first few rounds. Measure at the widest part of the hand; the mitten will hardly be able to be pulled wide later, and you want to be able to slip into it comfortably. It's best to keep the same number of st until you decrease toward the tip of the mitten. For my mittens, women's size S, I started with 36 st.

Close the ch row with a ss.

2 Starting now, you will stitch only with ss. For the cuff, stitch into the loop at the top or back; work five rounds in this pattern.

3 After working the cuff, insert the st into the lower or front loops. Continue crocheting with the same number of st until you reach the thumb hole.

4 For the **thumb opening**, skip six to eight st with the same number of ch. In the following round, crochet more ss into the ch from the thumb hole.

→ Building Instructions for Crochet Hook p. 291

→ Fulling Instructions p. 256

5 Continue this way until the index finger is covered. Then reduce stitches for the tip: Insert the crochet hook into the st, pull the thread through (two loops are on the hook), then insert the hook into the next st and pull the thread in one go through the st and both loops on the hook. Reduce by four for each round, distributed evenly.

6 When only four to eight st are left, pull the thread through all st, pull the opening together, and sew in the thread.

7 **Thumb:** Start with a new thread. One ss in each st of the thumb opening plus one st to the right and left. Continue crocheting until the bottom edge of the thumbnail. Bind off three times in the following round. Pull the remaining four stitches together and weave in the thread.

Instead of starting on the bottom edge, you can also create the mitten starting at the tip and working toward the opening. This way was typical in Finland in earlier times.

TIPS FROM THE CRAFT GROUP AT THE MÜNKEBOE VILLAGE MUSEUM

Stickbreyen (stick knitting) is an old East Frisian handicraft. It was used to make thick, warm mittens. Little is known about the history of *stickbreyen* in East Frisia. Unfortunately, neither old records nor *stickjes* nor original mitts have survived. Work was divided up: The women spun the wool yarn and knitted the cuff. The men then crocheted the mitten with a hook called a *stickje*. The women worked the thumb.

- For a mitten, knit the cuff with double pointed needles, knit one / purl one, and bind off loosely. Always insert the stickje into the front of the bound-off stitches and place the yarn around the stickje from the right side. Pull the yarn through the half stitch and the stitch on the stickje. You only ever insert the yarn at the front; patterns are not worked into these mittens.

- Continue working to the thumb. For the thumb opening, create nine chain stitches, skip the next nine stitches, and continue crocheting with the tenth stitch.

- Start decreasing for the tip of the mitten starting at the fingertip of your little finger. Pull the last six to eight stitches together and tie off the yarn.

- To finish, crochet the thumb into the thumb opening.

Courses in *stickbreyen* are offered at the Münkeboe Village Museum. Stickjes with crochet instructions can be bought in the museum shop.

Dörpmuseum Münkeboe
Lower Saxony, Germany

The Münkeboe Village Museum is a hands-on museum village. With its workshops and a windmill, it offers an insight into everyday life and work in a small moorland village.
www.doerpmuseum-muenkeboe.de

FULLING

Fulled wool clothing is particularly warm, windproof, and water repellent. In contrast to felting, the finished textiles are processed during fulling instead of the loose fibers.

In the past, many woolen fabrics and knitwear made of wool were intentionally matted. The wool was fulled in warm soapy water to shrink it and make it dense, then the nap was raised with weaving cards to give it a soft surface.

Sheep's wool is naturally water repellent and has an insulating effect thanks to its hollow fibers. These properties could be further enhanced by deliberately felting the individual hairs. Wool fibers have a scaly structure. When they are rubbed together when damp and warm, the fibers interlock and the wool becomes matted. This resulted in particularly dense and weatherproof garments. It also prevented the natural matting and shrinkage of clothing when worn.

One method that was already being practiced in ancient Rome is stamping the fabrics with the feet in water-filled basins. Rubbing wet wool with your hands also felts the material. Fulling with hands or feet is very strenuous. It is easier to have the work done by waterpower. Artificial water whirlpools or fulling mills with wooden beaters were used for this purpose. In addition to woven woolen fabrics, knitted woolen hats (well-known examples are the fez and Basque beret) and, above all, mitts and

The carder is equipped with the flower heads of fuller's teasel.

stockings were also fulled.

The fulling was followed by raising (teasing, napping) and finally shearing. During napping, the fibers were combed up with a special brush, the carder. This improved the wind- and water-repellent properties and also made the fabrics and garments cozier. During the final shearing process, the roughened surface was cut to a uniform height.

The flexible hooks on the flower head of the fuller's teasel (*Dipsacus sativus*) are ideal for combing up the wool fibers. Fuller's teasel, which originates from the Mediterranean region, is a cultivated form (i.e., it has been further developed by humans from the wild form). The wild form (*Dipsacus fullonum*) cannot be used for raising.

It is often said that fuller's teasel was used to loosen unspun sheep's wool. However, this carding is done with hand carders with metal hooks. Fuller's teasel is not suitable for this purpose.

102 At the *Kardenmuseum* (teasel museum) in Katsdorf in the Austrian Mühlviertel region, you can find out more about the cultivation and history of fuller's teasel: www.museum-katsdorf.at.

CULTIVATING TEASEL IN YOUR OWN GARDEN

Where can you get teasel? Real fuller's teasel can be found as a dried flower in flower shops. When occurring in nature, it can be found mostly as wild teasel. However, you may discover a spot where fuller's teasel has been preserved by garden escape. You can also easily grow it yourself; but first check to ensure it's not on your state's or region's invasive species list.

Only one rosette of leaves forms in the first year. Harvesting then takes place in the summer of the second year, when the teasel has almost or just finished flowering. Incidentally, the flowers of the fuller's teasel are a wonderful nectar source for bumblebees. When harvesting, about 6 inches (15 cm) of the stem should be left on the flowerhead. After harvesting, the teasels are dried. The numerous seeds can be shaken off or tapped out and stored for the next sowing or used as bird food. After drying, scrape off the spines on the stem with a knife and remove the bracts.

Fuller's teasel,
Dipsacus sativus

Wild teasel,
Dipsacus fullonum / D. sylvestris

Fulling in the sink

Small teasel holder for hand-raising mittens and stockings

FULLING AND RAISING

Any textile made of wool that does not have an antifelting finish can be fulled. You can try fulling with a knitted rectangle or one woven on a small loom. It is also suitable for self-knitted stockings or so-called felt socks. If you don't want to knit something, you can, of course, full any other textile made of feltable wool instead. The fabrics that have been introduced in this book that are most suitable are those done with nålbinding [Nålbinding: p. 197] and slip stitch crochet [Slip Stitch Crochet Mittens: p. 248]. The twined arm warmers and mittens [Twining Arm Warmers: p. 192] were also frequently fulled. However, if you are making a new textile for subsequent fulling, bear in mind that the material shrinks by up to 30 percent during fulling. You should therefore use a test swatch to determine the textile's shrinkage rate.

For fulling, the textile is moistened with hot water in the sink, rubbed with a little soap (simple curd soap or olive soap, which is gentler on the skin), and vigorously rubbed and pressed with the hands. An old washboard can be useful as a base for fulling. Ribbed, nonsplintering terrace boards are also suitable. Small corrugated boards for wet felting can be bought as "fulling blocks." Several times, hold the test piece under the hot-water tap, resoap, and fold it differently. After a few minutes, you will notice that the piece becomes smaller, and the stitch pattern or structure is no longer clearly visible. Then wash out the soap.

Before the fulled piece has dried, go over it lightly with brush (such as a nail brush or vegetable brush) to roughen it. You will see how the wool hairs stand up, creating a fluffy surface. If you have fuller's teasel heads, use these instead of the brush. You can hold the teasel in your hand or place it in a homemade holder.

Fulled hat made of thick wool yarn, excavated on Spitzbergen. It belonged to a Dutch whale hunter from the seventeenth or eighteenth century.

→ Nålbinding Mittens p. 197

→ Slip Stitch Crochet-Mittens p. 248

→ Twining Arm Warmers p. 192

TOOL WORKSHOP

INSTRUCTIONS FOR BUILDING TEXTILE TOOLS YOURSELF

TOOLS FOR

FIBERS AND THREADS

Flax Ripple, Flax Hackle, Spindles (Spinning Hooks, Dealgan, Diabolo, and Dumbbell Spindle), Rope-Twisting Paddle, Spinning Crank, Hand Winch

TOOLS FOR

BANDS AND BRAIDS

Bobbins, Weaving Bow, Rigid Heddle, Weaver's Shuttle, Weaving Sword, Weaving Tablets

TOOLS FOR

CLOTHING AND ACCESSORIES

Twining Form, Nålbinding Needle, Sprang Frame, Sprang Board, Crochet Hook

TOOLS AND MATERIALS

Tools: A basic set of tools is all you need. A pocketknife or carving (e.g., whittling) knife, a hand axe, and a pruning saw are essential. You will need a fretsaw to cut thin boards into the desired shape. A wood rasp is also useful for quickly removing large quantities of wood before using the sandpaper. Holes are drilled with a cordless power screwdriver, a drill, or, if you want to work without electricity, a hand drill. Holes can also be made in thin boards by using a pyrography pen or soldering iron. You should have at least three screw clamps to hold the workpieces in place. A useful addition to your tool kit is a chisel and a mallet. You will also have a lot of fun with a Japanese saw, which makes it easy to saw straight cuts. Use a yardstick or tape measure for measuring.

Here are the most important tools:

- carving knife
- axe
- saw
- wood rasp
- drill
- screw clamps

You should always have handy a ball of twine and sandpaper in various grit sizes, from 80 for presanding to 220 for fine sanding. I prefer to use rough horsetail for polishing. You can buy it in nurseries as a pond-edge plant. It grows well in its own container with sufficient moisture or freely in the garden, but then it is advisable to install a deep rhizome barrier.

Materials: If you want to start one of the following projects, you will need wood. You can either go to your nearest hardware store or use material that is available for free. Maybe you can find an old shelf in your basement or an unneeded wooden strip. Bulky waste on the side of the road is another good source for finding old wood. You can cut usable plywood boards from small fruit crates.

Green wood is the better choice for carving. It is much easier to work with than well-dried wood. You also need freshly cut branches (or branches that have been soaked in water long enough) for all parts that are to be bent or woven. Take care to follow the regulations for any public lands you may explore. You may find wood in your own yard. For example, you can cut individual branches from your hazel shrub in summer. But check first to make sure there are no nests in the branches. Nature reserves are of course off-limits all year round. In the winter months, trees and bushes in public green spaces and along roads and paths are pruned. If you save individual branches from the shredder, nobody will object. Just ask nicely. And finally, upcycling Christmas trees is also an environmentally friendly way of obtaining building materials.

All dimensions given in the assembly instructions are **only an approximate guide to size**. Modify the dimensions according to your wishes and the material available!

SPLITTING WOOD WITH A KNIFE: BATONING

You will need wooden boards for some of the following projects. You can buy these ready-made, saw them from solid wood, or split the wood with an axe. If you are not experienced with an axe, try splitting with a knife. If done correctly, it is a safe method. A sturdy knife is placed on the center of the upright stick and tapped into the stick with a mallet or heavy piece of wood until it splits (see photo on page 260).

TOOLS FOR

FIBERS AND THREADS

FLAX RIPPLE

Materials:

(Measurements are approx.; use what you have.)

- Wooden board, planed softwood (pine, spruce, or fir), 3.75 × 16 × 0.6 in. (9.5 × 41.0 × 1.7 cm)
- Wooden board (remnant) approx. 4 × 11.75 × 0.8 in. (10 × 30 × 2 cm)
- Square strip, 0.6 × 0.6 in. (1.5 × 1.5 cm), 7.5 in. long (19 cm)
- Carpenter's PVA glue

Tools: Saw, fretsaw, rasp, chisel and mallet, screw clamps, coarse and fine sandpaper

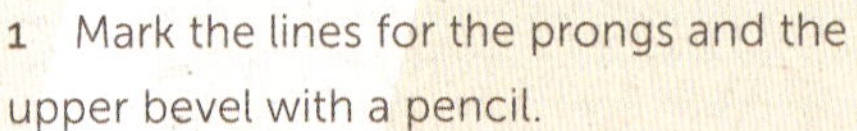

1 Mark the lines for the prongs and the upper bevel with a pencil.

2 Clamp the board in a workbench vise or with screw clamps. Work out the bevel with the rasp.

3 Saw the prongs: Cut the long saw cuts with the hacksaw or Japanese saw; cut off the remaining wood with the fretsaw.

4 Bevel the tips of the prongs slightly, first with coarse sandpaper and then with fine sandpaper.

5 Saw off the lower protrusion, each 0.3 in. (0.75 cm) wide.

6 Cut the square strip in half. Glue each 3.75-inch-long piece to the ripple board (see photo). Clamp with a screw clamp for at least thirty minutes, then leave to dry.

7 Chisel a rectangular recess in the support board. Check that the ripple sits well in the recess; if not, rework a little. Do not remove too much; otherwise the ripple will wobble in the holder.

8 Smooth all edges with sandpaper.

To use, the support board is attached to a tabletop or bench with two screw clamps. The ripple is inserted. Place a large cloth underneath to catch the flax seeds. Now the flax can be pulled through the prongs. Be careful; the seeds will bounce far!

FLAX HACKLE

You can often still find old hackles with forged teeth at flea markets and in antique stores. The teeth of our self-made hackle are not as sharp as those of their antique counterparts. This has the advantage that inexperienced people, such as school classes or youth groups, can work with them without any worries. The nails are sufficiently sharp to demonstrate the technique. If you use an original hackle with beginners, good instruction and supervision should be provided. It is not for nothing that many old hackles come with a protective cap for the hackle teeth.

Materials:

(Measurements are approx.; use what you have.)

- Rectangular wooden board; for example, 12 × 3 in. (30 × 7 cm), at least 0.75–1.2 in. (2–3 cm) thick, so that the nails have sufficient hold
- Approximately 30 nails, 3.1 in. (8 cm) long, 3.1 mm thick
- 1 sheet of graph paper (5 mm blocks)

The dimensions for the wooden board and nails may vary. Use what you have available. However, the nails should have a certain thickness and length.

Tools:

- saw, hand drill or electric drill, drill press (optional), awl/pricker
- 3 mm diameter drill bit, hammer, screw clamps

1 Draw a rectangle measuring approximately 2.3 × 2.3 in. (6 × 6 cm) on graph paper. Mark dots 0.4 in. (1 cm) apart for the drill holes: In the first row, six dots; in the second row, stagger the dots by 0.2 in. (0.5 cm).

2 Cut out the paper rectangle and affix it to the board with adhesive tape. There must be enough overhang on both sides to be able to clamp the board to a table later, using screw clamps.

3 Prepunch the holes for the nails at the marked points into the board, using an awl. Predrill the holes vertically (a drill press is handy). The drill bit should be slightly thinner than the nails. In my example, the drill bit has a diameter of 3 mm and the nails 3.1 mm.

4 Hammer the nails into the holes.

Attach the finished hackle to a tabletop or work bench, using screw clamps. If you use a large board (approx. 28 × 6 in. [70 × 15 cm]) and saw cutouts at both ends for the hand or foot, you can use the hackle comfortably while seated. One foot and one hand hold the board while the flax is pulled through the nails with the other.

SPINDLES

Materials: Branch fork or thick branches, depending on the spindle

Tools: Pruning shears or saw, hatchet or axe, carving knife or pocketknife, sandpaper. For diabolo or dumbbell: chisel and mallet, drill.

BRANCH FORK SPINDLE

1 Look for a forked branch about the thickness of a finger (yard, roadside). Cut off the forked branch with a pocketknife or pruning shears. Use a saw for thicker branches.

2 If you want the spinning hook to look particularly attractive, you can remove the bark and smooth the ends and surface with a knife. However, spinning also works with a stick with bark, fresh from the bush or tree.

DEALGAN SPINDLE

Cut a straight branch from a hedge, approx. 8 in. (20 cm) long, approx. 2 in. (5 cm) in diameter. Remove the bark.

1 Rough trimming: best done with a carving axe or hatchet (sharpened on one side), or with an axe or knife as a makeshift solution.

2 Use a carving knife or pocketknife for the following finishing touches. Round off the bottom end slightly. Cut two intersecting V-shaped notches into the bottom surface. Carve the wood thinner and thinner toward the top. Leave a knob at the top end to hold the thread.

3 Leave the spindle to dry for several days in a place that is not too warm, then smooth with sandpaper. Finish polishing with rough horsetail or very fine sandpaper. Rub with beeswax or linseed oil as desired.

DIABOLO SPINDLE

1 Debark a thick branch, about 6.25 in. (15 cm) long, 2 in. (5 cm) in diameter.

2 Mark the middle with a pencil. Saw along this line to a depth of approx. 0.7 cm to max. 1 cm all around.

3 Bevel from the ends to the center. To do this, use a chisel and mallet to remove first one side, then the other side, to create the shape of a diabolo.

4 Let dry and work the surface as desired (see Dealgan Spindle, step 3).

5 Drill a hole in the middle. Insert a small forked twig tightly into the hole as a hanger.

DUMBBELL SPINDLE

1 Debark a thick branch, about 6.25 in. (15 cm) long, 2 in. (5 cm) in diameter.

2 Mark a line with a pencil at both ends, approx. 1 in. (2.5 cm) from the end. Saw approx. 0.4 in. (1 cm) deep all around these lines.

3 Remove the middle area with a chisel and carving knife down to the depth of the saw cuts: two discs remain on the right and left.

4 Drill a hole in the center. Tightly insert a small, forked twig into the hole as a hanger.

ROPE-TWISTING PADDLE

Materials:

- 1 finger-width branch, 8 in. (20 cm) long
- 1 board, 2 in. (5 cm) wide, 10 in. (25 cm) long (approximate measurements)

Instead of the board, you can split a branch section with a diameter of 2 in. (5 cm) to obtain a board; see batoning above.
[Batoning Splitting Technique: p. 263]

(Alternative: 1 wooden dowel rod, 1 thick wooden bead with matching hole, 1 small board.)

Tools: Carving or pocketknife, saw, brace and bit hand drill or cordless drill, possibly carpenter's PVA glue

1 For the axle: Carve away enough wood from the 8 in. (20 cm) branch section so that a thicker knob remains at one end and a round piece of wood remains at the other end. Alternatively, glue a thick wooden bead to one end of the dowel or drill a hole and push a dowel through it.

2 For the swing weight: Debark the longer branch section and cut it at an angle with a knife. It should be wide and heavy on the outside and become narrower toward the axis. There must be enough width left after carving to drill a hole.

3 Drill a hole for the axle. Leave a little overhang. Cut a notch there to which the thread can later be knotted.

4 Push the wooden rod through. The board must be able to turn or swing easily around the axle. If it jams, widen the hole. It is not necessary to secure the board downward, since it is pressed against the knob at the end of the axle by gravity when swinging.

ROPE-TWISTING HOOK

Materials:

- 1 hazel rod (or willow)
- 1 wooden board
- Piece of thick twine

Tools: Pocketknife, branch or pruning shears, hand drill or electric drill

- Harvest a straight hazel rod about 5 feet (1. 5 m) long; no branches; about a finger width at the bottom and a little thinner at the top.
- Bend the thin end carefully multiple times over your knee to make it more flexible. If it starts to make soft cracking noises, stop bending and continue in another spot.
- Use a piece of twine on the thin end to form a U shape (see photo above).

The device can be used as it is. It then works like a natural branch fork. The hands have to constantly change their grip when turning the crank, which is not very comfortable.

It is easier with a rotating handle:

1 Make three holes in a wooden board (split from a thick branch yourself [Batoning Splitting Technique: p. 263] or a scrap piece from the workshop): Drill a large hole in the center through which the lower, thick end of the hazel rod fits. Drill two smaller holes to the right and left of it. (See photo below.)

2 Insert the hazel rod through the large hole. First push on a "washer" made from a perforated piece of wood or, more simply, from a piece of elderberry cane. Then secure the hazel rod against slipping through with a wooden or wire split pin or cotter pin (drill a hole).

3 For the hand loop, insert one end of an approx. 14 in. (35 cm) long thick cord into each of the smaller holes. Tie a knot in each end of the cord so that the rope does not slip through.

→ Batoning Splitting Technique p. 263

HAND WINCH

The hand winch is made of three parts: handle with axle, bow, and crossbar. For the bow, you need a wood that is easy to bend, preferably hazel or willow. The board for the crosspiece can be carved from a branch that has been split lengthwise.

Materials:

(Measurements are approx.; use what you have.)

- Round wood for the handle, about 12 in. (30 cm) long
- Flat wood for the crossbar, 1 in. (2.5 cm) wide, about 8 in. (20 cm) long
- Bendable wood for the bow, 0.75–1.0 in. (2–2.5 cm) in diameter, split lengthwise, about 18 inches (45 cm) long
- Possibly a tube made of elder wood, approx. 5 in. (12 cm) long
- Thin wooden sticks as splint pins; for example, blackthorn thorns

Tools: Carving knife or pocketknife, hand drill or electric drill

1 Wooden rod as an axle: Leave approx. 4 in. (10 cm) of the full thickness of the wood at one end as a handle. Carve the rest of the rod thinner all around. The adjustment to the hole size will be made later.

2 Crosspiece: Round off the board for the crosspiece at both ends. Cut notches in one end. The thread will be knotted there later when spinning.

3 Drill or cut a hole in the middle of the crosspiece. The wooden rod must be able to be easily inserted.

4 Drill two more holes to the right and left of the middle. The distance between the holes should be 4 in. (10 cm). The bow will be inserted into these later.

5 Bow: Leave the bark on the outer side. On the inside, mark two points 4 in. (10 cm) from each other. Use a handsaw or knife to remove enough material to create two 0.4–0.6 in. (1–1.5 cm) wide slits.

6 Bend the bow slowly up at these points until they form a right angle. The wood must not break.

7 Cut both ends of the bow so that they fit tightly in the holes of the crosspiece.

8 Drill or cut a hole in the middle of the crossbar of the bow. It must be big enough so that the wooden rod can be easily put through.

9 Place the crosspiece on the bow.

10 The wooden rod must protrude slightly from the top of the crosspiece. If not, remove some more material from the axle.

11 To secure the construction, drill a small hole in the end of the wooden rod poking out. Cut a small piece of wood so that it can be inserted into this hole as a splint pin.

12 If the bow gets wedged/stuck when turning the device, a washer secured with a split pin or cotter pin to prevent it from slipping downward will help.

13 Alternative for the handle: Attach a tube made from hollowed elder wood. Secure at the bottom with a split pin or cotter pin inserted through it. If you hold the winch by the elder handle, it should be easy to twirl in the tube.

TOOLS FOR BANDS AND BRAIDS

SIMPLE WOODEN BOBBINS

Materials (for four bobbins): Round or square length of wood, 20–24 in. (50–60 cm) long, 4 screw hooks

This project is well suited for recycling leftover wood, such as old shelf supports or branches from pruning. The wood should be thick enough to be easy to grip (try it out!).

Tools: Saw, sandpaper. Optional: chisel and mallet, knife.

Use the saw to cut the wood into four sections of equal length. Smooth all edges with sandpaper and screw a screw hook into the top of each.

Bobbins with a recess for winding the yarn supply are also practical. To do this, saw off four round pieces of wood (e.g., branches from pruning) to a length of approx. 6 in. (15 cm). Mark 2 circular lines: at 0.8 in. (2 cm) from one end and at 3 in. (7 cm) from the other. Saw along the lines to a depth of approx. 0.4 in. (1 cm). Chisel out a recess between the saw cuts with a chisel and mallet. Remove the bark from the bobbin. Use a carving knife or penknife to slightly taper all edges. If you like, finish the surface with a knife. If you don't want to chisel out or don't have a chisel, you can also make the recess with a sharp knife. However, this is recommended only for green wood; otherwise it is too much work.

NORWEGIAN BOBBINS

Materials (for four bobbins): Wooden board scrap, approx. 0.6 in. (1.5 cm) thick

Tools: Saw, pencil, sandpaper, hand drill or electric drill

Transfer the outline on this page (the template) four times onto the wooden board. Saw out the shapes by hand or with a bandsaw, round off all edges with sandpaper, and drill a hole for the thread at the marked point.

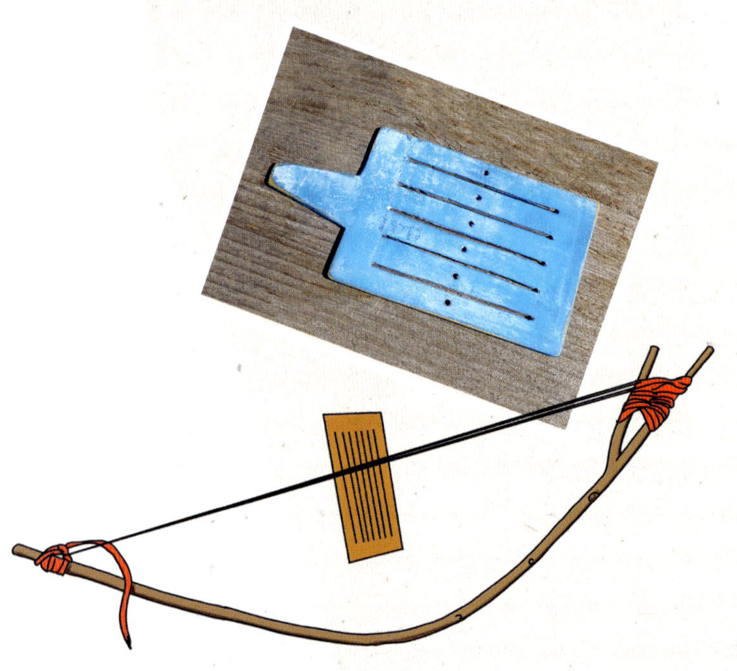

RIGID HEDDLE

The rigid heddle can be made either from one piece—traditionally from wood, bone, or antler, today also from plastic—or as a frame with inserted small wooden bars. You can easily make a one-piece heddle yourself.

Quick Method

Materials: Thin piece of wood or plywood, around 4 x 6 in. (10 x 15 cm)

Tools: Saw, fretsaw, hand drill or electric drill, pencil, possibly soldering iron or pyrography pen

1 Saw out a rectangle or square from plywood.

2 Make a paper template in the desired size (see photos) or draw directly onto the wood with a pencil. Seven to ten slits are sufficient to start with, since you can stretch double the number plus one warp thread.

3 Drill a hole at the end of each slit, through which the saw blade of the fret saw can be put. Cut out the slits.

WEAVING BOW

Materials: Forked branch, about 30–35 in. (80–90 cm) long, of bendable wood (hazel, willow)

Tools: Carving knife or pocketknife

Round off the ends of the branch slightly with the knife. Carefully bend the branch slightly round over your knee, little by little. The wood must not crack under any circumstances. Therefore, do not bend too much on the first pass; instead, repeat the bending several times.

To prevent the warp yarn from slipping off, make a notch all the way around the end that is not forked.

4 Either drill the marked holes to pull the threads through or burn them in with a soldering iron or pyrography pen. It is important to position the holes not exactly in the middle so that the part of the heddle below the holes is heavier than the upper part and the heddle hangs upright when weaving. Watch out: On photos or drawings you might run across, the weaving grids are often shown upside down!

5 Smooth all surfaces and edges with sandpaper.

6 If you'd like, decorate your rigid heddle.

Traditional Method

Materials: A short log. Birch, pine, or spruce are well suited. These woods are particularly easy to split into thin slices.

Tools: Axe or knife for splitting, saw, chisel, carving knife or pocketknife, pencil

1 Split a piece of wood out of the branch, using the axe or knife [Batoning: p. 263].

2 Saw out a rectangle or square from the piece of wood.

3 With a pencil, draw two lines across the board, marking off the area where the slits will be made. Do this on both sides of the board.

4 Cut these lines a few millimeters deep with a saw or a sharp knife. Using a chisel, deepen the area between the incisions on both sides of the board.

5 Mark the lines for the slits.

6 Use a sharp knife to run over the slit lines several times on both sides of the board until the slit is open.

7 Mark the holes to pull the threads through (slightly above the center so that the grid hangs well). Burn them in with a soldering iron or pyrography pen. In Sweden, this used to be done with a metal pin made red hot over a flame (e.g., a pointed knitting needle or bicycle spoke).

8 If desired, you can carve your rigid heddle to decorate it.

9 Smooth all surfaces and edges with sandpaper.

10 If you'd like, you can decorate the heddle, using colorful paints.

→ Batoning p. 263

GLUED RIGID HEDDLE

If you'd like to try band weaving as quickly as possible, or if you will be working with a group of children, you can also put together a rigid heddle by using glue.

Materials: Multiple popsicle sticks (from a craft store or collected), carpenter's PVA glue

Tools: 1–2 screw clamps or craft clamps, hand drill or soldering iron or pyrography pen

1 On a clampable work surface, arrange the popsicle sticks to form the heddle. For the crosspieces on the top and bottom, use two more sticks or thin pieces of wood each.

2 Thinly coat the connection points on both pieces of wood with glue.

3 Assemble the heddle and cover with a flat board. Carefully apply one or two screw clamps or craft clamps. The glued joints must not slip out of place! If you don't want to work with clamps, you can stack heavy objects, such as books, on the flat board.

4 When the glue has set after approx. thirty minutes, remove the clamps and allow the glue to completely cure.

5 Mark the holes slightly above the center and drill through them with a hand drill or burn them in with a soldering iron or pyrography pen.

6 Decorate the heddle as desired.

WEAVER'S SHUTTLE

To feed the weft thread through the shed, you can use a long weaving needle or wrap the thread around your fingers to form a butterfly or figure eight. A shuttle is not absolutely necessary for simple bands but makes the work easier. If one end is pointed, you can even use it to weave "pick-up" patterns.

Materials: Thin piece of wood, approx. 6 × 0.75 in. (15 × 2 cm), about 3–4 mm thick (plywood remnant or self-split wood; e.g., from a birch branch)

Tools: Fretsaw or scroll saw, pencil, sandpaper

1 Draw the outline on the board, either freehand or from a template (such as the one on this page).

2 Drill a hole in the marked opening at the top through which the saw blade can be threaded.

3 Cut out the shuttle.

4 Smooth all surfaces and edges with sandpaper.

5 A final rubbing with rough horsetail ensures a polished surface.

WEAVING SWORD

You can use a weaving sword to push down the weft threads. A sword can be made by sawing out a thin board. However, it then has relatively little weight, and all the power must come from the hand. The sword gains more mass if it has a thin "edge" but a thick back. The Anatolian swords for tablet weaving, which are made in this way, sometimes even have extra weighting in the form of embedded lead on the broad side.

Materials: Branch cutting, approx. 1 foot (30 cm) long

Tools: Axe or knife for splitting, saw, wood rasp, sandpaper

1 Split the branch twice (with axe or knife). [Batoning Instructions: p. 263] The first cut goes through the middle. With the second cut, a wedge-shaped "pie slice" is split off.

2 Prepare a handle with two saw cuts.

3 Carve out the handle with the carving knife. Round it off so that it is easy to grip.

4 Straighten all surfaces and edges with a rasp and knife. In particular, any protruding wood splinters must be removed.

5 Smooth all surfaces and edges with sandpaper. If desired, the finished weaving sword can be polished with rough horsetail.

→ Batoning Instructions p. 263

WEAVING TABLETS

In pattern instructions for tablet weaving, the individual tablets are numbered, and the holes are normally labeled clockwise from A to D. It's better, however, if you do not label your tablets, because that often just causes confusion. The wooden tablets look better unlabeled anyway.

CARDBOARD WEAVING TABLETS

Materials: Sturdy cardboard or old playing cards

Tools: Geo triangle, scissors, pencil, hole punch, corner punch (optional), possibly soldering iron or pyrography pen

A piece of sturdy cardboard is sufficient for your first attempts. Using a pencil, make a template (similar to the one on this page): a square with rounded corners and marked for four holes. Use your template to draw tablets on the cardboard, then cut them out. Punch out the holes with a hole punch.

It is quicker to use discarded playing cards, which you cut into squares. Such playing card "tablets" are surprisingly sturdy. The holes can be burned in with a soldering iron. Round off the sharp corners with scissors or a corner punch from a craft supply store.

WOODEN WEAVING TABLETS

Materials: Scrap cardboard (for the template); scrap wood, max. 4 mm thick

The material for these tablets is thin pieces of wood or plywood from the hardware store or hobby shop. A simple upcycling project can be done by taking apart an old wooden fruit or produce box. Another possibility is leftover thick veneer wood.

Tools: Scissors, geo triangle, saw, drill, awl, pencil, sandpaper

1 Cut out a square template from cardboard. All tablet sizes between 1.5 in. (4 cm) square and 3.25 in. (8 cm) square are easy to handle. I have relatively small hands, so tablets with a side length of around 2 in. (5 cm) are the most comfortable. Larger hands can also grasp larger tablets.

2 Mark the holes on the cardboard approx. 0.4 in. (1 cm) from the corners and pierce them with an awl or needle. Use a pencil to trace the outline and the holes on the wood for each individual tablet.

3 Saw out the tablets. If you are sawing several tablets from a longer strip, it is more practical to drill the holes first and then saw off the individual pieces.

4 Drill out the holes with a sharp drill bit. A drill press saves a lot of time here. Finally, smooth all edges and surfaces with sandpaper. The edges of the holes in particular must be rounded off well so that the yarn does not fray when the tablets are turned. This can be done with a needle file or more quickly with an electric mini sander.

5 The corners are first rounded off with coarse sandpaper, then with fine sandpaper. This is important so that the tablets can be turned easily.

Weaving tablets can also be made from self-split branches of hardwood; for example, birch or apple [Batoning: p. 263]. However, it is very difficult to get the wood slices only a few millimeters thick when splitting them. For historically correct bone weaving tablets, shoulder blades from cattle are used.

→ Batoning p. 263

TOOLS FOR CLOTHING AND ACCESSORIES

TWINING FORMS

FORM FOR BRACELETS

Materials:

- Softwood wooden dowel (or, as in the photo here, a recycled rolling pin), approx. 8 in. (20 cm) long. The diameter should be slightly smaller than the desired diameter of the bracelet (with a string placed around your hand or with a tailor's tape, measure so that you can just slip your hand through).
- About 50 nails, about 0.8 in. (2 cm) long. The quantity is dependent on the diameter. The nails protrude about 0.4 in. (1 cm) from the wood, and the warp thread is pushed up to the nailheads; therefore the circumference measured over the nailheads must correspond to the circumference of the bracelet.

Tools: Saws, hammer, pencil, ruler, coarse sandpaper

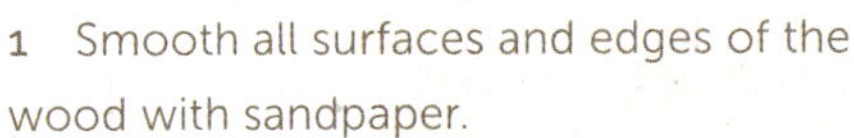

1 Smooth all surfaces and edges of the wood with sandpaper.

2 Use a pencil to draw two lines around the piece of wood, each 0.6 in. (1.4 cm) from an end.

3 Mark where the nails will be hammered in (with 0.3 in. [0.8 cm] distance from each other). If you'd like to work with a very thick yarn, the distance can be larger, about 0.4 in. (1 cm). For very thin thread, the nails should be closer together, about 0.2 in. (0.6 cm).

4 Hammer in the nails.

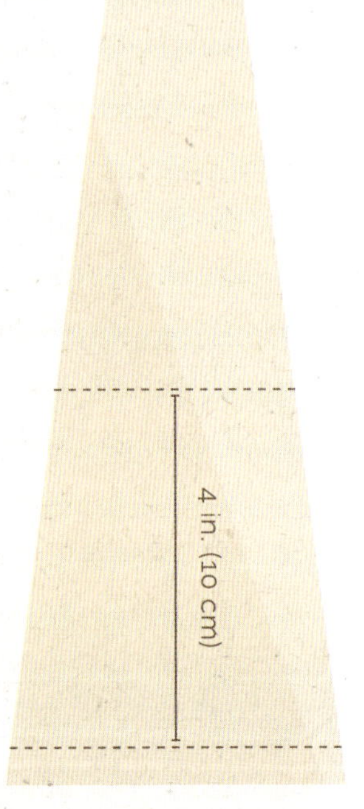

FORM FOR ARM WARMERS

Materials:

- Board of soft wood (pine, fir), approx. 7.8 × 4.7 × 1.0 in. (20 × 12 × 2.5 cm)
- Nails, 0.8 in. (2 cm) long: about 50 nails (for women's arm warmers). For men's arm warmers, you will need more.

Tools: Saw, wood rasp, hammer, coarse sandpaper

1 Mark a diagonal line (about 82 to 85 degrees) with a pencil on both sides of the board (see diagram).

2 Saw off the excess wood along both lines.

3 Round off the edges of the diagonal lines with the wood rasp.

4 Smooth all edges with sandpaper so that there are no splinters.

5 Hammer in one row of nails at the top and bottom, 0.4 in. (1 cm) from the bottom edge and 3.5 in. (9 cm) from the top edge. The distance between the nails in the top row should be 0.3 in. (0.8 cm). The number of nails must be the same at the top and bottom. The distance between the bottom nails is therefore greater (calculate this based on the circumference). The top nails can also be hammered into the top of the front side of the wood instead of around the outside of the edge.

Instead of the board, you can also use a log that tapers toward the top for the arm warmers. For example, a piece of a spruce trunk (discarded Christmas tree). You need to find a section that is about the thickness of your forearm. After debarking and smoothing the trunk, you can hammer in the nails as described above.

NÅLBINDING NEEDLE

These wooden needles are well suited for nålbinding and twining. If you would like to twine with them, you need to make two needles.

Materials: Small stick, about 6 in. (15 cm) long, freshly harvested

You need only a tiny amount of raw material. That's why carving a nålbinding needle is a great idea to get to know different types of wood. My favorite type of wood is spindle wood (*Euonymus europaeus*), which has a light-yellow color and is so fine grained that it has a perfectly smooth surface when carved. Its surface resembles bone. It is native to Europe and western Asia but grows in the US, having escaped cultivation. Incidentally, in the past, European spindle wood was often used for crochet and knitting needles and for spindles (hence the name). Boxwood can be worked in much the same way as spindle wood.

Barberry, privet, apple, or plum are also very suitable. Yew and the heartwood of black locust and walnut have beautiful colors. Birch, willow, hazel, poplar, boxwood, linden or lime, and fresh elder wood (it is very hard when dried) are easy to work with. In general, fresh wood, also known as green wood, is much easier to work with than dried wood. But dry wood can also have its advantages. For example, wood with fungal decay often looks very attractive with its colors and wavy patterns. You should therefore also experiment with dead wood, picked up from the ground or from dead trees. You can easily obtain the wood on a walk. However, you should not tear off branches but cut them off with a sharp tool so that you do not unnecessarily injure the tree or shrub.

Tools: Pruning shears, carving or pocketknife, sturdy knife for splitting, fine sandpaper or rough horsetail for polishing. If desired, beeswax, linseed, walnut, or hazelnut oil can be used.

1 Cut the stick approx. 6 in. (15 cm) long. The needle is only about 2.5–4 in. (6–10 cm) long; the excess length is used to hold it better and will be removed later.

2 Halve the stick lengthwise, preferably through the middle of the soft pith channel. You can halve it by carving, removing shavings. Or you can split the wood [see Batoning, p. 263], and two needles can be carved from one stick—one from each half.

3 Debark one-half of the stick and remove enough material from the rounded side to leave a flat, approx. 3 mm thick piece. The excess end is not processed.

4 Carve an elongated tip.

5 The excess wood is now cut away, leaving a needle length of approx. 3 in. (8 cm).

6 Round off the handle end.

7 Carve the eye of the needle: Make V-shaped incisions from both sides and gradually widen them. You can also burn the eye with a soldering iron or pyrography pen instead. Caution: Press only briefly on the wood at a time, then leave to cool again. Drilling does not work so well; the wood can easily break.

8 Let the needle dry overnight.

9 Smooth the needle with fine sandpaper. Depending on the type of wood, this step can be left out, and the needle can just be polished with extra-fine sandpaper. A wonderfully smooth finish can be achieved with rough horsetail.

10 If you wish, rub the wood with linseed oil or beeswax. This will give it a slightly darker and shinier surface. A crushed walnut or hazelnut, rubbed onto the wood with a cloth, also gives a nice finish.

→ Batoning
p. 263

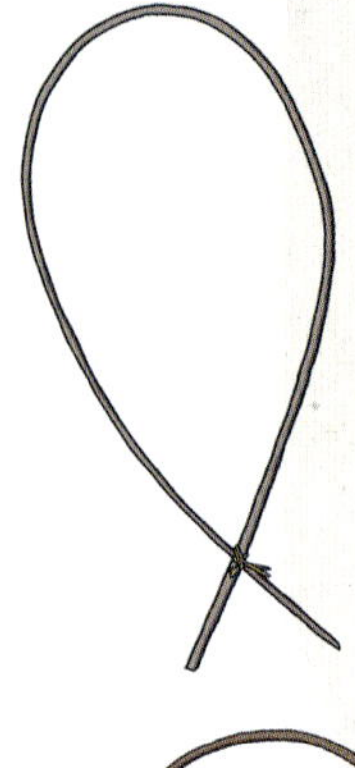

SPRANG FRAME

Sprang frames can be bought ready-made or are easily made yourself. Alternatively, you can use a large picture frame or something similar.

Materials: Branch of bendable wood (e.g., maple, hazel, willow), 8–10 feet long (2.5–3 m); twine or raffia; possibly a board, approx. 24 in. (60 cm) long

Tools: Carving or pocketknife

1 Cut the side branches flush.

2 If desired, debark from the branch (with the back of the knife or a dull knife).

3 Bend the wood into a round shape carefully with your knee.

4 Cross over the ends so that the frame has the form of a fish.

5 Tie at the crossing point with twine or raffia and fix it with a knot.

Another construction method: Bend the branch into a U and insert both ends into a predrilled board. Since the drill holes must have a large diameter to match the thickness of the branch, use a Forstner drill bit. Alternatively, you can drill several thin holes close together on a premarked circle. Remove the remaining wood with a chisel. Then smooth the resulting large hole with a round wood rasp. Because fresh wood shrinks as it dries, allow the wooden arch to dry thoroughly before determining the diameter of the drill hole. Otherwise, the arch could wobble in the board.

To use, place the board on the floor and hold it in place with your feet.

SPRANG BOARD

Materials: Wooden board or strip, 9–10 feet long (2.7–3 m), at least 0.6 in. wide, at least 0.4 in. (1 cm) thick; 3 sturdy nails or 3 wooden dowels

Tools: Hammer, possibly a drill for wooden dowels

1 Drive a nail into the center of the flat side of the wooden strip, around an inch from one end (or drill a hole and insert a wooden dowel so that it fits tightly).

2 Fasten two nails (or dowels) in a row at the other end, approx. 2 in. (5 cm) apart.

CROCHET HOOK

Materials:
Suitable materials are, for example, silver spoons or forks, single-use wooden spoon, a plastic comb, or a folder (of bone or plastic) from a drawing or book-binding supplier.

My favorite material is wood from the European spindle, or from boxwood. It can be easily polished and feels smooth and warm in your hand.

- branch (European spindle or boxwood), at least 1.25 in. (3 cm) in diameter
- paper

Tools: Saw, long sturdy knife or axe, pencil, scroll saw, carving or pocketknife, file, sandpaper or rough horsetail

1 Saw off the branch to length of 6 in. (15 cm).

2 Using an axe or knife, split a small board from the branch. [Batoning: p. 263]

3 Trace the template on this page onto paper, cut it out, and draw the outline on the wood with a pencil. Of course, you can also draw the shape freehand.

4 Saw out the shape with the scroll saw (choose a suitable saw blade).

5 Finish the surface with the carving knife or pocketknife.

6 Round off all the edges with a file and smooth.

7 Allow the wood to dry slightly.

8 Polish with fine sandpaper or slightly moistened rough horsetail.

→ Batoning p. 263

READING TIPS

The internet is of course a huge treasure trove, especially if you search not only in your own but also in different languages. The best first step is usually an image search. Try searching in Polish, Turkish, or Finnish. Once you have found interesting pages, an online translation program can help you overcome language barriers.

But my favorite source is still books. You can find my personal selection here.

ARCHAEOLOGY AND CRAFTSMANSHIP

I am a fan of Alexander Langlands. The British archaeologist, who is also involved in the Heritage Crafts Association, combines scientific research with personal experiences and hands-on experience. His films, such as the BBC's historical farm series, do not focus on textiles, but textiles do feature frequently. At https://alexlanglands.wordpress.com, for example, he shows how blackberries are used as twine for straw baskets.

Book tip: Alexander Langlands, *Cræft: An Inquiry into the Origins and True Meaning of Traditional Crafts* (New York: W. W. Norton, 2019).

FIBER MATERIALS AND ARCHAEOLOGY

Johanna Banck-Burgess and Lisa-Maria Rösch, eds., *Verknüpft und zugenäht! Bound and Stitched Up! Gräser, Bast, Rinde—Alleskönner der Steinzeit / Grass, Bast, Bark—Stone Age All-Rounders*, Archäologische Informationen aus Baden-Württemberg 82 (Heidelberg, Germany: Propylaeum, 2020). https://books.ub.uni-heidelberg.de//propylaeum/catalog/book/643.

The archaeotechnician Anne Reichert (1935–2022) was an expert in the processing of organic materials in prehistory. Her essay provides an insight into her work: "Zwirngeflechte in der Ausrüstung des Gletschermannes: zur Herstellungstechnik der Dolchscheide, des Umhangs und der Innengeflechte der Schuhe." *Zeitschrift für schweizerische Archäologie und Kunstgeschichte* 58 (2001): 61–66. Further articles by her can be found in the volumes of the series Experimentelle Archäologie in Deutschland-Bilanz and in the journal *EAS-Anzeiger*.

The following books deal specifically with stinging nettle as a useful plant:

Mechtilde Frintrup, *Das Brennnesselbuch: Die magische Nahrungs-, Heil- und Faserpflanze*, 4th ed. (Aarau, Switzerland, and Munich: AT Verlag, 2022).

Václav Michalička, *Die Brennnessel: Kleidendes Unkraut* (Klagenfurt, Austria: Wieser Verlag, 2021).

TEXTILE ARCHAEOLOGY

Margrethe Hald was a pioneer in textile archaeology. Almost all her publications can be downloaded on the Margrethe Hald Archive page from Copenhagen University as a PDF.

A terrific introduction can also be found in the book by Karina Grömer available as a PDF online: *The Art of Prehistoric Textile Making: The Development of Craft Traditions and Clothing in Central Europe* (Vienna: Natural History Museum, 2016).

The blog and website of textile archaeologist Katrin Kania is also worth reading: www.pallia.net.

TEXTILE SYSTEMATICS

Annemarie Seiler-Baldinger, *Systematik der Textilen Techniken*, Basler Beitrage zur Ethnologie 32 (Basel, Switzerland: Ethnologischen Seminar der Universität Basel and Museum der Kulturen Basel, 1991). Anyone who likes things sorted will enjoy this basic work. All the techniques are illustrated in sequence with simple, clear drawings.

SPINNING

Ulrike Claßen-Büttner, *Spinnst Du?—Na klar!* (Books on Demand, 2009). This work does not contain detailed instructions on hand spinning, but it does provide detailed and well-founded information on archaeology, history, and spinning equipment.

BRAIDING

Jacqui Carey, *Braids & Beyond: A Broad Look at Narrow Wares. A Braid Society Exhibition* (Ottery St. Mary, UK: Carey Co., 2003).

The Canadian Carol James is a globally in-demand expert for sprang and fingerweaving. Her introduction to fingerweaving is very good: *Fingerweaving Untangled* (3rd ed., Winnipeg: Fiber Arts, 2011). More information can be found on her website www.spranglady.com.

BAND WEAVING

Many examples of historical American bands from plant-dyed linen can be found in Susan Faulkner Weaver, *Handwoven Tape: Understanding and Weaving Early American and Contemporary Tape* (Atglen, PA: Schiffer, 2016).

Two books on the subject of pick-up bandweaving patterns: Heather Torgenrud, *Norwegian Pick-up Bandweaving* (Atglen, PA: Schiffer, 2014), and Irene Burchert, *Ostpreußische Jostenbänder* (Husum, Germany: Husum Druck- und Verlagsgesellschaft, 2007).

TABLET WEAVING

The booklet *Die Kunst des Brettchenwebens* by Karl Schlabow (Wachholtz Verlag Neumünster, possibly still available in antiquarian bookshops) offers a short, very clear introduction to the technique. More-recent books can be found under the search terms "card weaving" and "tablet weaving."

NÅLBINDING

The standard German work, from archaeologist Ulrike Claßen-Büttner, is self-published: *Nadelbinden, was ist denn das? (*Books on Demand, 2012).

Monika Künti, *Einhängen und verschlingen: Maschenbildung mit vorangeführtem Fadenende* (Bern, Switzerland: Haupt Verlag, 2014).

A very detailed Finnish site is www.en.neulakintaat.fi, by Sanna-Mari Pihlajapiha.

www.nalbound.com by Anne Marie Decker.

SPRANG

The ultimate sprang book is by British weaver Peter Collingwood,

The Techniques of Sprang. It is, unfortunately, available only second-hand or in libraries. A PDF format is at: https://taprootvideo.com

Carol James, *Sprang Unsprung: An Illustrated Guide to Interlinking, Interlacing and Intertwining* (Winnipeg: Fiber Arts, 2011).

SLIP STITCH CROCHET

If you would like to dive deeper into the theme of slip stitch crochet and textile loop techniques, I would recommend the website www.loopholes.blog by Cary Karp.

INDEX

THANK YOU

Many people have helped transform my idea into a book.
I would like to thank:

All textile enthusiasts, archaeotechnicians, archaeologists, textile craftspeople, and museum staff for informative, stimulating, and fiber-nerdy talks and tips.

Everyone who gave me access to their photos.

Gisela, Katrin, Ruth, and Sabine
for testing my instructions.

Günter
for his constructive craftsman point of view.

Gesa
for her work behind the camera in 97°F (36°C) weather.

Birthe, Helene, John, Katrin, Liam, and Volker
for their patient modeling.

The Dorenburg Open Air Museum in Grefath
for the perfect photo location.

My editor Ricarda Berthold,
who always finds the right words.

Carla Schmid from AT Verlag for the beautiful layout, and the whole publishing team for the pleasant working relationship.

DANKE, DANK OK, DĚKUJI, KIITOS, MÈRSI AND THANKS!

Image Credits

Archäologisches Freilichtmuseum Zeiteninsel, Susanne Gütter, pages 8–9, 170, 178, 179; Armémuseum (Sweden), page 223 top; Stephen Burton, page 70; Sylva Antony Čekalová, pages 219, 224, 236, 237; CETRAT–Center of Traditional Technologies (Czech Republic), Václav Michalička, pages 28, 37 bottom, 52, 53 top, 189, 194, 195; Ulrike Claßen-Büttner, page 62 right; Bernhard Dankbar, pages 210, 211 top; Susanne Fiedler, pages 34, 35 right; Mechtilde Frintrup, page 33; Glomdalsmuseet (Norway), page 223 bottom; Heimatmuseum Arosa-Schanfigg (Switzerland), Renzo Semadeni, page 187; Heimatmuseum Ratzenried (Germany), Hans Knöpfler, page 136 top; Wulf Hein, pages 36, 37 center, 175 bottom; iStock 1334668268, Castula, thread illustration; Katrin Kania, pages 112 both, 113; Gesa Kieselmann-Fricke, pages 22, 44, 64–65, 100, 132, 148, 182, 196, 214, 238, 252, 260; Gisela Mahnkopf, page 155 top; Gabriela Martin, page 147; McCord Museum Stewart (Canada), pages 59 top, 121, 175 top; Nordfjord Folkemuseum (Norway), pages 89, 93, 139 top; Norsk Folkemuseum (Norway), Anna Grostøl, pages 94 bottom, 205 top; Frank Peter, page 99 top; Rijksmuseum (The Netherlands), page 256 bottom; Astrid Rota, page 71; Megan Senior, page 242; Skansen (Sweden), Elisabeth Boogh, page 205 bottom; Alexandre Solliard, pages 123, 131; Sörmlands Museum (Sweden), page 202 top; Statens Historiska Museet (Sweden), page 139 bottom; Helene Staub, Katrin Staub, pages 114, 122, 164–165; Matthias Süßen, page 251; Hugo Sykes, page 206; Technisches Museum der Bandweberei Großröhrsdorf (Germany), Lutz Weidler, pages 117, 140 both; Textile Research Centre (The Netherlands), page 243 bottom; Silvia Ungerechts, page 155 bottom; Vänerborgs Museum (Sweden), page 198; Andrea Wagner-Neumann, pages 162, 163; Lois Walpole, page 172; Josefin Waltin, page 59 bottom.

All other photos and the drawings on pages 98, 99, 107, 108, 110, 116, 134, 142, 146, 151, 159–161, 185, 199, 209, 211, 217, 242, 268, 278, 290 by Doris Fischer.

Photo © Barbara Jopp

DORIS FISCHER

is an archaeological field supervisor specializing in the history and techniques of traditional fiber arts. With expertise in ancient methods like nålbinding, twining, and sprang, Fischer has dedicated her career to reviving and preserving these practices. Drawing from years of hands-on fieldwork and collaborations with reenactment groups and museums, Fischer's research emphasizes the cultural significance of fiber arts and their connections across time and cultures. Her passion is offering the understanding that people need in order to preserve this intangible cultural heritage.